Pressure Group Behaviour in Canadian Politics

McGraw-Hill Ryerson Series in Canadian Politics

General Editor—Paul W. Fox

Politics: Canada, 4th Ed.; P. W. Fox

Canada in Question: Federalism in the Seventies; D. V. Smiley

Canadian Foreign Policy; D. C. Thomson & R. F. Swanson

The Constitutional Process in Canada; R. I. Cheffins

Political Party Financing in Canada; K. Z. Paltiel

One Man–One Vote; W. E. Lyons

Nationalism in Canada; P. Russell

Political Parties and Ideologies in Canada; W. Christian & C. Campbell

Canada: A Socio-Political Report; R. Manzer

Pressure Group Behaviour in Canadian Politics; A. P. Pross

Pressure Group Behaviour in Canadian Politics

Edited by

A. Paul Pross

Department of Political Science

Dalhousie University

Pressure Group Behaviour in Canadian Politics

ISBN   0-07-082183-6

Printed and Bound in Canada

2345678910 D-75 432109876

for
FDMP
and
AWP

Contributors to this Volume

Peter Aucoin—Dalhousie University

Donald Barry—Dalhousie University

M. W. Bucovetsky—University of Toronto

D. A. Chant—University of Toronto

Helen Jones Dawson—University of Western Ontario

David Kwavnick—Carleton University

A. Paul Pross–Dalhousie University

CONTENTS

Pressure Groups: Adaptive Instruments of Political Communication*

A. Paul Pross

Canadian pressure groups live in the half-light of politics. Usually unobtrusive, and not always respectable, they serve as pervasive and necessary links in the processes of communication that bind government and people. Their many functions are often unrecognized and not always fully understood. Some represent elites, and thus use techniques and claim privileges denied the common man; consequently they are regarded by many with suspicion. The more vociferous enjoy exposing to general view the machinations of government policy-making, earning for themselves the low opinion of politicians, civil servants and competing interests. Yet pressure groups are an essential part of Canadian politics. They create day-to-day connections between public officials and private citizens, alerting both to new trends and facilitating the implementation of government decisions. Often considered illegitimate themselves, their advice and support contribute to the creation of acceptable public policy and give it legitimacy in the community. Their presence makes for a dynamic and healthy political system.

Their contribution to the Canadian political system is the concern of this book. The essays that follow attempt to determine the place pressure groups hold in the structure of politics in Canada, and to describe the role they play in political and administrative processes. To achieve this, the authors of this volume have tried to reach an understanding of the Canadian policy process; they have turned their attention to the impact major institutions—particularly Parliament and the civil service—have had on pressure groups, and they have noted the way in

* I should like to express my appreciation to Catherine Pross, Paul Fox and Geoffrey Burn for their helpful comments on an earlier draft of this paper, to Mrs. Carol Schenery for her patient typing and retyping of this and other papers in this book, and to Penelope Grows and Elizabeth MacLean for shepherding the manuscript into print.

1

which such groups have adapted to the requirements of the constitution. No uniform thesis emerges from this exercise, but there is agreement on some common features, notably the fact that Canadians have underestimated the importance of the role played by pressure groups; that the focal point for pressure group activity in this country is the civil service, which in turn tends to dominate the ensuing relationship; that Canada's pressure groups have proven to be remarkably adaptable instruments of political communication; and finally, that in recent years pressure groups have played an increasingly prominent part in political debate, a part that shows every likelihood of expanding. Before turning to these observations, however, it is important to clarify basic perceptions.

WHAT ARE PRESSURE GROUPS?

Pressure groups are *organizations whose members act together to influence public policy in order to promote their common interest.* The chief characteristic of the pressure group is the fact that it tries to persuade governments to pursue the policies it advocates. In doing so it uses various techniques of persuasion—the force of public opinion, the threat of economic sanctions, the logic of well-prepared arguments— which exert political pressure on government.

Pressure groups are not haphazard collections of individuals. They are organizations: groups of people associating together within the framework of a formal structure to share and promote a common interest.[1] This organizational quality grows out of the fact that pressure group activity must have continuity if it is to have lasting effect. Common objectives must be identified, strategies worked out, modes of procedure adopted, responsibilities assigned, and consistent positions formulated if a group is to persuade government to take specific action and if it is to watch over the development and implementation of supporting policies. These activities require organization, and it is the quality of organization that distinguishes the pressure group from the mob on the one hand and the movement on the other. The mob is an ephemeral thing, a product of chance. It may win clearly stated and immediately realizable goals. It cannot provide for the future because it cannot provide for its own continued existence. It lacks organizational capacity. In contrast, movements do exist over time, but they represent generalized progressions of public opinion. Organized groups participate in the progression, but the movement as a whole consists of too many distinct elements to be described as a coherent unit such as a pressure group. For this reason nationalist movements, for example, are not treated by most writers as pressure group activities, though we recognize that pressure groups take part in them.

Organizational capacity facilitates a third characteristic of the pressure group: the articulation and aggregation of common interest. Through discussion, group members identify the demands they wish to make upon government and explore the conflicts that arise because the objectives of some members clash with those of others. In the process some disaffected members leave the group, and newcomers may be attracted to it by the articulation of their own objectives. Debate brings the many demands together and achieves agreement on which they can be generally supported.

The possession of formal organizational framework, the ability to articulate and aggregate common interests, and the desire to act in the political system are characteristic of other groups beside pressure groups, notably political parties. What distinguishes the pressure group from these is the desire to influence power rather than to exercise the responsibility of government. It is this which permits pressure groups to focus on the special interests of a few and to avoid trying to engage the support of the mass public. In turn, the restricted role of pressure groups permits them to complement instead of rival the political party in the process of political communication.

Identification of the four prime characteristics of pressure groups establishes their broad outline. It does not offer a detailed view, nor does it qualify our description. Detail and restrictions will be developed more fully in this essay and in those that follow. At present it is necessary to note only two points. First, in these essays the terms "pressure group" and "interest group" will be used interchangeably. This may offend those who prefer the term "interest group" because it has fewer emotive connotations than the other and because it suggests the general, non-political, activities of such groups. However, "pressure group" is now so well entrenched in the vocabulary of the politics that it would be unrealistic to avoid the term here. Second, it is important to remember that for most interest groups political activity—activity carried on within the political system—is often a minor and unwelcome addition to more general concerns. Our interest in the political life of interest groups should not blind us to this fact, nor to the fact that general concerns will usually determine the form and extent of their political activities.

STUDIES OF CANADIAN PRESSURE GROUPS

Scholars frequently complain that very few studies of Canadian pressure groups exist. Less than a dozen articles address themselves directly to the subject, and until recently only one book-length study had appeared.[2] One writer has linked this to a common tendency amongst the general public to argue that pressure groups do not operate in Canada. To him, the rather thin literature is symptomatic of an attempt "to sublimate a process that seems functionally essential in any political system."[3] In reality, the literature is neither unduly limited by popular mythology, nor is it as sparse as it first appears. As well as the handful of items that focus explicit upon pressure group activities, unpublished dissertations present a variety of case studies. Biographies, histories, analyses of large-scale social phenomena and even government documents tell us a great deal about pressure group behaviour in Canada.

3

The articles that follow testify to their usefulness, and the bibliography at the end of the volume gives some idea of their extent.

The real problem in the study of Canadian pressure groups lies not in the paucity of the literature, but in the poverty of its analytical approach. There have been two basic difficulties: with a few important exceptions[4] we have not moved beyond descriptive, historically oriented case studies, and we have not worked within the context of a conceptual framework for the analysis of the Canadian policy process as a whole. A third, less significant problem stems from an uncritical adoption of the analytical perceptions of American scholars. The majority of existing studies of Canadian pressure groups explain in detail what pressure groups do. Many explain how they carry on their activities. Very few explain why pressure groups should exist in the Canadian political setting or why some methods of organization should be functional in the setting, but not others. In short, there has been little probing analysis of the roots of pressure group behaviour.

Two attempts have been made to tackle this analytical problem.* Engelmann and Schwartz, in studying the relationships between Canadian political parties and interest groups, undertake a far-reaching discussion of the role groups play in the business of expressing and drawing together the demands of special interests. Their basic assumption is that "the aim of interest articulation is to affect governmental outputs. Any interest system must, therefore, be oriented toward the maximization of access to governmental structure and, therefore, be adapted to this structure."[5] Their terms of reference preclude an extensive exploration of this theme, but their useful review of pressure group relations with various decision centres in the Canadian system concludes with the observation that there is "a tendency among organized interest groups to transmit their demands directly to the governmental structure, and not to parties."[6] The form of adaptation that has developed to maximize access has tended to exclude the political party from the pressure group's area of interest. The investigation of this exclusion reveals a great deal about the Canadian policy system.

In 1971 Van Loon and Whittington published the first attempt to analyze the behaviour and structure of interest groups in the context of a general discussion of Canadian political life. The presentation is important for its synthesis of the then existing literature and its treatment of the input activities of interest groups, especially their methods of influence and the determinants of group success. The importance of output functions is also stressed, particularly such activities as self-regulation of members by professional groups, the dissemination of information

* Robert Presthus' recent two-volume study of elite accommodation in Canada may be counted as a third attempt. However, although its sophisticated and often illuminating analysis contributes to our understanding of pressure group behaviour in this country, its focus on established, or institutional groups means the study does not address itself fully to the issues raised in the preceding paragraph. See Presthus, *Elite Accommodation in Canadian Politics*, (Toronto: Macmillan, 1973), and *Elites in the Policy Process*, (Toronto: Macmillan, 1974).

concerning policy and regulation, and the actual administration of government-authorized programs.

Unfortunately, while Van Loon and Whittington recognize that "the location at which pressure is applied, and the channels of communication on which a group concentrates are related to the structure of the government and its decision-making processes, and to the structure of the pressure group itself,"[7] the conceptual framework they apply does not go beyond a simple input-output scheme. Reference is made to theoretical literature developed elsewhere, chiefly in the United States, and a typology of groups is suggested, but both discussions are only peripherally related to their analysis of Canadian interest group behaviour. By way of explanation it is suggested that "about all that one can assert with certainty here is that if groups are to be effective in politics, they must have access to the political system. The more channels of access they have, and the closer these bring them to the men who actually make decisions, the stronger their influence will be. That is about as much as can be said at present. Further information on the effect of governmental structure on group activity will have to await considerable further comparative research."[8]

More *can* be said, but our capacity to say it depends upon our ability to devise a framework for analyzing the relationship between the structures and behaviour of Canadian pressure groups and the conditions of political life of the Canadian political system as a whole. Such a framework may be inspired by international comparative literature, but it will depend principally upon an understanding of Canadian political life if it is to achieve a theoretical synthesis capable of relating a typology of pressure groups to the observed realities of the Canadian policy process. In the next few pages an approach to such a framework will be attempted.

THE SYSTEMIC ROOTS OF PRESSURE GROUP BEHAVIOUR

Though pressure groups are an almost universal phenomenon, their characteristics and behaviour patterns vary according to the environment in which they are found. This has led Henry W. Ehrmann to observe that "the methods by which pressure groups penetrate parliament will in part be conditioned by the nature of constitutional processes; a parliamentary system, a system in which the separation of powers prevails, a federal system, and a unitarian system will of necessity place the organized interests in a different position."[9] In other words, the structure and behaviour of pressure groups are functions of the political systems in which they are located. The Canadian scene is no exception. Both Engelmann and Schwartz, and Van Loon and Whittington have noted the adaptive propensities of Canadian pressure groups, and their observations are corroborated by case studies. Johnson, for example, concluded that the Union of Nova Scotia Municipalities could not act as a "common" pressure group because the political durability of the provincial government and the undifferentiated nature of the decision-making structure "made it relatively immune from political embarrassment and a potential pressure group found that it . . . had to be invited in to the sphere of government."[10] Manzer found that the development of Canadian teachers' associations confirmed Eckstein's view that "pressure-group politics is a function of political culture and the policies of government."[11] Similar findings are reported upon in this volume.

If the pattern of pressure group life is a function of the political system in which it is observed, it seems appropriate to examine Canadian pressure groups from the perspective of functional analysis, using as a base the widely accepted view that it is the function of the political system to oversee the authoritative allocation of value. That is, government, exercising the coercive power bestowed upon it by the community, achieves the ordering of values that cannot be attained through the economy or the social system. It may decide, for example, that Canadian natural resources are too valuable to be exported to other countries in an unprocessed state, or it may attempt to determine when the life of a human foetus may be ended. The intense competition to manipulate or to influence this powerful instrument of community control is manifested in various ways, the most notable in western systems being the operations of political parties. Only slightly less significant are the activities of other governments, the public service and pressure groups.

Primarily, pressure groups perform communication and legitimation functions. Secondly, they act to regulate their members and to supplement governmental administration.

The communications function is central. It embraces the transmittal of every type of politically relevant information, from highly technical data to the protestations of an outraged citizenry. Because these communications activities are usually initiated by groups outside government, we tend to think of pressure groups as devices for transmitting demands *to* government. But they also help government identify the interests of particular sectors of the community and so channel communications *from* government and offer a means through which government can test opinion. Hence a two-way flow of communication can be created in which the pressure group and government representatives can discuss matters as divergent as national policy and administrative detail. A continuing relationship is established through which both parties obtain information vital to policy-making and administration and through which each can register demands upon the other.

The legitimating functions of pressure groups are by-products of their communications activities and supportive of them. Group involvement in policy discussions not only expands the range of information available to government—it can be used to neutralize group objections to proposed legislation and to engage support for it. Government thus finds in the pressure group system a device for testing policy proposals and a means of eliciting support for them. As we shall see, this doubly supportive function has encouraged some agencies to stimulate pressure group activity within the community. The relationship is equally rewarding to compliant pressure groups since government recognition enhances their own stature and guarantees a measure of influence over policy decisions that are of concern to them. Above all, the relationship may serve the function of keeping the political system abreast of changes within the social system as a whole and in so doing promote general political stability. The successful performance of this last function, however, will depend on the sensitivity of the governmental and pressure group sub-systems to changes in their own and immediate environments. Closed and captive agencies and groups through their failure to absorb external demands, may compound rigidities existing elsewhere in the system.

Quasi-judicial tribunals, such as motor carrier boards, frequently encounter this problem. By defining very narrowly the public's right to intervene in regulatory hearings and by depending upon the information resources of the groups they are meant to control, they lose the capacity to assess the broader public interest.

Finally, pressure groups frequently act as the agents of government. Their role in the regulation of professional activity is perhaps the best-known example of this function,[12] but there are many other occasions when their work supplements that of government agencies. Hawkins, for example, has noted that "over the whole post-war period . . . voluntary agencies have given considerable (and largely unpaid) service to the government in the reception, welfare, settlement, and adjustment of immigrants."[13]

Inevitably, the fact that pressure groups share many of their functions with other actors in the political system induces considerable competition. Political parties, the media, private individuals, and others vie with pressure groups for the privilege of interpreting the public will to key decision makers. Distinguishing their respective roles is often difficult; none more so than those of pressure groups and political parties. Some observers feel that pressure groups are partially responsible for the recent apparent decline in the role of political parties in the Canadian system.[14] Others argue that they are complementary, with pressure groups undertaking the communication of unaggregated demands and parties aggregated demands.[15]

In practice, unfortunately, the distinction is not as clear as this suggests. Unaggregated demands can come from many sources. Many individuals, for example, have been credited with exercising considerable influence in the making of specific policies. If the pressure group is not the sole source of unaggregated demand, the party is not alone in aggregating demand. The majority of established groups find themselves drawing together smaller groups, compromising positions in order to retain the support of diverse memberships and engaging in alliances with likeminded organizations to influence government. The Consumers' Association of Canada, like many organizations, frequently acts in concert with other groups, particularly those associated with its advisory board. In order to co-operate with such groups, the association has from time to time had to modify its own policy positions.[16] It is the scale, not the fact, of aggregation that distinguishes political parties from pressure groups; that, and the fact that pressure groups, unlike parties, aim to exercise influence, not wield power.

So far we have considered pressure group functions that are systemic and general. We must also look at functions which are performed within the organization and which create the internal conditions that determine whether or not it will have the inner resources needed to achieve its objectives.

These are the services that pressure groups perform for their supporters. They include the benefits won through negotiation with governments, such as tariff concessions, tax incentives, professional recognition, and so on, and also the "non-political" services any group with sufficient resources can offer its members. Teachers' associations, for example, negotiate with Canadian provincial governments to obtain "collective benefits" related to salaries, professional status, policy influence and so on.[17] They also, however, "provide protective services, assistance in professional development, and social incentives which are clearly selective benefits,"[18] that are not enjoyed by those outside the organization. Selective benefits are positive incentives encouraging individuals to obtain and maintain membership in associations. Frequently they are far more powerful incentives to membership than are collective benefits. For this reason the capacity of the organization to provide its members with "selective inducements" may be a critical factor in determining the degree of support the organization can count upon when it acts as a pressure group.

The provision of selective benefits for the membership at large helps determine the internal resources available to the leadership.[19] Equally important are the benefits the organization proffers its leadership and its permanent staff. These are often intangible and range from the personal gratifications of leadership to the advantages career officials see in working for particular organizations. David Kwavnick has pointed out that:

> One of the major prizes in the struggle between competing interest groups for organizational maintenance and enhancement is tangible recognition by government of the status and representative capacity claimed by interest group leaders for their respective organizations. Such recognition is conferred when government canvasses interest group leaders for nominations to official bodies and when government calls a group's leaders into consultation on legislative or administrative matters which fall within the class of matters on which the group's leaders claim to speak in a representative capacity.[20]

Kwavnick argues that interest group leaders may feel that it is more important to obtain government recognition of the group than to win concessions on specific issues, since recognition acknowledges the group's right to have its views considered by government.[21] The thrust of pressure group activity is consequently likely to be modified by the organization's need to satisfy the demands made upon it by its own leadership and permanent staff.

In summary, pressure groups perform communications and legitimation functions within most political systems. Their particular importance stems from their capacity to transmit to the political system the demands of special interests, an activity that is carried out through bringing about a degree of aggregation amongst those special interests anxious to influence public policy yet too weak to act independently. As a channel of communication, the pressure group is capable of carrying messages in various directions and is consequently also a means whereby the demands of government are conveyed to the private sector. The performance of these systemic functions has tended to allocate to pressure groups a role complementing that of the political party. As well as performing general systemic functions, pressure groups must be seen as bodies providing benefits of various sorts for their members, their leaders and their permanent staff members. These functions are frequently indispensable—some, at least, provide the organization's *raison d'être*—but collectively they modify the roles played by voluntary associations in carrying out pressure group activities.

TYPES OF PRESSURE GROUPS

Earlier we stressed the role of organizational characteristics in determining the capacity of pressure groups to develop the coherence and continuity necessary for negotiating with government over a period of time. We argued that while not all pressure groups possess highly developed organizational capacity, none lack it completely. In the following paragraphs we shall use a particular concept of organizational capacity to suggest a typology of pressure groups that is designed to relate varieties of such groups to one another and to the policy system at large.

Our approach is suggested by Philip Selznick's concept of the institutionalization of organizations, a process through which an organization, a "technical instrument designed as a means to definite goals,"[22] becomes an institution—"a responsive, adaptive organism."[23]

> Beginning as a tool, the organization derives added meaning from the psychological and social functions it performs. In doing so it becomes valued for itself. To be sure, the personal and group bonds that make for institutionalization are not wholly separable. As the individual works out his special problems . . . he helps to tie the organization into the community's institutional network. Personal incentives may spark this absorption, and provide the needed energy; but its character and direction will be shaped by values already existent in the community at large. Similarly . . . the internal struggle for power becomes a channel through which external environmental forces make themselves felt. This is, indeed a classic function of the American political party system; but less formal and recognized groupings . . . follow the same pattern.

9

Organizations do not so much create values as embody them. As this occurs, the organization becomes increasingly institutionalized.[24]

The fact that "as institutionalization progresses the enterprise . . . becomes peculiarly competent to do a particular kind of work,"[25] suggests the applicability of a sequence, or continuum, to the classification of pressure groups, positing at the one extreme "issue-oriented" groups (a designation we shall elaborate below,) and at the other, "institutionalized" or "institutional" groups. We shall describe the institutional groups first:

(1) *They possess organizational continuity and cohesion.* There will be fairly clear delineation of responsibility and well defined channels of communication throughout the organization. These permit the orderly flow of information within the organization and ensure that individuals carry out the tasks assigned to them. Usually this will involve elaborate organizational structure since that is needed to carry out the many specialized functions that are involved in preparing briefs, organizing representations to officials, sitting on advisory boards, rallying membership support and creating a positive public image, to say nothing of the many non-political activities engaged in by most large interest groups. Continuity is essential to ensure the long-term implementation of favourable policies and to maintain a watchful eye on the evolution of new policies.

(2) *They have extensive knowledge of those sectors of government that affect them and their clients,* and enjoy easy communications with those sectors. The organization's officials have ready access to government officials and are aware of the procedures necessary to bring their views to the attention of appropriate officials.

(3) *There is a stable membership.* Attracted in large part with secondary inducements, it generally acquiesces in the policy directions taken by career and elected leaders and is willing—within limits—to assign them the resources needed to carry out the group's political objectives.

(4) *Operational objectives are concrete and immediate.* General philosophies are usually broad enough to permit each group to bargain with government over the application of specific legislation or the achievement of particular concessions. In consequence, the tactics of negotiation are devised pragmatically.

(5) *Organizational imperatives are generally more important than any particular objective.* It is better, most leaders of institutional groups seem to feel, to return to bargain another day than to risk the "credibility" of the organization in the eyes of those whose decisions may in the future make or break the group and its clients. Hence the reluctance of most institutional groups to avail themselves of the wide range of pressure techniques—particularly the manipulation of public opinion—that exists in most western systems. The degree of manoeuverability open to groups varies, of course,

between political systems and is one of the determinants of the characteristics of pressure group behaviour within specific systems.

The ideal institutional pressure group depicted here rarely exists, and is probably non-existent in Canada. As Helen Jones Dawson points out in her description of contemporary national pressure groups, most Canadian groups, even those such as the Canadian Manufacturers' Association, that we would consider highly institutionalized, are required by their supporters to operate with extremely limited resources.

Our analytic approach suggests that we see issue-oriented groups as having the reverse characteristics of institutional groups. They have limited organizational continuity and cohesion; most are very badly organized.[26] Their knowledge of government is minimal and often naive. Their membership is extremely fluid. They encounter considerable difficulty in formulating and adhering to short-range objectives and they usually have a low regard for the organizational mechanisms they have developed for carrying out their goals.

This is because such groups possess a limited organizational base, focusing usually on the resolution of one or two issues or problems. The magnitude of the issue is of little consequence. As long as the group's concern is narrowly defined, then that concern will dominate the group's organizational arrangements, producing the characteristics we have just described. This will occur whether the group's concern is with material benefits or is ideologically or attitudinally based because the group's preoccupation with one or two issues prohibits it from developing selective inducements other than the largely psychological rewards it can offer the leadership and a small group of supporters for whom the organization is a centre of social life.

Their weak base does not in itself render issue-oriented groups ineffective, nor does it necessarily cause an early death. Ideologically oriented groups often exist for years on miniscule resources, attempting to contribute to the development of public opinion. Many groups concerned with preventing action can achieve their objectives using techniques that institutional groups consider crude and self-defeating. As Donald Barry points out in his analysis of the Biafra issue, they can do this because they have no commitment to the future, and thus are not bound by the considerations which often render institutional groups powerless. Nevertheless, many more issue-oriented groups die in infancy than survive. Many succumb to discouragement, others cannot muster sufficient resources to hold together even a small group of dedicated supporters, and a few disappear because they have achieved their goal. Of those that survive many remain much as they were originally created, but others broaden their base, form coalitions with like-minded groups, create selective inducements and become institutionalized.

The conditions under which institutionalization occurs will vary a great deal but will usually depend on the capacity of the group to accept the extension of its concerns and activities in order to attract new membership, the acquisition of permanent staff, and the relegation to it of an increasingly influential role in the management and leadership of the organization. Accompanying these developments will be a heightened understanding of public policy processes, a growing sophistication and specialization in techniques of communication with official bodies—though probably with an atrophication of communication links with the general public—and governmental recognition of the group's claim to speak on issues of interest to it. Finally, not all issue-oriented groups that broaden their bases develop into institutional groups of the conventional type. An extremely small number are able to retain the public interest and achieve sufficient cohesion to develop into political parties.[27]

Despite their usually insignificant size, issue-oriented groups frequently serve important functions in the political system. Their chief advantage lies in their flexibility. Because they develop extremely quickly and are unencumbered by institutionalized structures, they are excellent vehicles for generating immediate public reaction to specific issues.[28] Because their stake in the future is usually limited, they can indulge in forms of political communication that institutional groups are reluctant to use. This is particularly true in Canada where established groups tend not to resort to publicity for fear of disturbing relations with administrative agencies. Issue-oriented groups are seldom constrained in this fashion and consequently are able to embarrass governments into taking action. On occasion institutional groups avail themselves of the services of issue-oriented organizations, allowing members to work with their more radical counterparts in the hopes of winning through publicity what conventional methods have failed to achieve. In general systemic terms, issue-oriented groups enhance the adaptive capacity of the over-all system, permitting a responsiveness to emergent issues that is not easily achieved by more cumbersome mechanisms of political communication. So, for example, the early environmental groups were loosely structured organizations that emerged to protest particular abuses. Few survived for very long, but they were highly successful in drawing public attention to the need for more effective methods of environmental protection.

The categorization of pressure groups and the definition of their ultimate relationship with the political system has caused analysts considerable difficulty.[29] The institutional continuum model presented here does not overcome all of those difficulties, but it attempts to meet some. In particular, the organizational base of the model provides a means of considering all pressure groups within a single framework: something that ordering groups according to their attitudinal or materialistic bent fails to do. The possibilities of comparative analysis of groups are consequently enhanced and hence the likelihood of achieving general statements about the characteristics of pressure groups operating in different environments. The last point underlines the most important feature of the continuum model, the fact that it can be used to relate pressure group behaviour to the structures and processes of the policy system. When we recall that the points of contact between groups and governments are organizational, it seems sensible to use organizational characteristics as a base for categorization and eventual analysis.

A graphic representation of the continuum framework appears in Table I. To avoid complexity only four points on the continuum have been identified—groups are treated as either issue-oriented, fledgling, mature or institutionalized—and three chief descriptive categories are selected. Within each of the latter, however, a further categorization is attempted so that the objectives of groups are classifiable as single and narrowly defined ("Stop Spadina"); multiple but closely related (those of the Indian-Eskimo Association); multiple, broadly defined and collective (those of the Canadian Civil Liberties Assocation) or multiple, broadly defined and both collective and selective (those of the Canadian Automobile Association). Organizational features have been confined to four, the least sophisticated level being that of the small group that relies on its own membership to do the office work, meet with officials and the media, and to prepare briefs and press releases as well as performing leadership and aggregation functions. At the other extreme is the large multi-faceted organization that at times appears to be run by its professional staff rather than by the membership. Its employees man offices in major centres and provide services that are often quite unrelated to the group's political activities. Labour unions and large religious denominations possess organizational structures of this sort. Levels of communication are divided into two broad groupings that relate to groups' approach to the question of influencing public opinion in order to win government concessions and to their orientation towards non-public communication with officials. Media-oriented categories include, predictably, publicity stunts and protests designed to draw public attention to an issue, public presentations of prepared briefs to officials, commissions of inquiry, regulatory boards and so on, and finally the discreet attempts of well-established organizations to cultivate a favourable climate of public opinion. These techniques will include public service advertising and the range of public relations gimmicks. Media-oriented communication attempts to influence public opinion generally as well as to win specific decisions from government officials. Access-oriented communications, on the other hand, focus on generating a receptive attitude at the political and administrative levels, as well as on achieving more narrowly defined goals. Confrontation is at one extreme of this continuum, but a more frequently used technique is the cultivation of regular and private meetings with officials and politicians. At the other extreme such contact leads to the infiltration of group members into the public establishment, and vice-versa. Mrs. Beryl Plumptre, for example, was a leading figure in consumers' associations for many years prior to her appointment as chairman of the Prices Review Board. At lower levels there is a continuous flow of personnel

TABLE I   THE CONTINUUM FRAMEWORK

CATEGORIES	GROUP CHARACTERISTICS							
	Objectives				Organizational Features			
	single, narrowly defined	multiple but closely related	multiple, broadly defined & collective	multiple, broadly defined, collective & selective	small membership/ no paid staff	membership can support small staff	alliances with other groups/ staff includes professionals	extensive human and financial resources
Institution-alized				▓				▓
Mature			▓				▓	
Fledgling		▓				▓		
Issue-oriented	▓				▓			

CATEGORIES	LEVELS OF COMMUNICATION WITH GOVERNMENT					
	Media-Oriented			Access-Oriented		
	publicity-focused protests	presentation of briefs to public bodies	public relations; image-building ads, press releases	confrontation with politicians, officials	regular contact with officials	regular contact, representation on advisory boards, staff exchanges
Institution-alized			■			■
Mature		■	■		■	
Fledgling		■		■	■	
Issue-oriented	■			■		

between the public bureaucracy and interest groups. A former official of the Canada Council may become executive director of a private foundation promoting public-policy research. Organizations active in the field of international aid, such as Canadian University Service Overseas or World University Service, often lose their career staff to government agencies like the Canadian International Development Agency. In this fashion group interests and public policies are integrated and become mutually supportive.

Analyzed in the context of our previous discussion of the continuum framework and in the light of the studies presented in this volume, Table I suggests that a left to right upward movement will occur as the characteristics of each type of group are identified and located within the table. Generally this movement will occur whether the characteristics identified are group objectives, organizational features, or levels of communication with government. The blocked sections of the table illustrate this tendency. (It should be remembered that the distinctions between each category of group are not clear-cut. Given different resources, different concerns and the variation in the levels of political communication that occur within any complex political system, it is inevitable that few groups will conform exactly to the pattern described here. The pattern is a mean, a central tendency.)

Before leaving this effort to develop an analytical framework for studying pressure groups and before we attempt to apply it to the study of Canadian groups, we shall give it a little more substance by considering it generally in the context of the women's movement, a movement rich in examples of the various types of pressure groups. Women's liberation organizations seem to have started generally as isolated groups concerned with discrete issues related to the role of women in modern society. Small self-help organizations worked to deal with the problems of one-parent families; impediments to career advancement concerned others, and the unequal rights of women before the law still others. Some of these, such as women's business and professional groups, were well established long before women's liberation was labelled as a movement. It was the simultaneous appearance of numerous loosely organized groups of women protesting cultural stereotyping and strict abortion laws that brought public attention to the women's movement and gave these many organizations sufficient sense of common cause to create a movement. Except for a few of the longer established associations, the membership of most of these groups was small and their activities were organized by volunteers. These activities tended to be oriented to attracting public concern for specific issues through stunts, such as bra burning, and demonstrations. Many of these "issue-oriented" groups attained sufficient organizational sophistication to remain active over a period of time, often through the hiring of one or two full-time staff members who provided secretarial, and occasionally professional, assistance and lent continuity to the organization.

Maintenance of an organization of this sort requires a sound financial base and this was usually obtained by extending the membership or by obtaining governmental assistance for specific aspects of women's movement goals—for example, the elimination of job discrimination. Usually the quest for financial security brought a modification of group objectives, when, for example, additional members were obtained by amalgamating two or more groups with similar objectives into one organization pledged to promote those goals all the confederating groups could agree upon. Other members might be attracted by the formulation of a more inclusive statement of goals and removal of goals—such as abortion on demand during the late stages of pregnancy —that were unacceptable to large groups of women. For similar reasons the style of communication changed. Demonstrations still occurred but they were more orderly and less flamboyant, and increasingly they were supplemented or replaced by careful documentation of women's grievances and reasoned discussion of proposed solutions. Confrontation with officials has become less common. As these changes occurred women's lib groups ceased to be issue-oriented and became fledgling and then mature organizations. In the latter stage a few have adopted quite broad goals and have acquired the financial resources needed to support a professional staff capable of recruiting women to the organization, negotiating with public and private agencies, and producing journals such as Ms. that are intended to promote the aims of the movement throughout the population and to encourage women to identify themselves with those aims. At this stage some groups have become institutionalized.

The women's movement illustrates not only pressure group institutionalization but also offers an opportunity to speculate on group reversion. Doubtless many organizations participating in the movement will continue to survive at one stage of development or another. Those concerned with continuing problems or able to provide desirable selective benefits will be the most likely to survive at the institutional or mature level. As the objectives of the movement are attained—or if society as a whole should lose sympathy with those objectives—membership in many groups will decline, forcing consolidation with other organizations, fragmentation into smaller groups concerned with single issues, or complete dissolution.

Table I and the example of women's liberation organizations illustrate a tendency of pressure group development, not an unalterable pattern. Many variations in behaviour occur because groups differ from one another in terms of human, financial and organizational resources. There are many issue-oriented groups that boast competent staff and access to influential politicians and bureaucrats simply because they are supported by people who are themselves influential. In a number of communities, for example, small groups concerned with preserving important landmarks have been remarkably successful for this reason. Again, not all institutional groups have mass memberships, though they pursue broad objectives and enjoy ready access to government. Some learned societies fall into this category. In general, however, it is the contention of this paper that the majority of pressure groups display the characteristies we have attributed to them.

PRESSURE GROUPS IN THE CANADIAN POLICY SYSTEM

Applying general concepts to the real world is never easy, and it is particularly difficult when there are large gaps in our knowledge of that world. Nevertheless, as long as both reader and theorist bear in mind the fact that the exercise is intended only in a limited way to test a hypothesis, then it helps to expose the weaknesses in both theory and data and offers a spring-board for further development. In the following discussion, the exercise also allows us to suggest interpretations of the material presented in the other contributions to this volume, though it is important to point out that the interpretation is that of the present writer and not of his colleagues.

One of the most striking features of current writing on Canadian politics is the continual reiteration of concern at the lack of openness in the policy system.[30] Whether it be a discussion of the structures of central policy making or a study of citizen participation, an investigation of parliamentary procedure or a review of recent developments in Canadian party organization, the limited capacity of the system to absorb and act upon demands generated by the public is a common theme. The root of the problem may lie in the fact that the policy process appears to operate principally through two relatively closed structures, the party system and the bureaucracy, both of which achieve an apex in the Cabinet. A similar, though not identical, process operates in each of the provinces, with the informal but influential network of intergovernmental committees and conferences providing a counterpoise to the authority of any one executive. Although by many standards these structures are considered "open" and "democratic", they may be termed "closed structures" here for two reasons. First, both are hierarchically organized systems which maintain a considerable degree of discipline. In the bureaucracy each officer is expected to report to his immediate superior, and he to his, and so on. There are strong formal and informal sanctions inhibiting him from taking his views to the public and seeking support for them in the newspapers or amongst pressure groups, although such behaviour is not unknown. Discipline is less strict within party structures, but it is nevertheless a potent force. Few backbenchers in the government and opposition parties have persistently challenged the leadership in recent years; the authority of the Cabinet or the leadership is usually cited as the reason for this. At lower levels similar constraints appear.

Equally important, however, is the fact that the Canadian political system is based only to a limited extent on a pluralistic, competitive, approach to decision making. Some competition exists, of course— intergovernmental rivalry arises out of the concurrent exercise of power or the unclear definition of jurisdiction—but within each government there is relatively little of the functional rivalry which typifies inter-agency competition in the United States. Similarly, the fact that the executive operates within a cabinet and parliamentary system of govern-ment means that rivalries between legislators cannot be readily ex-ploited.

The consequence is that the Canadian system places a good deal less emphasis on issue generation than does the neighboring United States system. Instead it places a premium on access, and access need not be a function of publicity. Depending on the strength of the source of a demand, inputs may be channelled through a broad range of commun-ications facilities or through very few, regardless of the importance of the issue. In fact the system presents great impediments to those who want to raise new issues and who lack either the knowledge or the power to command access. They find it difficult to locate the most effective channel through which to communicate with politicians or ad-ministrators. Consequently, if the public authorities are unreceptive to an issue, it may be years before it is considered, if it is discussed at all. However, if the public authority is receptive to an issue, it can act with despatch. Information can be made to move quickly within the system and resolution of conflict can be restricted to a small group of actors. The Canadian policy system, then, tends to favour elite groups, making functional accommodative, consensus-seeking techniques of political communication, rather than conflict-oriented techniques that are directed towards the achievement of objectives through arousing public opinion.

The effect this has on pressure group behaviour is not hard to imagine. Generally the operation of the policy system indicates that we should expect to find that those groups that have maintained a fairly consistent level of success in achieving their political objectives, have done so because they have maintained close connections with one or other of the principal policy structures and because they have avoided jeopardizing the intimacy of those connections through appealing either to Parliament or to the public at large. Effective interaction with the Canadian policy system then, depends on the cultivation of access to those public decision makers having influence in the policy area of greatest concern to the pressure group, and a willingness to accept short-term defeats of specific proposals in the interests of continuing favor-able relations over the long run. Consultation and the search for accommodation and consensus become the outstanding characteristics of government–pressure group relations, with some students of the relationship arguing that government is nearly always the dominant partner, and several pointing out that it is not unusual for Canadian governments to create pressure groups in order to foster relations with "special publics" and to promote a demand for policies which particular departments are anxious to adopt.[31] It follows that groups that are not accommodative and consensus-seeking (issue-oriented groups) have very little chance of achieving desired changes in government policy. They

19

may, through their use of the media, achieve some short-term modifications of policy, but they are limited by their organizational weakness,
by the inability of the general public to maintain interest in an issue,
and by the fact that established groups tend to avoid publicly endorsing
their causes for fear of antagonizing influential public officials.

To examine these propositions more clearly we shall look at the
pressure group behaviour patterns that have been identified by the
contributors to this volume as occurring at the Cabinet, parliamentary
and administrative levels. We shall also consider their reports of the
fashion in which the operation of the federal system seems to affect
pressure group behaviour, noting that to some extent it encourages
activity that varies from the norm that prevails in other parts of the
policy system.

Turning first to the Cabinet influence on pressure group behaviour,
we are struck by the similarity between Donald Chant's conviction that
"one should approach the real centers of power: Cabinet members . . .
and other political leaders," and R. MacGregor Dawson's view that the
Cabinet is the "centre of gravity" of the Canadian political system.[32]
For as long as they have been studied in Canada, pressure groups have
attempted to work by appealing primarily not to the voters in general,
nor even to their representatives in Parliament or legislature, but to the
Cabinet. As early as 1900, officials of the Canadian Manufacturers'
Association believed that they "should have influence with whatever
government may be in power."[33] Though its early lobbying activities
embraced "interviewing Cabinet ministers, members of the House of
Commons and Senate, and . . . distributing pamphlets," the CMA
seems to have focused its attention fairly quickly on the Cabinet.[34]
Analysis of H. G. Thorburn's study of the revision of combines legislation, carried out half a century later, reveals that the majority of
representations concerning the legislation were made to the responsible
ministers.[35] Some twenty groups made 28 formal representations to the
government. Only twelve appeared before the Commons Committee
on Banking and Commerce when it reviewed the proposed legislation in
1960. An even clearer indication of pressure groups' appreciation of the
contemporary federal power structure was suggested by the fact that
only one group accepted an invitation to appear before the parallel
Senate Committee hearing,[36] and only one group attempted to solicit
the support of private members.[37] The studies in this volume suggest
that the Cabinet continues to occupy this central role. The Cabinet is
the final decision-making authority in the political system and the
pressure groups, whether issue-oriented or institutional, behave accordingly, attempting either to secure access or to embarrass ministers
into compliance.

It is in their approach to the administrative arm of government that
institutional and issue-oriented groups differ most markedly in perception and technique. The former take to heart the fact that Cabinet
authority necessarily devolves upon the public service, bringing with it

considerable responsibility for the formulation and implementation of policy. The power this bestows upon the administrative arm is augmented by the practice in Canada of conducting policy discussions away from public view. In a system which emphasizes the political responsibility of the minister, the pressure group and civil service participants in policy formulation prefer to avoid public discussions of issues, relying on co-operation and consultation, rather than on conflict, to achieve their objectives. The extent of their interaction is illustrated below in Helen Jones Dawson's description of the consultations which take place during policy formulation. She concludes that "the number of times that groups are consulted or may make an opportunity to exercise influence is considerable." Her description makes it apparent, however, that such frequent and ready access to administrators is largely the privilege of institutional groups.[38] Issue-oriented groups lack the knowledge, the resources and the longevity to influence officials on a day-to-day basis over an extended period.

Influence and access are double-edged instruments, however, as Barry shows in his discussion of the attempts made by institutional groups to change Canada's policy toward Biafra. He concludes that because institutionalized groups have committed themselves to non-public discussions of policy, they can, when governmental opinion differs from their own, have much less political effect than issue-oriented groups commanding broad public support. The high costs of maintaining access are also reflected in J. E. Anderson's observation that "in Canada the relations between civil servants and pressure groups are usually dominated by civil servants."[39] His point is supported by Pross and Barry whose analyses suggest that government agencies can withstand considerable input pressure from the external environment, and that they may significantly influence that environment, if not dominate it. The fact that external pressure for or against a particular policy is seldom unanimous, even within a specific group, and that such divisions can be exploited by an agency, enhances its power. The preservation of the capacity to communicate easily and effectively with bureaucracy, and the legitimation that governmental recognition implies is often achieved at the expense of organizational freedom of action, sometimes even of perverting the original role of the organization.[40]

Students of Canadian pressure group behaviour have traditionally argued that the logic of the country's parliamentary system forces lobbyists to focus on Cabinet and bureaucracy, rather than on House and Senate, if they wish to achieve their objectives.[41] "Working in a parliamentary system", Helen Jones Dawson has observed, "it is inevitable that Canadian organizations find it essential to influence policy and legislation before the parliamentary stage is reached."[42] Because bills can be substantially amended only with considerable embarrassment to the government, concessions to pressure groups have to be won before the parliamentary stage is reached. Lacking an incentive to use Parliament, most groups have tended to ignore it. In fact, the very nature of the parliamentary process has acted to discourage consultation between groups and members since it involves airing in public differences with government concerning proposed legislation, and the co-operative and consensus-seeking approach that typifies pre-legislative consultation is thus endangered.

Recently, there has been some debate over the extent of pressure group neglect of Parliament and the provincial legislatures. Presthus has suggested that pressure groups interact with legislators rather more frequently than has been generally supposed.[43] His view receives some support from Barry's contribution to this volume. Barry shows that the co-operation of Parliament and the media had a great deal to do with the prominence achieved by the pro-Biafra groups, and suggests that because issue-oriented groups are likely to utilize a wider range of communications devices than institutional groups, they are more likely than the latter to enhance the role of Parliament in policy formation. His analysis also demonstrates, however, the limitations of the parliamentary forum as a vehicle for influencing policy, for while Parliament and the media responded to the issue and Parliament in particular placed the government under considerable pressure, the lack of general support from the public convinced the government that it did not have to modify its position substantially. In the end, despite intense activity on the part of all pressure groups, the advice of the administrative arm, chiefly the Department of External Affairs, was followed. The uncertain outcome of exerting parliamentary influence leads Dawson in this volume and elsewhere to continue to argue that pressure groups do not spend a great deal of energy influencing legislators. Byers's recent study of changes in defence policy endorses her view.[44] On the other hand, it is possible that recent changes in parliamentary procedure and the strengthening of the committee system have forced pressure groups to play a more public role in recent months, a possibility that is considered by Aucoin in his article on pressure groups and recent changes in the policy-making process. Should such changes be taking place, it is possible that institutional groups will become more adept at promoting and participating in public debate and that the position of issue-oriented groups will be considerably strengthened.

The role of pressure groups in federal-provincial relations is the least distinct of those discussed thus far. Some writers, notably Simeon, have found evidence suggesting that the role is minimal.[45] Kwavnick and Bucovetsky in their essays in this collection question this view. David Kwavnick, examining the experience of organized labour and students' associations, contends that since the distribution of powers does influence "the structure, cohesion and even the existence of interest groups," then such groups "may attempt to influence the distribution of powers between . . . governments." While Kwavnick's investigation does not go beyond establishing the fact that some groups participate in the division-of-powers game, Bucovetsky's examination of the tax reform debate demonstrates that the mining and oil interests successfully exploited federal-provincial relations. Endowed with considerable economic and institutional power, these industries also dominate specific regions and constituencies. Pressure from the regions coupled with economic might created an "inexorable pressure" that provincial leaders could not resist. They in turn persuaded Ottawa to abandon important elements of its proposed tax reforms.

These studies, however, make only a small dent in our ignorance. We need to know a great deal more about the operation and structure of provincial groups, their influence on provincial governments and their utilization of the processes of federal-provincial diplomacy. Similarly, as Dawson indicates, we need a firmer understanding of the structure and behaviour of federated groups and their role in the creation—and dissolution—of national goals. For the moment we know only enough to suggest that federalism is both an important influence on pressure group behaviour and that group manipulation of intergovernmental relations may have a significant effect on the policy process.

Our discussion thus far has emphasized the role the policy system plays in promoting pressure group activity that is consultative rather than conflict-oriented, and supportive of public bureaucracies rather than openly critical. We have argued that institutional groups more than issue-oriented groups flourish in this system. We have also, however, cited some evidence that occasions arise—and they may be increasing—when it is advantageous for pressure groups to defy the accepted norms of pressure group-agency relations and to encourage public review of issues. The success of Pollution Probe in exploiting public concern for environmental deterioration has encouraged many issue-oriented groups to seek public exposure. The Biafra debate saw an interesting extension of this: when an established group found that it could not influence policy but dared not publicly press its view, some members affiliated with more radical, publicity-oriented groups. Such alliances are extremely informal and if unsuccessful can be broken off at will. They offer the possibility, however, that public pressure may succeed where behind-the-scenes efforts have failed.

Problems in obtaining access or a failure to influence decision makers are the chief factors encouraging pressure groups to find alternative access points to the decision system and to "go public." But they are not the sole factors. Aucoin's review of recent trends suggests that parliamentary and Cabinet reforms will encourage greater public activity on the part of institutional, as well as issue-oriented groups. The issue explored by Pross suggests that external support may be helpful, perhaps even necessary, in specific policy discussions and thus may be encouraged by the agency. Finally Bucovetsky's analysis points out the fact that because bureaucracy is not monolithic the objectives of one agency may be thwarted by alliances between other agencies, and the affected interest groups. The complexity of the political communications process is thus considerably enhanced, and we are left with the impression that while agencies may dominate relations with specific groups, fragmentation of interests prevents their complete control of entire policy arenas. Consequently a place exists for issue-oriented groups, a place which from time to time gives them considerable influence and possibly growing prominence.

CONCLUSIONS

In defining pressure groups as organizations whose members act together to influence public policy in order to promote their common interest, we have suggested that their chief characteristics are the possession of a formal organizational framework, the ability to articulate and aggregate common interests, and the desire to act in the political system through exerting influence rather than exercising the responsibilities of government. Working from this base we have attempted to construct an analytical approach to pressure group behaviour that is applicable in various political systems, but particularly in the Canadian political system.

Our analysis identifies four chief functions of pressure groups—communication, legitimation, self-regulation, and quasi-official administrative functions—as well as numerous sub-systemic functions which help determine the extent of the resources the pressure group has to deploy in acting in the political system. As well, our analysis has used the organizational base of pressure groups to establish a typology that permits us to consider all pressure groups within a single framework. Application of this framework—or continuum model—in the context of the Canadian policy system suggests that issue-oriented groups, though they have a well-defined role in the system, tend to be considerably less favoured by the relatively closed nature of the Canadian policy structures than are the more fully institutionalized groups.

Earlier we confessed that much of our analysis of the role of pressure groups in the Canadian policy system rested on a very insecure data base. In particular, though we do know a great deal about the relations between groups and governments, our knowledge has not been systematically gathered, nor has speculation been convincingly tested, though recent work by Presthus, Kwavnick and Manzer has brought us a long way towards methical documentation of data. We still need to know a great deal more about the intra-systemic functions of Canadian groups. Why do people join them? Why do some groups and some people prefer certain types of action to others? What resources are available to different types of groups? Does an issue-oriented group select certain tactics of communication out of necessity or predilection? What happens to its membership if and when the group becomes institutionalized? Do institutionalized groups occasionally become issue-oriented? If so, how and why? These and many other questions must be answered before we say authoritatively whether the sort of speculation that has been indulged in throughout this discussion has any utility in the analysis of Canadian political life.

NOTES

1. This view contrasts with that of David Truman, *The Governmental Process*, (New York: Knopf, 1951), p. 36, but is supported by J. D. Stewart, *British Pressure Groups: Their Role in Relation to the House of Commons*, (Oxford, 1958) and W. J. M. Mackenzie, "Pressure Groups in British Government," (*British Journal of Sociology*, June, 1955).

2.* Clark, 1939. Recent monographs include Dion (1967), Presthus (1973, 1974) and Kwavnick (1972).

3. Presthus, 1971, p. 446.

4. Notably Dion (1969, a and b), Manzer (1969), Porter (1965), Kwavnick (1972), Presthus (1973, 1974), Engelmann and Schwartz (1967), and Van Loon and Whittington (1971).

5. Engelmann and Schwartz (1967), p. 96.

6. *Ibid.*, p. 113.

7. Van Loon and Whittington (1971), p. 305.

8. *Ibid.*, p. 317.

9. Henry W. Ehrmann, ed., *Interest Groups on Four Continents*, (Pittsburgh: University of Pittsburgh Press, 1958), p. 5.

10. Johnson (1970), pp. 2, 5.

11. Manzer, (1969), p. 106.

12. Taylor's recent (1972) discussion of Quebec health policy offers an interesting illustration of the conflicts that arise when the state extends its activities in a field that has traditionally been supervised by professional groups.

13. Hawkins (1972), p. 301.

14. See Meisel (1965).

15. Ehrmann, *op. cit.*, pp. 3–4.

16. Dawson (1963).

17. Manzer (1969), p. 104. Collective benefits may be enjoyed regardless of an individual's membership in an organization. Selective benefits can only be obtained through membership.

18. *Ibid.* See also Clark (1939), pp. 40–63.

19. When we refer to the determination of the resource base we recognize that the political activist in the group leadership will find the presence of selective inducements a mixed blessing. They attract members whose attitudes may impede resolute, unequivocal action. Furthermore, some forms of political action may have to be modified because they could threaten continuation of certain services. These and other politically dysfunctional effects will be examined later in this discussion.

20. Kwavnick (1970), p. 58.

21. *Ibid.*, the case is developed more fully in Kwavnick (1972).

22. Phillip Selznick, *Leadership in Administration*, (New York: Harper and Row, 1957), p. 21.

23. *Ibid.*, p. 5.

24. *Ibid.*, p. 20.

25. *Ibid.*, p. 139. Particular competence has, as Selznick suggests, the corollary of particular incompetence, a factor which explains inflexibility in many institutions. A pressure group that is adept at quiet diplomacy often lacks the institutional capacity to undertake a publicity campaign.

26. Freda Hawkins' description of voluntary groups working in the immigration field could be applied to many other issue-oriented groups. They "do not have an office, never keep records, and simply respond to the needs of the

---

* Complete bibliographical information for this and all other short entries will be found in the "Selected Bibliography" at the end of the book.

moment. Their program, objectives, and performance may change totally from year to year. Only a very few officials and experienced community workers in a particular city who have been working with these agencies, committees, and groups for some time can really assess the quality and usefulness of the work they do." (1972, p. 294.)

27. See, for example, Hagy, 1969.

28. Pollution Probe offers an excellent Canadian illustration.

29. Space prohibits adequate discussion of these problems. Francis G. Castles illustrates them when he suggests that though the categories of 'interest' groups (which protect shared sectional interests) and 'attitude' groups (which promote shared attitudes about common causes or specific objectives) overlap considerably, "one is able to assign a group to one or the other category quite easily." *Pressure Groups and Political Culture* (London: Routledge and Kegan Paul, 1967), p. 2. As long as one is content only to label groups, Castles' approach suffices. Once one attempts to describe relations between groups and their place in the political system, the typology is more hindrance than help because it is static and imprecise. Again Castles' study offers an illustration.

30. See, for example, Ronald S. Ritchie, *An Institute for Research on Public Policy* (Ottawa: Information Canada, 1971); the recent work (unpublished) by Stephen Clarkson dealing with Liberal party; C. E. S. Franks, "The Dilemma of Standing Committees in the Canadian House of Commons," *Canadian Journal of Political Science*, IV, No. 4 (December, 1971, pp. 461–476, and John Sewell, *Up Against City Hall* (Toronto: James Lewis and Samuel, 1972).

31. For example, the complaint of Anthony Adamson, an official of the Community Planning Association of Canada, that that organization "was called into being by government subsidy as a stooge of the government to sell town planning to the inexpert." *Civic Administration* (June, 1970), p. 2. This practice has a long tradition in Canada—early farmers' organizations offer a good example—but its increasing use as a means of encouraging issue-oriented groups has far-reaching implications for the policy system and deserves further research.

32. *The Government of Canada* (Toronto: University of Toronto Press, 1954), p. 197.

33. Clark, (1939), p. 16.

34. *Ibid., passim.*

35. Thorburn (1964).

36. *Ibid.,* p. 172.

37. *Ibid.,* p. 160–162.

38. See also Dawson (1960) and Taylor (1960).

39. Dawson (1967).

40. See, for example, Johnson (1969).

41. Engelmann and Schwartz (1967), Van Loon and Whittington, (1971), Dawson (1967), and Anderson (1970).

42. Dawson (1967), p. 454.

43. Engelmann and Schwartz, *op. cit.*

44. Byers (1971).

45. Richard Simeon, *Federal-Provincial Diplomacy: The Making of Recent Policy in Canada* (Toronto: University of Toronto Press, 1972), pp. 280–283.

2.

The preceding paper suggested a framework for analyzing pressure groups as political communication mechanisms capable of adapting to the policy system within which they are located. The discussion, somewhat general and theoretical, posited an organizational continuum for categorizing pressure groups and suggested a number of structural and behavioural characteristics of the extremes—institutional and issue-oriented groups. The two following articles present an opportunity to examine each type more closely and to weigh the validity of the suggested conceptual framework.

The first of these discussions, by Helen Jones Dawson, is concerned almost exclusively with the type of group that has been identified as institutional, particularly the institutional group operating at the national level. The analysis concentrates on the structure and behaviour of the groups as they are influenced by Canada's federal system of government, and by relations with the Cabinet, Parliament and the federal civil service.

Viewed in the light of the continuum model, Professor Dawson's analysis makes it extremely clear that very few Canadian pressure groups possess all the features of the model institutional group. Many are strapped for funds; only a handful maintain a large and specialized supporting staff, and most have been slow to avail themselves of the full range of political communication devices—appearances before parliamentary committees, cultivation of interest on the part of MPs, etc.— that they might use. At the same time, however, the analysis shows that established Canadian groups demonstrate many classic features of institutional pressure groups, particularly in their tendency to avoid open conflict with associates in the civil service, and in the inclination of long-established representatives of some groups to share the points of view of the officials with whom they must work.

There is no doubt that the Canadian political system has been the single most important influence on the structure and behaviour pattern of institutionalized pressure groups in this country, despite a tendency on the part of both practitioners and analysts to look to the U.S. for models. As Professor Dawson points out, "those groups which have operated effectively over a prolonged period have had to tailor both their method and organization in order to maximize their impact on the political institutions". Numerous examples are cited to establish this point, but the most conclusive evidence is found in the relations between pressure groups and Cabinet and in the impact of the Canadian federal system on the structure of national pressure groups. The friendly relations frequently existing between Canadian Cabinet ministers and pressure group representatives, the relatively easy access to ministers, and sometimes to the entire Cabinet, even the availability of the Prime Minister—all these are factors which distinguish Canadian pressure groups from those of other countries. Similarly, Canada's federal system appears to have had the effect of weakening the structure of many pressure groups, making it more difficult to organize concerted and sustained influence on federal decision-making. It would be interesting to speculate on the extent to which such organizational barriers have impeded free-flowing political communication in this country, perhaps thus exacerbating regional alienation.

Helen Jones Dawson has written a number of articles on Canadian pressure groups, and lectures on political parties and pressure groups at the University of Western Ontario.

pressure groups for guidance. Although some of the tactics adopted by pressure groups in Canada are similar to those in other countries, the Canadian groups emerge with distinctive personalities and habits.

THE IMPACT OF FEDERALISM

Canada's brand of federalism has put its stamp on the character of Canadian pressure groups. It affects their structure and frequently their ability to represent their clientele effectively in Ottawa. This is most noticeable in groups concerned with problems where jurisdiction is shared by both federal and provincial governments such as agriculture, labour and fisheries, or where the jurisdiction is not yet clear, as in consumer protection and environmental control. Groups with widespread interests have in common a great variety of weaknesses in terms of organization, financing and difficulty in formulating policy[1], which in turn impede their ability to influence government.

The first and most obvious effect of the federal system of government is the adoption by most of the national organizations of parallel federal structures. They must operate at least on federal and provincial levels. Most are weak federations whose component parts, the provincial organizations or branches, and in some cases functional affiliates as well, tend to dominate national headquarters in policy determination. This gives rise to serious problems when provincial branches have reservations about national policies. The fact that the national organization's executive or board of directors or both is often composed of regional or provincial representatives, (usually branch presidents), means that the achievement of a consensus on desirable national, as opposed to regional or provincial, policies often verges on the impossible. Consequently the national headquarters is frequently unable to present a vigorous, consistent, or sometimes even united front to the federal government. Furthermore, for reasons that are not always clear, provincial branches and other affiliates tend to keep re-electing the same personnel to the national executive, board of directors and committees. Not surprisingly, many organizations have the same personnel for years at a stretch. This has two consequences: an ageing executive body and difficulty in initiating policy changes. This may not have been too serious, and may possibly have had some advantages when the same people remained in the Cabinet, often in the same portfolios, for many years, but when governments, portfolios, and the whole style of politics change rapidly, it leaves the groups in a vulnerably static position. A further complication of the federal structure of the groups is that increased national membership is dependent to a large extent upon the popularity of the provincial organizations. These latter, if they are to operate effectively and to attract local support must reflect the needs and aspirations of their provincial clientele[2], and in many cases this will also involve tailoring their policies in order to gain utmost acceptability by provincial governments. For example, the attitudes of the Social Credit government in Alberta, the New Democratic Party government in Saskatchewan and the Conservative government in Ontario toward producer-controlled marketing boards or the regulation of trading stamps were all different. Provincial organizations are apt to reflect these attitudes as opposed to the national organization's avowed policy. Thus many national pressure groups are frequently confronted with the following paradox: if a provincial organization permits its policies to be too profoundly influenced by national as opposed to local considerations, it will lose support among its local clientele, and this in turn will diminish the national organization's political impact; whereas, if the provincial organizations adhere too rigidly to policies approved at the local level, it may be impossible to achieve any kind of national policy at all. Although this is not uncommon, it rarely becomes public knowledge as it did in one case where a group official informed a House committee that his organization was unable to achieve a national policy due to "the variety of views among the member organizations."[3] Another important factor in this equation is an apprehension at the national level that in case of disagreement between the policy of the national organization and provincial government policy, the provincial organization may support the provincial government. Two important consequences stem from this difficulty. First, the public disagreement of a provincial branch, especially an important one, as with the Ontario branch of the Consumers' Association on the issue of trading stamps, can severely damage the impact of the national stand[4]. Second, unpopular or ineffectively pursued policies on the part of the national organization have an adverse effect on membership which in turn also affects its political impact and financial stability.[5] The later discussion of the way in which groups mobilize help from provincial governments[6] and the way in which the representative nature of the Cabinet affects the behaviour of the groups, makes the apprehension of the national organization seem realistic.

Federal organizational structure does not have as many difficulties for groups whose major concerns lie within either provincial jurisdiction, such as the various teachers' associations, or federal jurisdiction, like the Royal Canadian Legion. However, the latter type at least shares to a certain extent another problem which is of almost equal importance to their effectiveness in Ottawa. That is that the national executive is bound by the decisions of the non-expert general meeting. This does not permit group officials any flexibility in discussions with government officials. If a new proposal is put forward by the central government between general meetings, there must of necessity be a long wait while provincial branches are consulted. The additional restrictions imposed on the national organizations in attempting to influence government decisions affecting their clientele by delay or inability to reach a consensus of its regional or provincial branches have very serious repercussions on their effectiveness and sometimes on their working relationship with government officials. This becomes startlingly obvious when Canadian groups are compared with similar organizations in the United States and Great Britain.[7]

Confusion over legislative jurisdiction produces a number of problems for the groups. The most notable are the difficulties that arise out of the search for *intra vires* legislation. It is not always easy to achieve legislation that the courts will accept. A well-known instance of this is the difficulty Canadian governments have experienced in establishing regulatory control over the marketing of agricultural products. After thirty or forty years of controversy in and out of the courts, the issue is by no means settled. Conversely, judicial decisions have sometimes upset established patterns of regulation, causing problems for groups with clientele whose interests overlap jurisdictions. The decision in the case of *Attorney-General of New Brunswick vs. Winner* in 1954, for example, meant that trucking concerns and bus lines operating across provincial boundaries would be subject to federal regulation, whereas previously they had been regulated only by the provinces concerned, putting some concerns in a disadvantageous competitive position.[8]

Perhaps the pressure groups find that the most frustrating political outcome of the Canadian constitutional structure is the fact that both the federal and provincial governments often justify inaction on the grounds that each lacks jurisdiction.[9] On the other hand, some pressure groups damage their credibility at both levels of government by their insensitivity to the constitutional realities or simple ignorance of the barriers which stand in the way of their proposals, as in the case of one group spokesman who advocated giving "authoritarian" powers to federal agencies to control provincial boards.[10] Politicians complain that some of the most peculiar proposals are put forward by militant organizations which deliberately ignore the constitution in their attempts to rally vociferous support from their members.

The task of persuading several governments to enact uniform legislation is often just as difficult as that of persuading one or more to accept responsibility for a field of action. Yet lack of uniformity between the legislation of different governments can cause considerable hardship for the clientele of groups with interests that straddle jurisdictions. Conservation of the Atlantic salmon fisheries was hindered by the inability of the federal government to persuade provincial governments to pass uniform regulations.[11] Moreover, organizations which have a clientele basically affected by provincial laws must nevertheless try to exert influence at the federal level when legislation affecting them conflicts with provincial law. Because such organizations do not maintain close contact with the federal capital they find this a difficult endeavour. The National Association of Canadian Credit Unions encountered this problem between 1969 and 1971 because the federal government's comprehensive tax reform legislation threatened to impose guaranteed reserve requirements different from those authorized by some provincial governments, the traditional regulator of credit unions.[12]

Further problems arise from the complications of co-operative federalism. The necessity of keeping in close touch with both levels of government on the myriad programs operating under joint control has proved a difficult and frustrating task as indicated by a brief from the Saskatchewan Wheat Pool.

> It [the Agricultural and Rural Development Act] started out to offer a programme and federal money to assist the provinces in matters of resource allocation. However, we see very little of that . . . programme in operation. The fault may lie . . . with the federal programme . . . although we suspect the programme and the ideas behind it are good. The fault may lie with the provincial governments . . . some . . . have acted with more vigour than others. And some fault may lie with organizations like the Pool which might have done more. We suspect that . . . farmer organizations have been less at fault than the others . . .[13]

Also, the amount of coordination in which farm organizations are involved, as a result of the ARDA program, is immense for it is necessary to stimulate action at both federal and provincial levels as well as to keep track of individual agreements that the federal government undertakes with provincial governments.[14] Since the provincial governments are responsible for administering the agreed-upon programs, the close involvement of the groups in offering advice on the administration of these complex programs tends to bring provincial organizations into closer alliance with the philosophy of the provincial administrations. There are apt to be sharp differences of opinion between provincial and federal governments as to priorities, and these frequently are reflected in the attitudes of the relevant national and provincial organizations.[15]

The problems associated with unclear constitutional jurisdiction and group difficulty in aggregating client demands into cohesive country-wide policies are the cause of major weaknesses in pressure groups claiming national support. They affect not only the groups' ability to perform effectively their role in influencing federal government policies, but have also led, as noted earlier, to financial instability.[16] The problem is most serious for groups which depend upon "voluntary assessment" from component organizations whether of a geographical, commodity or functional variety. The financial weakness is exacerbated by the necessity of maintaining well-staffed offices at both levels, and it also has an adverse effect on the frequency of board and executive meetings, thus compounding the normal communication problems extant in large national organizations. Lack of money has led to restriction of activity at the national level or to acceptance of a government subsidy or grant[17]. The latter can threaten the independence of the groups in question. The Consumers' Association, which until 1971 got more money from the federal government than from membership fees, maintains that there has been no interference, and this is supported by statements of government officials[18]. Nevertheless, the long-term viability and continued influence of organizations in receipt of government money is open to doubt.

Possibly these financial problems may help to explain one of the most distinctive features of the Canadian groups, and that is their attitude toward national headquarters. There is reluctance to have a national office at all, more than reluctance to locate it in Ottawa, and determination to keep it small and poor. Indeed group officials complain that chronic poverty leads to understaffing, and thus prevents their organizations from providing proper services for clientele.[19]

This is one of those areas in which it is only possible to advance educated guesses about the underlying reasons. In any case the result of this attitude is lack of professionalism and expertise. Unlike their American and British counterparts, very few of the groups have developed a large, specialized headquarters staff capable of arguing every case or problem effectively with their thoroughly professional and well-briefed opposite numbers in the civil service. Professionals do not expect, as the clientele sometimes does, to sway anyone with passionate but unsupported cases. Instead, they develop a widespread network of contacts throughout all levels of government. They know better than to waste a minister's time with a problem the senior civil service can handle, and they also know which problems they can take to a branch or divisional head, rather than bother a deputy minister or one of his assistants. Even organizations of moderate size, like the Federation of Agriculture, the Consumers' Association or the Canadian Trucking Association, can establish a moderately satisfactory set of relations with the civil service. They cannot, however, provide specialized exepertise or well-documented briefs on a wide range of subjects of varying degrees of importance to their clientele. Astonishingly few organizations, notably the Canadian Medical Association, the Canadian Legion, the Canadian Federation of Mayors and Municipalities, the Canadian Labour Congress, and the Canadian Council on Social Development, maintain large staffs with some pretence of expertise.

A series of interrelated attitudes lie behind membership approach to the subject of national headquarters. Fear of being or acting like a pressure group or lobby, which will be discussed at a later stage, is a factor. Moreover, rank-and-file members see local and provincial activities as being more interesting and more worthwhile. There is unwillingness to invest money in something for which the membership can see no tangible benefits.[20] In addition, members feel that they may lose control of policy formulation to "national", as headquarters is often called. This is partly due to provincial[21] or regional feeling which causes local membership to regard Ottawa as remote, and perhaps hostile. As mentioned earlier, the federal-style structure of the organizations' governing bodies does not promote the development of a national outlook. There is also apprehension that large national office would be just as bureaucratic and unfeeling as the government, plus a definite suspicion that pressure group officials, elected or appointed, who are in constant contact with government officials ultimately come to think more like the officials they deal with than like the membership.[22] However, the groups which have been effective in influencing government policies over a prolonged period reject this attitude in favour of a staff with widespread connections in Ottawa.

Clearly Canadian federalism has had, and continues to have, a formidable impact upon the organization and behaviour of the pressure groups. It has complicated and confused their tasks while increasing their expenses and policy formulation problems. Although the resulting lack of cohesion gives the general impression of ineffectiveness and confusion,[23] it is possible that this is the result of both their clientele and governments expecting federated groups to perform too many functions at too many levels. At any rate, few national pressure groups have broken out of the vicious circle involving finances, membership and effectiveness, and as a result they are unable to offer services to their clientele which would demonstrate their usefulness. It seems as if the centrifugal forces of federalism may have been more important to Canadian groups than to similar American ones[24], although admittedly not all the reasons are as yet clear.

Relations with the Cabinet

Groups which aspire to continuing influence have to master the art of bringing their views to the attention of the Cabinet as a whole, and to the sometimes even more important and more subtle endeavour of persuading influential ministers to take a sympathetic attitude toward the needs of their clientele. While the existence of a cabinet-parliamentary system in Canada means that the Canadian groups face an entirely different set of circumstances from those of their American counterparts, it does not mean that they are carbon copies of British groups. The Cabinet, as in Britain, is responsible for co-ordinating policies, initiating legislation, for ensuring that it progresses through the legislative process, and for overseeing the administration of the multitude of statutes and regulations which affect the everyday lives of all citizens. These factors alone would make the Cabinet an important point of attack for the groups. Add to this the fact that once the government's bills are introduced into Parliament, they are generally ensured of passage with only minor changes in detail, and it becomes apparent that it is necessary for organizations which hope to shape government policies in general to make their views known to Cabinet members long before the parliamentary stage is reached. Aside from that basic and very important similiarity, Canadian groups face problems and opportunities somewhat different from the British ones. These differences not only determine which points of attack the groups find most useful, but also influence the structure of the groups.

One important difference is the fact that the Canadian Cabinet is more accessible. Its annual sessions with major pressure groups to discuss their policy recommendations[25] contrast strongly with practice in Britain, where, according to G. Wootton, "In all probability no Cabinet has ever received a deputation from a pressure group . . ."[26] Although the British consider this particular Canadian foible a waste of time, it provides the Cabinet with an opportunity to expose each group to the searching and sometimes hostile questions of ministers who are interested in other projects or policies or perhaps preoccupied with problems of a regional or provincial nature. The Canadian Prime Minister has also been more accessible to pressure groups and their delegations.[27] Many Canadian groups regarded him as a court of last resort; it remains unclear why they should expect him to persuade his colleagues to reverse a decision already made public. Individual ministers are also more accessible. Any organized interest group of stature can usually find a federal minister to speak to its annual meeting; some attract several. Some ministers, indeed, are expected to attend the meetings of organizations with which their departments have close contact.[28] Similar occasions in Britain are both rare and more formal.[29] Although Canadian ministers sometimes are cool towards groups which organize protest demonstrations, they usually try to accommodate groups which give them sufficient warning. This is in contrast to Britain where ministers may refuse to see groups if their protests are considered extreme or if they have not yet been accorded what is usually described as "official recognition".[30] Furthermore, it appears to be easier for pressure group officials in Ottawa to see ministers on an informal basis and thus develop personal contacts which sometimes help to ease difficult discussions or misunderstandings. However, easier access does not necessarily mean that it is easier to influence a minister or the Cabinet in determining policy. Indeed there is considerable informal evidence to indicate that ministers are very hard-headed in assessing not only the merits of the arguments advanced but also a group's popularity with the public, and whether or not it speaks for those persons or interests it claims to represent.

The other major difference encountered by the Canadian groups, as compared to the British ones, is the representative nature of the Cabinet. The possibility of applying pressure not only on the minister responsible for a given policy, but also on the provincial or regional representatives in the Cabinet is open to British groups only under very unusual circumstances. Canadian pressure groups can and do appeal to these representatives for both aid and advice. They also ask provincial governments, regardless of their political affiliation, to use their influence. Although one might assert that this type of approach is an "almost daily" occurrence, it is extremely difficult to document. The following examples can at least demonstrate the type of activity that occurs. One involves the Hon. George Nowlan, Minister of National Revenue 1957–62, sitting for a Nova Scotia constituency, who indicated that he had received a deputation from local mining interests, and telephone calls from the Nova Scotia premier in regard to increased subsidies for the Nova Scotia coal mining industry.[31] In another case, the British Columbia Cattlemen's Association described how the then Minister of Justice, representing Kamloops, British Columbia, had intervened on its behalf with the Minister of Finance.[32] Early in 1972 the Vancouver Board of

Trade boasted that it had been able to get the Canadian Development Corporation's headquarters situated in that city by speaking to British Columbia ministers in the federal Cabinet.[33] Although this type of approach is much used in Canada, there is no way of determining the frequency of its success. A careful look at the composition of delegations when presenting their annual briefs reveals that they usually display a careful geographical distribution; so does the group of Cabinet ministers facing them.

This technique can have both advantages and disadvantages. The advantages lie in friendly interchanges between ministers and delegates from the same region. However, dissension within the group membership is apt to lead to embarrassing questions. It seems not to matter whether disaffection stems from one particular sector of a trade association, an affiliated organization or a provincial or regional branch in a federal-type organization; the merest hint that the national organization does not really speak for all of its membership weakens its case before the Cabinet. This can have serious repercussions, ranging all the way from a decision to ignore the group completely to a division within the Cabinet which could delay a final decision. The usefulness of exerting pressure through the provincial governments is variable and depends upon a large number of intangibles among which the most prominent would be the general state of relations between the federal and provincial governments, or the assessment of the provincial or regional representatives in Cabinet of how an issue might affect the number of seats gained or lost in their areas.

Another important factor for the groups to consider is the ability of a minister to persuade Cabinet to accept, or even to consider, policy changes advocated by the pressure groups most frequently concerned with matters under the jurisdiction of his development. Although the Canadian pressure groups, unlike the British groups, have not had to worry about whether or not "their minister" is a minister in the Cabinet or outside the Cabinet, they share with their British counterparts some concern about the ranking of certain departments and certain ministers.[34] The personality and prestige of a minister are important to the groups in both countries. His usefulness as a group ally depends on a number of quite intangible factors, such as his relationship with caucus, the degree of formality which he desires in his relationships with groups, and in some cases, his relations with his senior civil servants. On the whole, ministers welcome pressure group submissions as yet another source of information upon which to base decisions; they occasionally use them as a countervailing argument against their civil servants and also as ammunition in parliamentary committees and against the opposition parties.[35]

Against this background, it is interesting to look at some of the methods which pressure groups in Ottawa use in trying to influence the Cabinet. There is the presentation of a formal brief containing either general policy recommendations or points on one specific issue—this is not necessarily limited to one occasion per year. Briefs may be presented to the Cabinet, to a small group of interested—and perhaps even sympathetic—ministers, or to a single minister. In some instances a joint brief may be submitted by a conglomeration of pressure groups which have banded together on one issue.[36] The formal brief, especially if presented at a public meeting with Cabinet, appears to have become a sort of ritual which does not have much significance aside from publicity for the organization concerned. It should be noted, however, that the conglomerate approach has proven effective on a number of occasions. In any case, formal briefs are effective only when preceded by advance discussions with the responsible ministers and their senior civil servants, and when they are followed up with the same group.

There are also informal consultations with ministers; direct personal contact is certainly not eschewed.[37] Because these informal consultations take place out of the limelight they can be among the most effective means of influencing policy. Here two very important factors come into play. First, the group must be sufficiently well informed to know or make educated guesses about which ministers, aside from the ones obviously concerned, will be most sympathetic to their general line of approach. Second, the groups which are reasonable in their demands and sensible about recognizing that the Cabinet must deal with many conflicting pressures[38] in reaching decisions will be most successful in the long run. An ancilliary point is that when a group takes a stance openly hostile to government, the latter is very apt to win, for a complete breakdown in communication means the group is unable to exert influence of any kind.[39]

An entirely different situation may arise when a minority government holds office. Armstrong, in his article on collective bargaining for the public service, intimates that a majority government withstood pressure in favour of it whereas a minority government did not because it had to be "careful to work out a consensus".[40] Can this assessment be broadened to support the speculation that minority governments are generally more susceptible to pressure groups? Interviews in Ottawa suggest that it can. Politicians in both major parties agree that under these circumstances the Cabinet listens more carefully to caucus and generally is more willing to make concessions to minor parties. This, at the very least, provides two new points of access to decision-making for outside organizations. It is difficult to judge just how important this has been in fact. Judy LaMarsh, who had problems with the Canada Pension Plan during a minority administration, attributes a major share of those problems to negotiations with the provinces rather than to the insurance lobby. She does not complain of direct pressure on her or her colleagues by this lobby, which she describes as "well-financed"; but she does seem aggrieved that the lobby should chose to exert its influence through provincial premiers.[41] Since the advent of another minority government in late 1972, there has been ample evidence that pressure groups, as well as provincial governments, regard the situation as one providing them with greater opportunities for achieving their aims.[42] Another speculation which arises in regard to pressure groups during minority governments concerns the reformed legislative committees. A minority government being unable to control the majority of committee members creates the possibility that a pressure group could bring about considerable changes in proposed legislation, delay, or perhaps even prevent its passage, by simple dint of cultivating back-bench members of the opposition parties. It need hardly be said, however, that much of the foregoing is at the time of writing (1973) highly speculative.

Other comparatively recent developments are also affecting the type of methods which the groups find useful. First, the government appears to be trying to force group approaches out into the open and the Prime Minister is not as accessible as he used to be to group delegations. His office is much more reluctant to have him hear these last minute appeals by pressure groups, or even conglomerates of groups, and except in unusual circumstances,[43] they are generally refused. Taken together, these may point in the direction of disengagement or more formal relations. Second, the growth of staff and specialized functions in the Prime Minister's office, the proliferation of executive and administrative assistants around other ministers, and the use of Task Forces all tend to confuse or bypass the time-honoured channels of communications. Third, during the past decade, the use of Cabinet committees has become both more common and more effective. Some groups find it difficult to determine which ministers are on which committees or what their jurisdiction is.[44] It has become an arduous, and not always successful, endeavour for pressure groups to discover the locale of decision-making so that they can seek to exert influence in the appropriate quarter. Increasingly pressure group relations with the Cabinet, as a whole, and with its individual members, should be viewed as a constantly shifting arena where changing personnel and interests add an extra dimension of unpredictability.

Relations with the Legislature

Traditionally Canadian pressure groups have not paid much attention to Parliament, its institutions, or its private Members. Groups used to regard the opportunity to appear before a parliamentary committee as a good occasion to publicize their views, but they did not expect to affect legislation[45]. Since virtually all legislation and estimates are now sent to committees for examination and the committees have shown a willingness to amend government legislation, the groups have become much more interested in obtaining an opportunity to make their views known to them. They also have reason to hope that they may obtain some concessions. However, as long as ministers are determined to retain the principle[46] behind a bill, it is extremely unlikely, except in the event of a minority government, that a committee would recommend major changes or if it did, that the government would accept them. Although this situation has some of the same elements as the American committee system, the total effect is quite different, largely because of the strong party discipline which enables a majority government to ensure passage of its legislation. Canadian groups, unlike American ones, cannot normally hope to kill legislation, but must confine their activities to proposing modifications or to asking for delay to permit further study. It should be noted that when the government introduces a bill for discussion and then subsequently withdraws it, as in the case of the 1971 amendments to the labour code or the Competition Bill of the same year, groups may claim credit. Sometimes, on the other hand, even a majority government does withdraw a bill, like the Young Offenders Bill, when the controversy is too intense. Only a careful examination of *Hansard* and committee reports can assist in an attempt to determine whether or not withdrawal was an avowed governmental aim in the first place. Such investigation may also help to pinpoint the source of modifications if and when the bill is re-introduced; it may also be helpful in determining the rationale behind amendments introduced in and accepted by committees.[47] At any rate, the groups realize that they cannot hope to persuade any significant number of government Members to bolt the party either in committee or on the floor of the House. Perhaps more unusual, the groups have not yet mastered the technique of getting Members to raise grievances for them when estimates are considered in committee.

Committee hearings quickly establish the weaknesses of group presentations. Legislators are irked by organizations which are caught lying or present briefs which lack supporting facts, research or realism;[48] groups which organize demonstrations or "marches", or assume an aggressive stance;[49] and groups which employ some of the more ebullient American pressure group techniques;[50] as well as those group which have been invited, and have then failed to appear before the hearings. An organization which cannot prove its sole right to speak for clientele, whether because of internal dissension or the existence of a rival in the same sphere, often encounters a lively time when appearing before a committee, for there are usually Members present who have some interest in undermining their credibility. In fact, a committee sometimes spends more time discussing the internal dispute than it does the contents of the organization's brief. Established groups currently being challenged by temporary or permanent rivals may find their well-prepared cases undermined by one or more committee members. It is notable, however, that the committee report usually leans more heavily on the views of the established organizations[51] than on those of their attackers. The financial resources of the organizations also appear to affect the methods they employ. In the copious presentations made on the amendment to the Combines Act and the tax reform legislation of 1971 for example, the poorer organizations did not usually submit proposed legislation or amendments, which they regarded as a function of the law officers of the Crown. Instead they suggested general changes and described the probable effects of the legislation on their clientele.

The wealthier organizations, especially those accompanied by legal counsel, submitted specific and detailed proposed amendments. Now that committees travel outside Ottawa, it is necessary for national groups to arrange with their branches to present briefs, and this provides opportunities to try out new techniques, such as slide presentations, inviting Members to attend annual meetings or to go on conducted tours, and more use of hospitality.[52]

Despite some well-publicized examples, it seems that groups rarely feed information and technical details to spokesmen in committees;[53] certainly this technique has not been developed to the same extent that it has in either the United States or Great Britain.[54] The increased interest in standing committees has led to some apprehension that pressure groups would use the hearings as a device for delaying legislation[55], and the length of time that both the tax reform proposals and the Farm Marketing Products Bill spent in committee lends some weight to this view. However much the activity has increased, it is still true that group relations with committees and their chairmen are quite formal, and the groups in most cases still do not pay much attention to individual committee members.

In general, Canadian groups do not pay much attention to private Members, but this is unfortunately an area in which it is necessary to resort to educated guesses based upon evidence of inconsistent reliability. Some organizations, like the Canadian Federation of Agriculture, do not, as a matter of policy, lobby Members. Although others send periodic delegations to Ottawa with instructions to visit their local Members, this does not appear to be a very common practice[56]. Indeed, a high proportion of Members say that they do not have pressure group officials come to their offices much oftener than twice in the life of a Parliament. Apparently it is even rarer for delegations organized by a pressure group to visit them at home in their constituencies.[57] Some organizations, such as the Consumers' Association of Canada, the Canadian Medical Association, the Royal Canadian Legion and the Canadian Labour Congress, can count on sympathetic Members to act as their spokesmen in the House. Members can sometimes be found publicly acknowledging past or present connections with pressure groups.[58] Relatively few bills are introduced by Members at the behest of pressure groups.[59] The "planted" question is not very common, although, not surprisingly, it appears occasionally from the opposition benches. Groups, of course, send Members copies of their publications, petitions, resolutions, and most are willing, even anxious, to supply Members with information upon request. It is hardly surprising, in view of the lack of research facilities for private Members in Ottawa, that the Members, and especially those of the opposition parties, make copious use of such material, generally in a somewhat cynical fashion, citing those portions which happen to suit their purposes at any given moment.[60] A few groups advise their clientele to write to their Members about certain issues. This is normally one of the least successful techniques available. Members, for the most part, confess that they pay little attention to mail from outside their own constituencies and indicate that form letters, clip-out coupons, and so on, even from the constituency, impress them very little. However, if a Member receives a considerable volume of correspondence from his constituents with all the appearance of genuine concern, he quickly develops a profound interest. This is apparently what occurred when John Bulloch, a Toronto businessman, ran a series of newspaper advertisements urging people to ask their Members how the tax reform proposals presented by the government between 1969 and 1971 would affect them. The consequent flood of mail caused serious unease among government Members in committee and, reputedly, in caucus as well. However, it should be noted that the vigorous publicity campaign over Biafra did *not* result in a similar flood of letters so it would seem that the success of this technique is dependent upon being able to arouse public concern to the extent that people will actually sit down and write to their Members.

It is necessary to be a good deal more cautious in trying to assess pressure group contact with or influence on caucus. Certainly some groups meet with one or more of the party caucuses.[61] Interviews with both politicians and pressure group officials give the impression that this tactic is not apt to be productive unless there is widespread and obvious public support of the view being advocated. The re-structured organization and status of the Liberal caucus[62] in which back-bench Members are no longer faced with a *fait accompli* but have some opportunity to influence policy before it is publicly unveiled may mean that caucus, and indeed individual Members, will become much more important in the eyes of the pressure groups. Even now a close scrutiny of committee minutes indicates that caucus is exerting some influence on the course of events in that quarter.[63] Again, it should be said that even these beginnings may change radically in a minority situation when the government does not have a majority of Members in standing committees. The strong suspicion is that pressure groups will begin to pay a great deal more attention to the Members of the various opposition parties. At any rate Canadians have not yet seen a pressure group bring about a massive back-bench revolt of the kind that occasionally occurs in Britain.[64] On the whole, when the Canadian scene is viewed in comparison with Westminster or Washington, the only fair conclusion is that Canadian pressure groups do not devote much time or effort to influencing private Members.[65]

The general lack of interest in private Members may provide at least a partial explanation of the attitude toward opposition parties and parliamentary secretaries. Although, as mentioned above, Members of the opposition parties frequently use pressure group information to belabour the government, there is little significant contact between them and the groups. Certainly very few groups regard even the Official Opposition as the formulator of alternative policies which in the long run might come to affect them significantly.[66] A large proportion of the group officials interviewed expressed a positive reluctance to become too closely connected with opposition policies or attacks for fear this might endanger their working relationships with ministers and senior civil servants. Perhaps more surprising is the fact that few groups bother to retain special contact with former ministers after a change of government. In Britain, groups use them as well-briefed spokesmen who have a working knowledge of their former ministries. In Canada, this rarely occurs,[67] and organizations rarely mention the presence of former ministers or "shadow" ministers at their conventions. Some organizations, however, have tried to get policy commitments from various parties prior to general elections.[68] There is some recent evidence to indicate that organized interests ask opposition parties to speed up or delay passage of bills.[69] Equally the credit unions and co-operatives went to unusual lengths to determine the positions of the opposition parties on tax reform and to brief them on even the most technical aspects of the legislation. This, however, is not a common gambit in Ottawa. Although groups sometimes use the opposition parties as a means of getting questions asked, there is rarely a serious relationship of any kind.

Parliamentary secretaries don't see many more delegations of pressure group officials than do the ordinary back-bench Members. Any extra contact appears to occur because the responsible minister asks the parliamentary secretary to receive a group on his behalf or to fulfill a speaking engagement for him. Certainly the Canadian groups have not had as much contact with the parliamentary secretaries as the British groups have.

Little hard information is available about pressure group relations with the Senate or Senators. Unfortunately most of the widely publicized information has been of a rather sensational nature.[70] A more balanced assessment has only recently become available.[71] Not surprisingly, it finds that most informal "lobbying from within" in the Canadian Senate is done on behalf of the financial and business communities. It also finds that Senators rate organized interests as a good source of information on which to base decisions. This is directly contrary to the impression gained by this author over a twenty-year period of interviews with both Senators and pressure group officials.[72] There is little evidence that Senators endeavour to use their influence on civil servants.[73] On the more formal legislative side, the groups have long been aware that the Senate rarely makes major alterations to bills already approved by the Commons and, that until the late 1960s, very few government bills originated in the upper chamber. Accordingly the groups, in general, appear to look upon the Senate and its committees primarily as a public forum which discusses issues and hears groups which might otherwise be ignored. Possibly, now that more government legislation is being introduced in the Senate, a wider range of pressure groups will be more interested in it and will maintain closer contact with its members.

Why are the group contacts with Members of both Houses so super-ficial? A major factor is that groups generally recognize that private Members do not have the power or influence of ministers or senior civil servants. Possibly it also has a great deal to do with the attitude toward "lobbying" and "pressure groups" in Ottawa. The following analysis certainly comes under the category of educated guessing for the only thing that is clear about the subject is that it is impossible to find any two people who will agree upon a definition of these terms. There are some organizations which, while making policy recommendations to government on a regular basis, will deny with their utmost vigour that they are pressure groups.[74] Some people appear to draw a distinc-tion between pressure groups, which they usually regard as well-known organizations which defend the legitimate interests of their clients, and lobbies, which appear to have a universally bad reputation. If the question is pursued beyond this point, there is only complete confusion about distinction between the two terms. Some of the confusion seems to arise from the fact that the word "lobby" has connotations of venal lobbying in the United States.[75] However, it is unlikely that any group is either sufficiently politically influential or wealthy to sway any significant number of legislators away from the party line. In fact, it is difficult to see just how the old-style American lobby could operate successfully in the Canadian context. If nothing else, the restricted budgets of most Canadian pressure groups, even of those whose clientele should be able to provide substantial sums, make the idea of bribery seem ludicrous; although admittedly, venal lobbying involves more than bribery. Whatever may occur at the provincial or municipal levels of government, no cases have yet come to light at the federal level in which a pressure group (as opposed to a single company or an in-dividual), has been accused of attempting to exercise the traditional venal methods in regard to public officials.

It might be more useful to get away from these highly emotive words and try to describe some of the techniques used occasionally in Ottawa which verge on the above description. There have been rare allegations that Members have accepted payments from outside organizations for their services in making representations to various government boards and to ministers.[76] Organizations which can afford it, such as the Legion and the Labour Congress, occasionally invite Members, ministers and senior civil servants to receptions; they seem to do little, except the Legion, in the way of entertaining small groups of Members at more intimate gatherings where general policy issues are discussed. Now that the legislative committees travel, pressure groups appear to be making use of the opportunity to provide Members with various forms of entertainment.[77] Sometimes groups do indulge in "lobby-type" tactics. For example, in the cases of the Pharmaceutical Manufacturers' Associa-tion of Canada and the various producer groups, companies and other industries involved in the "Tobacco Lobby," there was active lobbying of Members, open feeding of information to Members in committee, threatening letters, and so on. There were loud complaints from Members about these tactics.[78] All of which leaves unanswered the question as to what constitutes "lobbying" in the context of the Canadian parliamentary system.

Relations with the Administrators

The pressure groups which operate effectively are aware that consultations with government can and do shift rapidly from the political level to the administrative level and back again; indeed sometimes they are carried on simultaneously at both levels. Competence under these circumstances requires good staff work and a considerable degree of agility. The groups know that they can maximize the long-term benefit to their clientele by influencing regulations proclaimed under various pieces of legislation and, of course, their application. Thus they have a two-fold reason for cultivating their relationship with the civil service. They stand a better chance of influencing the content of new legislation in its formative stages, and providing the relationship is a good one, they will be consulted later about the content of regulations. This relationship is a frustrating mechanism to try to describe, largely because civil servants desire anonymity and secrecy.[79] It is highlighted by close and continuous consultations.[80]

Perhaps a short summary of the various opportunities for groups to influence legislation and regulations will be helpful in outlining the importance of the relationship. Regardless of whether the action is initiated by civil servants as a result of administrative experience and discussions with affected outside interests, (and these preliminaries are often vitally important), or at the political level, the serious work begins when a Cabinet Minute is issued defining the general principles to be embodied in legislation. At this stage the minister will likely ask the major organizations interested to prepare private briefs for him. When these replies have been received drafting will begin, with frequent consultations over particular points. Before drafting instructions are sent to the Department of Justice, a further communication, which is nearly as detailed as the drafting instructions, may be sent to all interested organizations. Although this stage, or indeed any of the others outlined here, does not always occur, it may be the source of the allegation that pressure groups are shown bills before they are introduced in Parliament.[81] However, the following ministerial statement puts matters in a different perspective:

> We did not produce a bill to these groups because that insults Parliament. Parliament was the first to see the Bill. However, we did show many of these groups very carefully, specifically worded sort of drafting instructions.[82]

After this stage, organizations make detailed representations as a result of which some adjustments in the bill are likely to be made. After the bill has been given first reading, copies of it are sent to all possibly interested organizations soliciting their comments. The groups then approach the department with further detailed suggestions. Discussions between organization officials and civil servants produce further changes which the minister or deputy minister introduces before serious discussion begins in the legislative committee.[83] After the bill has been enacted, the civil servants and group officials settle down to discussions regarding the regulations emanating from the new Act. One new piece of legislation even provides the "statutory right" for a pressure group to make its suggestions felt in the process of drafting regulations. From the foregoing description it is apparent that the pre-legislative stage may be a prolonged process, perhaps stretching over more than a year; the discussion about regulations goes on over an indefinite time. The number of times that groups are deliberately consulted or may take an opportunity to exercise influence is considerable.

Several factors determine the amount of influence a group may have with the bureaucracy as opposed to its influence with politicians. It if is to be at all effective, its officials must know a great many civil servants, especially at the branch-head level and above in the department concerned, and preferably in a wide range of departments. A wide network of acquaintances, and even friends, within the bureaucracy is essential for utilization of all the opportunities outlined in the preceding paragraphs. The group and its officials must have a reputation for expertise, reliability and political non-partisanship. They should be able to provide accurate information quickly; they must be reliable about keeping confidences; preferably they should try to restrain their clientele from great public excesses. If the relationship is working properly there is a constant two-way flow of information.[84] After years of exchanging information and chatting together over general policy problems, the relationship becomes so intimate that each one will be able to make a very good estimate of the other's likely reaction to any given development. This type of close relationship is particularly helpful when relations with the minister or the department are strained over some incident. One thing is clear: groups which do not have full-time staff in Ottawa cannot develop this type of relationship. The groups which depend on sending periodic delegations to see the Cabinet, the minister or the deputy minister will normally be listened to with attention, but their views are hardly likely to carry the weight of those of persons who are well known and respected. The relationship develops further through informal encounters such as when civil servants attend annual meetings or participate in panels and seminars sponsored by pressure groups. The relative smallness of the setting in Ottawa also contributes to the air of informality.[85] Personal friendships and even civil service membership in pressure groups also contribute to this atmosphere. This is particularly noticeable where there is a clientele-type of relationship between a department and a group,[86] or where civil servants have helped to establish a number of pressure groups whose recommendations they sometimes use to bolster their own views.[87] As with politicians, those groups which attempt to be understanding about the conflicting pressures[88] which civil servants must resolve are the ones with which a good, long-term relationship will prosper. Public criticism of civil servants is, of course, deleterious to the development of this type of relationship.[89]

As noted earlier, few groups in Ottawa have a sufficiently expert staff to be able to face departmental experts on an equal basis. Occasionally civil servants complain even publicly that organizations do not have sufficient expertise in order to present their cases properly.[90] The groups are sometimes consulted about appointments outside the merit system, but there are far fewer of these than there would be, for example, in the United States.[91] It is by now abundantly clear that such consultation is not tantamount to acceptance of advice given, and groups which wish to foster a close relationship must be prepared to accept this.[92] There is virtually no opportunity for a pressure group to endanger a civil servant's tenure, although it may have some influence on re-appointment to or extension of those relatively few positions not covered by the merit system.[93]

Possibly the importance of close and continuous relations with civil servants is an important factor in the determined adherence of Canadian pressure groups to the principle of political non-partisanship. This prickly subject also involves educated guesses, although the conclusions here are on firmer ground than in some other instances. Leaving aside the marriage of the Canadian Labour Congress and the New Democratic Party,[94] Canadian groups are almost obsessed with the desirability of remaining aloof from any hint of involvement in partisan politics. Perhaps this can be attributed to past experience. The demise of the old Canadian Council of Agriculture after its close involvement with the Progressive Party taught the agricultural organizations not to take that particular route again. Indeed, the Progressive Party provides a good illustration of what can happen to interests which try to elect their own group to or to organize a group within Parliament; unity is virtually impossible except on a very narrow range of issues.[95] The Canadian Manufacturers' Association early in its history found that open association with the losing political party carried at the very least the penalty of distrust[96], and it still maintains a public attitude of political neutrality. Most groups, therefore, confine their political activity to urging their membership to vote for the candidate who appears to be the most friendly to their interests.[97] Although they sometimes request parties or candidates to make commitments during election campaigns,[98] they generally refrain from endorsing candidates or party platforms; many will not even discuss party policies relevant to their membership. Some force their officials, appointed or elected, to resign from office as soon as nominated for political office; others after their election.[99] It has been many years since any major groups have been implicated in partisan politics at the national level. Some organizations carry this so far that they try to avoid dealing with government officials who are "too political" in their views.[100] There is as yet no evidence to indicate that pressure groups per se contribute to party compaign funds.[101] Clearly there is a close relationship between the Labour Congress and the New Democratic Party, but while the former goes further than most other groups in urging its membership to support the latter at the polls, it denies that it contributes to the party's campaign funds.[102] Other organizations also deny such activity, but some are not prepared to guarantee what their affiliates, in some cases much more affluent than the national organization, may or may not do at the provincial or constituency level. Groups appear to have come to the conclusion that threatening politicians with exercise of the franchise is a useless manoeuvre. Even the labour unions, where there is a tradition of solidarity and disciplined behaviour, have virtually abandoned the vote as a political weapon.[103] In fact, the groups try to avoid any discernible leaning toward a political party for fear of encountering difficulties when their favoured party is not in power. The groups almost universally say that a minister's party label is not important to them.

The pressure groups also have an important set of relations with the various Crown corporations, independent and semi-independent boards and commissions. Aside from the material published on broadcasting and on the National Research Council, little is known about the range, extent or intimacy of these relations in Canada.[104] The Royal Canadian Legion, which for many years was entitled to have an observer on every civil service examining board, built up a very close relationship with the Civil Service Commission. Also after a long-term joint sponsorship of Farm Radio Forum, the Federation of Agriculture built up a close relationship with the Canadian Broadcasting Corporation and especially its farm service. Occasionally, it is possible to discern the influence of groups in appointments to these bodies. In view of Doern's analysis of science policy, it would seem that some groups exert influence on these bodies in an attempt to affect their policy and also with the hope of indirectly influencing the direction of government policy. Not only are these bodies subject to pressure, but they themselves also make recommendations to government which in many cases reflect the submissions which they receive.[105] The President of the Export Credits Insurance Corporation, a government agency, sounded more like a pressure group leader than a Crown employee when he appeared before a parliamentary committee to urge passage of a bill "this Session".[106] However, very little is known about pressure group activity in regard to a whole range of establishments, such as the Canadian Transport Commission, Central Mortgage and Housing Corporation, the Copyright Appeals Board, and so on. The whole area needs more case studies and much more careful analysis before any firm conclusions should be attempted.

INFLUENCING PUBLIC OPINION

The techniques which Canadian pressure groups use in order to attain a favourable climate of public opinion through long-term publicity or to create or change opinion by short-term campaigns are much the same as in the United States and Britain. It should be noted, however, that the Canadian groups are not very adept at using these techniques and do not often resort to them. An interesting if not helpful aspect of this is that some publicity efforts, like the campaign against tax reform or the copious publicity about pollution control, have evoked considerable public support and subsequent politicial action; others, just as vigorously pursued, like the Biafra campaign, have not. Many groups still rely solely on a house organ which has little if any circulation outside their own membership. The concept of reaching out to a larger audience is not yet common. Naturally the press receives copies of formal submissions to Cabinet or to ministers, but the groups seldom pursue the matter further unless a reporter or newspaper requests further information. Rarely do the groups indulge in special briefings for selected journalists.[107] Nevertheless, some members of the Press Gallery appear to be worried about the presence in their midst of lobbyists paid by outside interests.[108] A few organizations practice a dual approach to public relations: provide all kinds of information freely and willingly in order to educate outsiders; but exercise very great restraint in reacting to published criticism.[109] Groups participate widely in meetings, seminars and panels of other groups in the community, even those sponsored by organizations which might be thought hostile.[110] Various types of antics, ranging from mass protest demonstrations, boycotts, strikes and tractor parades through to people chaining themselves to the seats in the gallery of the House, have been used to attract publicity. The tone of the articles and editorials provoked by such tactics give rise to doubt that they achieve the objective of a favourable climate of public opinion.[111] Moreover, many politicians have come to regard these demonstrations more as stunts designed to attract publicity for the organizers than as a means of attracting their attention. If this attitude continues, groups which indulge in them will have to find other means of communicating their views to government.

One of the interesting things about the Canadian groups is their early and continued interest in radio, and later television, as a medium of reaching both their own clientele and the rest of community.[112] Now some groups also appear to be sponsoring paid advertisements.[113] Some organizations have begun to use the "open-line" programs as a means of stimulating public attention to or sympathy with their causes. American and British groups do not appear to have become interested in radio at such an early stage and with such limited financial resources. One can only speculate about the reasons. Possibly the British groups relied on the printed word because of access to a national press—something which Canadian and American groups both lack. The Canadian groups, unlike the American ones, have had access since the mid–1930s to a publicly owned nation-wide network which carries a number of public service programs. The only fair assessment is that while Canadian groups are just beginning to develop a more sophisticated approach to the use of the printed word, they are perhaps even ahead of their British counterparts, at least, in the use of radio and television.

SUMMARY

The Canadian pressure groups attack where there is the best opportunity to exert influence, and there seems little doubt that the most fruitful points are the Cabinet and the senior civil service. Indeed those groups which have operated effectively over a prolonged period have had to tailor both their methods and organization in order to maximize their impact on the political institutions. For example, despite the manifest problems imposed on them by their distribution of legislative powers, they make good use of the propitious circumstances arising from the federal nature of the Cabinet and the political prestige of the provincial premiers. Also, the increased attention to legislative committees as a result of the change in their status would lead one to suspect that if the groups are to be successful they must react to the institutions which confront them and to the changing points of access and decision-making which are open to them. Indeed, continued success depends on their willingness or ability to adapt their techniques to changing institutions and centres of decision-making.

The Canadian groups are clearly still evolving and somewhat immature although they have increased in number and variety. The newer ones are still learning the rules of the game while the older ones are gradually becoming more sophisticated. It is interesting to note that Canadian groups have not tried adopting as many American techniques as the British groups.[114] Recently they have begun mounting massive attacks on several points in which a conglomerate of several organizations combines to approach government separately or together, or both, with similar recommendations. This is reminiscent of what V. O. Key describes as the "inter-group lobby."[115] Some of the trade associations have adopted the attitude of their American counterparts, in that they speak only on issues on which all their affiliates are agreed, and for the rest act in a co-ordinating capacity for the various interests under their umbrella; they leave affiliates free to pursue their own concerns at any and every level of government. There seems to be a more active interest on the part of both ministers and civil servants in using pressure group emanations to bolster their own views. At the same time, the government appears to be endeavouring to shed more light upon the demands of the groups and government reaction. It is not yet clear whether this is an attempt to de-emphasize the importance of the groups in policy determination or merely a desire to make the whole process of consultation and negotiation more public.

NOTES

1. *Canadian Public Administration*, Dawson, H. J., "The Canadian Federation of Agriculture" in vol. III, no. 2, June 1960; "The Consumers' Association of Canada" in vol. VI, no. 1, March 1963; "Relations between Farm Organizations and the Civil Service in Canada and Great Britain" in vol. X, no. 4, December

1967; hereafter cited respectively as Dawson, (1960); (1963); and (1967). However, the Canadian Medical Association, a federation of provincial organizations, does not appear to have been seriously affected due to its members' similar professional backgrounds. *Ibid.*, M. G. Taylor "The Role of the Medical Profession in the Formulation of Public Policy", in Vol. III, no. 3, September 1960 (hereafter cited as Taylor), p. 235, and pp. 237–8.

2. Dawson, (1963), p. 99.

3. *Minutes*, House of Commons Standing Committee on Agriculture, March 17, 1970, 17:11.

4. Dawson, (1960, 1963 and 1967). Equally interesting is the Minister of Agriculture's statement that organized agriculture was not represented on a new Task Force because the National Farmers' Union and the Federation of Agriculture could not agree on a nomination. *Minutes*, H. of C., Standing Committee on Agriculture, December 5, 1968, p. 231, and October 22, 1964, p. 302; June 8, 1969, pp. 1898–90.

5. Dawson, (1960), pp. 135–137; (1963), pp. 96–99.

6. M. W. Bucovetsky, "Tax Reform in Canada: A Case Study of the Mining Industry", an unpublished Ph.D. dissertation, University of Toronto, 1971, at pp. 48–9, the Minister of Finance as saying that some major changes in the mineral tax proposals were the result of "inexorable pressure from the provinces."

7. V. O. Key, Jr., *Politics, Parties and Pressure Groups*, (4th ed.), (New York: Thomas Y. Crowell Company, 1960), p. 49; A. Potter, *Organized Groups in British National Politics*, (London: Faber & Faber, 1961), pp. 97–180; and P. Self and H. Storing, *The State and the Farmer*, (London: George Allen & Unwin Ltd., 1962), pp. 50–53.

8. The Canadian Trucking Association told a Senate committee the decision in the Winner Case meant that truckers who carried on interprovincial operations were subject to the more stringent Canadian Labour Standards Code, whereas those operating within a single province under the various provincial acts could operate under comparatively lax regulations, and that within the larger provinces, like Ontario and Quebec, these companies provided major competition over large areas. *Minutes*, Senate Standing Committee on Banking and Commerce, March 1965, p. 31.

9. Examples of this include: trading stamps, highway safety, humane slaughter of animals, and many problems associated with environmental control. The following exchange is an illustration of the positions adopted on occasion at both levels: in the case of trading stamps, a government supporter maintained that the matter fell purely within provincial jurisdiction and an opposition spokesman quoted two provincial attorneys-general to the effect that responsibility fell within federal jurisdiction. *Debates*, H. of C., February 4, 1960, 726 and 740. Note the submission of the Canadian Federation of Humane Societies, *Minutes*, H. of C., Standing Committee on Agriculture, April 28, 1959, p. 168; and various submissions of the Farmers' Union, especially, *Ibid.*, July 6, 1967, p. 159.

10. *Ibid.*, July 6, 1959, p. 159.

11. *Debates*, H. of C., May 17, 1961, 4948.

12. *The Globe and Mail*, October 15, 1971.

13. *Minutes*, H. of C., Standing Committee on Agriculture, Feb. 8, 1967, p. 1225.

14. Dawson, (1967), p. 454.

15. *Minutes*, Sen., Standing Committee on Banking and Commerce, May 31, 1961, 11 and 28; H. of C., Standing Committee on Finance, Trade and Economic Affairs, March 5, 1970, 26:5; *The Globe and Mail*, October 2, 1968.

16. Dawson, (1960), p. 137; (1963), pp. 98–99.

17. The Canadian Forestry Association, the Consumers' Association, the Canadian Safety Association, the Canadian Council on Social Development, and the John Howard Society are but a few examples.

18. The Deputy Minister of Consumer Affairs told a parliamentary committee: ". . . We exercise no control whatever over the policies of the organization or

the use to which these funds are put." *Minutes*, H. of C., Standing Committee on Health, Welfare and Social Affairs, November 14, 1968, 73. Perhaps more convincing is the fact that none of the Association's spokesmen in the House, even those belonging to opposition parties, have complained about attempted government interference.

19. Generally speaking, they each have a staff of half a dozen, or less, and budgets which run between $130,000 and $350,000. Officials from the following organizations were interviewed: Canadian Council on Social Development (formerly the Canadian Welfare Council); Canadian Association of Broadcasters; Grocery Products Manufacturers of Canada; Canadian Federation of Agriculture; Canadian Trucking Association; Executive Consultants; Canadian Bar Association; Consumers' Association of Canada; Canadian Federation of Mayors and Municipalities; Canadian Construction Association; Royal Canadian Legion, and Canadian Manufacturers' Association.

20. Dawson, (1960), p. 137; (1967), pp. 452–3.

21. The files of the three organizations which the author has examined in depth, and interviews with the officials of other organizations, indicate that the British Columbia provincial organizations have been consistently the most troublesome. This has even been acknowledged in the House of Commons: "We raise more hell in British Columbia than in any other province. Even the Canadian Legion feels that way about us." *Debates*, H. of C., July 10, 1959, p. 5787. See also Dawson, (1963), p. 469.

22. *Minutes.*, Sen., Standing Committee on Legal and Constitutional Affairs, March 11, 1970, 1:8. The President of the National Farmers' Union, in explaining why his organization was establishing its headquarters in Winnipeg, said: "A feeling expressed by our people that it was . . . just as well to sort of stay outside of Ottawa because when you get into Ottawa you get so close to the machine that you have a different perspective on things." The Canadian Manufacturers' Association has retained its headquarters in Toronto for the same reason.

23. One can find examples of: groups demonstrating in the wrong capital (*The Globe and Mail*, October 5, 1968); a provincial pressure group appealing to the federal government for help (*Ibid.*, November 16, 1971); and the federal government subsidizing a pressure group operating at the municipal level. (*Ibid.*, November 16, 1971).

24. Compare H. Zeigler, *Interest Groups in American Society*, (Englewood Cliffs, N. J.: Prentice-Hall Inc., 1964), p. 27, p. 48 and p. 58, with J. LaMarsh, *Judy LaMarsh: Memoirs of a Bird in a Gilded Cage*, (Toronto: McClelland and Stewart Limited, 1969), ch. V.

25. The Canadian Labour Congress and the Cabinet have met in public for many years. The Federation of Agriculture met the Cabinet in private until 1969 when this meeting also became public. Some organizations, like the National Council of Women, still meet the Cabinet behind closed doors.

26. G. Wootton, *The Politics of Influence*, (London: Routledge and Kegan Paul, 1963), p. 128.

27. *Canadian Journal of Political Science*, vol. III, no. 1, March 1970, D. Kwavnick, "Pressure Group Demands and the Struggle for Organizational Status", pp. 65–69; hereafter cited as Kwavnick. The Canadian Labour Congress had no reservations about communicating with the Prime Minister frequently and they obtained an interview with him. The widespread nature of contacts with ministers is noted in Dawson, (1963), *passim*. Wootton states that groups do not normally communicate with the British Prime Minister and only very rarely are they granted interviews. This assessment is confirmed by H. Eckstein, *Pressure Group Politics: The Case of the British Medical Association*, (London: George Allen & Unwin, Ltd., 1960), p. 84; and A. Potter, *op. cit.*, p. 204; as well as the *British Farmer*, January 7, 1961, and *The Times*, March 18, 1965.

28. *Debates*, H. of C., November 7, 1957, p. 861. The contact is even closer in the case of the Minister of Veterans Affairs who sometimes even attends meetings of the Executive Committee of the Canadian Legion. *The Legionary*, August 1944, p. 27.

29. Potter, *op. cit.*, p. 204 and p. 206, says that a ministerial address to a pressure group is usually regarded as "official recognition" of the group, like an invitation for its leaders to a garden party at Buckingham Palace. Certainly the groups do not *expect* the minister to appear at their annual meetings, even informally.

30. The Hon. J. J. Green, then Minister of Agriculture, refused to see a protest delegation organized by the Farmers' Union because it insisted upon bringing its demonstration to Ottawa at a time when he had other commitments. *The Globe and Mail*, May 10, 1967. For comparison see Potter, *op. cit.*, p. 204, and Wootton, *op. cit.*, p. 216. A British minister may either refuse outright to see a group or he may pass it along to a junior minister or his parliamentary secretary.

31. *Debates*, H. of C., January 28, 1958, p. 427; January 29, 1959, pp. 4595–99.

32. *Minutes*, H. of C., Standing Committee on Finance, Trade and Economic Affairs, Sub-Committee A, July 23, 1970, 78:90.

33. *The Globe and Mail*, March 14, 1972.

34. Eckstein, *op. cit.*, p. 54; *Yearbook*, National Farmers' Union, 1941, pp. 23–24; 1942, p. 28; 1943, p. 4. The *Legionary*, August, 1957, pp. 5–6, noted that both the Prime Minister and the Minister of Finance rank ahead of the Minister of Veterans Affairs in getting things done for ex-service personnel; it also noted that the Minister of Veterans Affairs cannot always persuade Cabinet to accept requested changes. *Ibid.*, November 1960, p. 8.

35. *Debates*, H. of C., February 3, 1948, p. 795; June 29, 1951, p. 4952; March 28, 1952, pp. 922–23; April 21, 1953, p. 4143; September 28, 1961, p. 9207; *Minutes*, H. of C., Standing Committee on Banking and Commerce, March 10, 1961, p. 12; and on Finance, Trade and Economic Affairs, May 12, 1970, 42:80.

36. *Canadian Journal of Economics and Political Science*, vol. 30, no. 2, May 1964, H. G. Thorburn, "Pressure Groups in Canadian Politics: Recent Revisions of the Anti-Combines Legislation", p. 160; (hereafter cited as Thorburn); Dawson, (1963), p. 113 and p. 115.

37. *Legionary*, December 1935, p. 6; October 1939, p. 3; Taylor, p. 241; G. B. Doern, "Pressure Groups and the Canadian Bureaucracy: Scientists and Science Policy Machinery" in W. D. K. Kernaghan, ed., *Bureaucracy in Canadian Government*, (Toronto: Methuen, 1961), p. 115.

38. See *Minutes*, H. of C., Standing Committee on Health, Welfare and Social Affairs, November 25, 1968, p. 94. In another case, concerning cigarette advertising, the briefs presented to the House Committee were nearly all previously presented to Cabinet; their contents make clear the kind of conflicting demands which the Cabinet faced. See *Ibid.*, May 13, 1969, p. 1065.

39. The Canadian Labour Congress concluded that if it refused to re-establish a working relationship with the government it would be bypassed completely. Kwavnick, p. 70.

40. "Pressure-Group Activity and Policy Formation: Collective Bargaining in the Federal Public Service", by Robert Armstrong in Kernaghan, *op. cit.*, p. 493.

41. LaMarsh, *op. cit.*, pp. 88–92.

42. The following examples are among the most interesting: the reaction of the People or Planes group in *The Globe and Mail*, November 1, 1972; and a spokesman for the Federation of Automobile Dealer Associations who said "We'll be reaping benefits from the weak government" in *Ibid.*, November 29, 1972.

43. *Ibid.*, March 14, 1969; *Debates*, H. of C., October 23, 1968, p. 1936. However, he did grant special interviews to a group of industrialists and later to some union leaders late in 1971.

44. British pressure groups sometimes meet with Cabinet committees or selected members of them. *Yearbook*, National Farmers' Union, 1943, p. 3; 1952, pp. 74–5; and the *Landworker*, January 1963, p. 2. This constitutes the nearest equivalent to the Canadian practice of groups meeting with Cabinet.

45. *Minutes*, Sen., Standing Committee on Banking, Trade and Commerce, June

24, 1969, p. 211. The Canadian Life Insurance Association tacitly admitted that it had already gotten all the concessions it was likely to get.

46. Note the statements by the Ministers of Health and Welfare, Labour, and Consumer Affairs, indicating willingness to accept amendments to controversial legislation before Parliament, but indicating that they would not back down on the basic principles contained in the legislation. London *Free Press*, September 22, 1971; Ottawa *Citizen*, October 20, 1971; *The Globe and Mail*, November 20, 1971.

47. *Debates*, H. of C., July 13, 1957, p. 6293; September 6, 1958, p. 4705; March 2, 1971, p. 3865; November 22, 1971, p. 9763; March 29, 1972, p. 1268; *Minutes*, H. of C., Standing Committee on Banking and Commerce, June 28, 1960, p. 38; on Finance, Trade and Economic Affairs, February 17, 1970, 21:70; on Agriculture, January 30 to February 12, 1960; on Finance, Trade and Economic Affairs, December 4, 1968, p. 861; on Justice and Legal Affairs, December 21, 1971, 45:4; Sen., Standing Committee on Banking, Trade and Commerce, June 25, 1969, p. 4709.

48. *Debates*, H. of C., June 14, 1965, p. 2372; *Minutes*, H. of C., Standing Committee on Finance, Trade and Economic Affairs for June 1967, and also on Agriculture, March 12, 1957, p. 46; February 8, 1967, p. 1207; July 6, 1967, pp. 165–8; January 20, 1970, 2:13–4.

49. *Ibid.*, June 30, 1960, p. 306. "If we are going to call the farm unions here to make representations . . . , then the Members from western Canada might just as well throw in the towel and suggest that the farm unions take over our work." and also *Ibid.*, June 3, 1969, p. 1828: "I reject your inference that any of those elected [Members of Parliament] are scum. A brief like this does not embarrass this Committee so much as it embarrasses the author . . . and the people . . . whom you are supposed to represent." See also *Ibid.*, March 6, 1969, pp. 854–5; and also on Finance, Trade and Economic Affairs, December 1966 and January 1967; June 24, 1967, p. 2587; *Debates*, H. of C., December 19, 1967, p. 5594; February 12, 1968, pp. 6640–2; March 28, 1969, p. 7277.

50. *Minutes*, H. of C., Standing Committee on Agriculture, October 29, 1964, p. 377; July 6, 1967, pp. 146–47; on Banking and Commerce, June 22, 1960, p. 258.

51. *Report*, H. of C., Standing Committee on External Affairs and National Defence, Second Report in Proceedings #13, especially pp. 13–7.

52. *Minutes*, H. of C., Standing Committee on Finance, Trade and Economic Affairs, March 3, 1970, 24:7, and various references in the *Minutes* of the House Standing Committee on Agriculture between 1968 and 1970.

53. *Parliamentarian*, January 1970, pp. 15–6.

54. J. D. Stewart, *British Pressure Groups: Their Role in Relation to the House of Commons*, at the Clarendon Press, Oxford, 1958, pp. 77-8. British legislative committees do not normally hear witnesses; instead the groups which wish to influence the details of legislation send counsel to brief Members who will move amendments and speak on their behalf.

55. *Minutes*, H. of C., Standing Committee on Agriculture, January 30, 1969, p. 471; May 26, 1970, 34:15.

56. Members occasionally mention private contacts with groups or delegations present in Ottawa. See *Debates*, H. of C., December 20, 1957, p. 2675; *Minutes*, H. of C., Standing Committee on Finance, Trade and Economic Affairs, December 5, 1968, p. 407; on Agriculture, May 6, 1969, p. 1377.

57. One Member, with twenty-five years parliamentary experience, said that he could not recall more than two or three such occasions. The Legion is an exception to this rule for it has sometimes encouraged its local Branches to visit Members at home when there is important legislation pending. The *Legionary*, July 1951, p. 7; September 1951, p. 4. The rather different situation which prevails in Britain is described in H. H. Wilson *Pressure Group—The Campaign for Commercial Television*, (London: Secker & Warburg, 1961), ch. IV; also the *Economist*, March 14, 1964.

58. *Debates*, H. of C., June 9, 1961, pp. 6124–25; *Minutes*, H. of C., Standing Committee on Agriculture, June 18, 1964, p. 63; November 10, 1964, p. 359; February 8, 1967, p. 1194; on Finance, Trade and Economic Affairs, October 29, 1968, pp. 29–30.

59. *Debates*, H. of C., February 13, 1959, p. 1023: Dr. H. M. Horner sponsored a bill to change the constitution of the Canadian Medical Association. *Ibid.*, May 19, 1959, pp. 3808–11: an ex-service Member, and former Legion executive, introduced a bill to change the name of the Royal Canadian Legion. *Ibid.*, May 7, 1970, p. 6701: Mr. A. B. Douglas introduced a bill to incorporate the National Farmers' Union.

60. *Ibid.*, November 7, 1959, p. 825; p. 872; January 23, 1958, pp. 3711–12; June 6, 1958, p. 897; July 10, 1959, pp. 5781–95; February 4, 1960, pp. 720–29.

61. Dawson, (1960), p. 148; *Minutes*, H. of C., Standing Committee on Banking and Commerce, 1960, pp. 147–51 and 621–23.

62. A. Westell, *Paradox: Trudeau as Prime Minister*, (Scarborough: Prentice–Hall of Canada, Ltd., 1972), p. 102.

63. *Minutes*, H. of C., Standing Committee on Finance, Trade and Economic Affairs, Jan. to Sept. 1970.

64. Both *The Times*, February 10, 1964, and the *Economist*, March 14, 1964, indicate that pressure group activity at the constituency level caused twenty-one government Members to vote against a bill dealing with resale price maintenance while twenty-five others deliberately abstained.

65. Stewart, *op. cit.*, pp. 205–37; S. E. Finer, *Anonymous Empire*, (rev. ed.), (London: Pall Mall Press, 1966), pp. 45–64. Group spokesmen, although in reduced numbers, still exist in Parliament; groups interview prospective candidates to ascertain their views; some groups maintain Parliamentary Committees at the County level to keep in touch with Members when they visit their constituencies. Key, *op. cit.*, p. 149; A. Holtzman, *Interest Groups and Lobbying*, (New York: The Macmillan Company, 1966), p. 100.

66. One well-known exception to this general rule is described by Thorburn in regard to consultations between the Retail Merchants' Association of Canada and the Opposition on resale price maintenance prior to the 1957 election.
    Another exception is the occasion when two opposition Members moved amendments to a veterans bill which were based on Legion proposals. *Legionary*, September 1946, p. 19.

67. Only very occasionally does an ex-minister even acknowledge close contact with a group. See statement by the Hon. Paul Martin regarding the Public Health Association in *Debates*, H. of C., February 26, 1960, pp. 1519–20.

68. Thorburn, p. 160; R. Armstrong, p. 488; see also *Debates*, H. of C., December 10, 1957, pp. 2127–28, when the Minister of Justice revealed prior consultation over the Bill on the Humane Slaughter of Animals.

69. For example, the National Farmers' Union sent a telegram to the Leader of the Opposition urging "cooperation of your members on the agriculture committee" in facilitating the passage of the Canada Grain Bill. See *Minutes*, H. of C., Standing Committee on Agriculture, May 26, 1970, 34:60; June 23, 1970, 44:106–7.

70. *The Globe and Mail*, March 14, 1969, and *Weekend Magazine*, September 25, 1971.

71. "Canadian Senators as Appointees to a National Legislature: Group Consultants, the Lobby Within, and Social Reforms" by Colin Campbell, S.J., an unpublished paper presented to the Canadian Political Science Association in June 1972.

72. Some groups do not even approach Senators who have in previous years been actively involved in their organizations. Others have occasional contacts on specific isues. Some maintain an informal relationship with certain Senators which involves a two-way exchange of information.

73. Interviews with civil servants indicate that their contacts with Senators are pretty much restricted to appearing to give evidence before Senate committees. Senators who are lawyers sometimes represent clients before various government boards and commissions.

74. Dawson, (1963), p. 97, 103 and 116. Other examples: *The Canadian Grocer*, November 21, 1951, as quoted in *Debates*, H. of C., February 4, 1960, p. 751; and the Retail Merchants' Association, *Minutes*, H. of C., Standing Committee on Banking and Commerce, June 17, 1960, pp. 146–47.

75. *Annals*, American Academy of Political Science, vol. 319, September 1958, pp. 3–4; E. Cellar, and Holtzman, *op. cit.*, pp. 77–81, indicate that this is no longer common. Note that it is considered libellous by some in Canada to refer to a Senator as a lobbyist. *The Globe and Mail*, March 14, 1969.

76. *Debates*, H. of C., February 2, 1968, p. 6329.

77. When the House Committee on Agriculture went on tour in April 1969 it was entertained by the British Columbia Broiler and Turkey Marketing Board, the British Columbia Federation of Agriculture, the Portage LaPrairie Chamber of Commerce and Campbell Soup Company executives, and the Selkirk Mayor and Council. After being entertained at a reception given by the British Columbia Broiler and Turkey Marketing Board, the committee heard briefs describing the effects of American imports on the local poultry industry. The Committee, without waiting to question witnesses, passed a unanimous resolution urging the government to consider the establishment "of tariffs and other protective measures" in regard to the importation of eviscerated or dressed poultry. Only one member had the temerity to point out that this was quite outside the committee's terms of reference as it was supposed to be investigating problems affecting the grain trade. *Minutes*, H. of C., Standing Committee on Agriculture, April 12, 1969, pp. 1056–58.

78. *Parliamentarian*, January 1970, pp. 15–16.

79. *Canadian Journal of Economics and Political Science*, vol. XXIII, no. 4, November 1957, "The Civil Service and Policy Formation" by J. E. Hodgetts, 467; J. E. Andersen, "Pressure Groups and Canadian Bureaucracy" in W. D. K. Kernaghan and A. M. Willms, *Public Administration in Canada: Selected Readings*, (2nd ed.), (Toronto: Methuen, 1970), pp. 370–72.

80. Andersen, pp. 370–79; Taylor, p. 237, pp. 242–43, 249–50; and Dawson (1960, 1963, and 1967).

81. F. C. Engelmann, and M. A. Schwartz, *Political Parties and the Canadian Social Structure*, (Scarborough: Prentice-Hall of Canada Ltd., 1967), p. 103.

82. The Hon. R. S. Basford: *Minutes*, H. of C., Standing Committee on Health, Welfare and Social Affairs, January 14, 1971, 4:18. See also: *Debates*, H. of C., November 6, 1957, p. 834; March 17, 1971, p. 4358; *Minutes*, H. of C., Standing Committee on Agriculture, June 4, 1970, 33:38.

83. Although ministers and officials in the past introduced amendments to proposed bills as a result of outside submissions, the opportunities for groups to exert effective influence at this stage has increased immensely. For a good example of how this technique used to operate, see several statements by the Hon. E. D. Fulton on the Humane Slaughter of Animals Bill, *Debates*, H. of C., November 6, 1957, p. 834; and September 6, 1958, p. 4705; see also the statement by the Toronto Board of Trade on the re-drafted Combines Investigation Bill, *Minutes*, H. of C., Standing Committee on Banking and Commerce, June 28, 1960, p. 38.

84. Andersen, p. 371; Taylor, p. 238; and Dawson, (1960, 1963, 1967).

85. It appears to be more informal than similar relationships in Britain. See Stewart, *op. cit.*, p. 7; Finer, *op. cit.*, p. 25.

86. Andersen, 373–4; R. J. Van Loon, and M. S. Whittington, *The Canadian Political System*, (Toronto: McGraw-Hill Company of Canada Limited, 1971), 312; Dawson, (1960), p. 145, and (1963), p. 111; and Taylor, *passim*. The Royal Canadian Legion and the Department of Veterans Affairs provide a good example: for many years, a former Legion official, Lt. Col. Lucien Lalonde was Deputy Minister of Veterans Affairs and a former Legion Dominion Secretary was Chairman of the Veterans Allowance Board; in 1970 the Legion's Dominion Secretary resigned to become Chairman of the Canadian Pensions Commission. In addition, the Legion has access to the Department's files. *Legionary*, February 1937, p. 18.

87. Reading together Andersen, pp. 377–78, Van Loon and Whittingdon, *op. cit.*, p. 302, and the *Parliamentarian*, January 1970, pp. 15–16 leads to speculation that civil servants may employ this technique on legislative committees and perhaps even on ministers.

88. *Legionary*, December 1948, p. 11. See *Minutes*, Sen. Standing Committee on Banking and Commerce, November 22, 1967, p. 82, statement by the Deputy

Minister of Health and Welfare: "We in the department realize that we are probably going to suffer more than anybody else from this sort of legislation (Control of Hazardous Substances), because no doubt we will be subject to all kinds of pressure from sincere people who have strong views about certain substances they think should be removed . . . or controlled . . . , and we may not agree. . . . We will just have to brace ourselves to withstand this sort of pressure. . . ." See also *Minutes*, H. of C., Standing Committee on Finance, Trade and Economic Affairs, April 15, 1969, p. 2069. The Deputy Minister of National Revenue, in explaining the application of taxes to prefabricated closets, cabinets, etc., indicated that presentations on the subject had been made by the Construction Association, many individual builders, as well as furniture people and concludes: ". . . The real problem boils down to what the government is going to endure by way of dissatisfied people for whom equity is the removal of the tax on theirs as well."

89. *Minutes*, H. of C., Standing Committee on Agriculture, March 12, 1957, p. 49.

90. *Minutes*, H. of C., Standing Committe on Finance, Trade and Economic Affairs, December 3, 1968, p. 831; December 4, 1968, p. 888; and December 5, 1968, p. 903. The Assistant Deputy Minister of National Revenue said that the Canadian Shoe Manufacturers' Association would "help itself by coming to us with cases of real injury, rather than with general statements. . . . I would like to appeal with them to come to us with well documented cases. . . ." The following day, the Assistant Deputy Minister of Finance said of agricultural producers: "The problem always is that we are not provided with sufficient factual information. I must say that the Canadian producers (faced with representatives of the exporting countries) were revealed to be remarkably ill-informed and unable to make a case."

91. D. F. Hadwiger, and R. B. Talbot, *Pressures and Protests*, (San Francisco: Chandler Publishing Co., 1965), p. 35; Zeigler, *op. cit.*, pp. 287-88; Holtzman, *op. cit.*, pp. 122–23; and "The Bureaucracy in Presure Politics" and "How Pressure Groups Operate" in the *Annals*, September 1958.

92. *Minutes*, H. of C., Standing Committee on Agriculture, May 21, 1970, 32:12, p. 28, 38; Kwavnick, *passim*.

93. *Ibid.*, p. 64.

94. Gad Horowitz, *Canadian Labour in Politics*, (Toronto: University of Toronto Press, 1968), pp. 140–41 and 200, indicates that the alliance may not be very satisfactory. Certainly Kwavnick's article, indicates that the Labour Congress has encountered some hostility on the part of politicians because of it. Note that during the 1972 general election, the St. Jean Baptiste Society of Montreal abandoned political neutrality for the first time in 140 years. *Globe and Mail*, October 25, 1972.

95. P. F. Sharp, *Agrarian Revolt in Western Canada*, (Minneapolis: University of Minnesota Press, 1948), and Dawson, (1960), pp. 134–38; (1967), p. 450; and "Agricultural Interest Groups in Canada and Great Britain", unpublished thesis, Oxford University, 1966, pp. 25–30. For a similar British experience see Self and Storing, *op. cit.*, 42–47.

96. S. D. Clark, *The Canadian Manufacturers' Association*, (Toronto: University of Toronto Press, 1939), pp. 18–19.

97. Dawson, (1960, 1963, and 1967).

98. Armstrong, 123; London *Free Press*, September 26 and October 19, 1972; *The Globe and Mail*, October 10 and 11, 1972.

99. Officials of the Federation of Agriculture and the Consumers' Association resign upon nomination or after election. The Legion's literature is very outspoken about the dangers of partisanship. *Legionary*, July 1944, 17; June 1956, p. 3. On at least one occasion, the Legion was undoubtedly relieved to be able to sit determinedly on the fence. Its national treasurer ran against a provincial president and a branch president in a federal by-election. *Ibid.*, pp. 147, p. 27.

100. Interviews reveal that this attitude is usually applied to ministerial aides, but it may also include civil servants.

101. *Report of the Committee on Election Expenses*, (Ottawa: Queen's Printer, 1966); *Studies in Canadian Party Finance*, (Ottawa: Queen's Printer, 1966).

102. *The Globe and Mail*, September 22, 1972.

103. Horowitz, *op. cit.*, 51; Taylor, (1960), 241.

104. Frank W. Peers, *The Politics of Canadian Broadcasting, 1920–51*, (Toronto: University of Toronto Press, 1969); and G. B. Doern, "Scientists and Science Policy Machinery", in Kernaghan, *op. cit.*, pp. 112–19; F. Lemieux, "Lobbying Plus . . . the CMA" in *Politics: Canada*, (Toronto: McGraw-Hill Company of Canada, 1966), p. 35; Kwavnick, p. 68; Dawson, (1960), pp. 144, 147; and (1963), p. 105.

105. Other examples can be found in *Minutes*, H. of C., Standing Committee on Agriculture, May 14, 1970, 31:19; May 19, 1970, 32:9 and May 26, 1970, 34:15.

106. *Minutes*, H. of C., Standing Committee on Finance, Trade and Economic Affairs, May 8, 1969, pp. 2309–10.

107. *Parliamentarian*, January 1970, 15–16.

108. *Minutes*, Special Senate Committee on the Mass Media, December 11, 1969.

109. Taylor, (1960), pp. 254–55.

110. Dawson, (1960), pp. 139–40; and (1963), pp. 112–14.

111. "Watch the Rebound" by Bruce West, in *The Globe and Mail*, June 22, 1966; London *Free Press*, April 8, 1967; Halifax *Chronicle-Herald*, May 29, 1967; *The Globe and Mail*, October 2, 1968; May 12, 1970; October 16, 1971, and November 2, 1971.

112. For years the Federation of Agriculture spent over half its annual budget on Farm Radio Forum; the Alberta Farmers' Union in the first year of its existence spent nine-tenths of its budget on radio. An interesting side effect of Farm Radio Forum is that the Federation of necessity produced over the years a group of competent performers who were in turn invited to appear on other panels and programmes thus exposing the Federation's viewpoint to a much wider audience than Farm Radio Forum. Other organizations with restricted financial resources, such as the Consumers' Association, also use radio and television.

113. Van Loon and Whittington, *op. cit.*, p. 314.

114. British groups have tried to organize bi-partisan committees or blocks, within Parliament; have kept and distributed to membership, the voting records of Members; have indulged in considerable informal entertainment; have made use of private Members, of all parties, to move amendments to Bills. See Wootton, *op. cit.*, pp. 147–48, 152–54, 178–83; G. Wootton, *The Official History of the British Legion*, (London: MacDonald & Evans Ltd., 1956), 131; *Yearbook*, National Farmers' Union, 1921, pp. 69–72; 1923, pp. 47–48; 1926, p. 259; 1944, p. 51; 1947, p. 24; 1949, p. 102; *British Farmer*, January 6, 1962, p. 28; January 12, 1963, p. 35.

115. Key, *op. cit.*, 156–67.

3.

How do issue-oriented groups come into being? And once created, how do they develop a capacity to influence government? In 1970, D.A. Chant published the following description of the birth and partial institutionalization of one of Canada's most successful issue-oriented groups, Pollution Probe. His description still serves as an excellent guide to the process.

The "spontaneous" emergence of Pollution Probe, in February 1969 is typical of many issue-oriented groups, as is the fact that the group originally came together in response to a particular event, the investigation of an anti-pollution television program. Its survival is not as characteristic, however, and to account for it, one should note the climate of opinion in which its founders decided to act. Increasing coverage of environmental problems by the media had led to a heightened awareness of and concern for the issue on the part of the general public and particularly members of the university community. It was probably the conjunction of this climate of opinion and the specific event that gave Pollution Probe both its initial start, and the momentum to survive as an organization. Perhaps many issue-oriented groups have only a short existence because they lack this opportunity to relate concern for a specific problem to a broader but less clearly defined cause. Conversely, as Chant points out, it is equally important that a newly formed group focus its general concerns on specific issues "with which the public can readily identify before moving on to larger issues of more far-reaching importance."

Pollution Probe's experience also suggests a good deal about the way an issue-oriented group becomes a force to be reckoned with on an extended basis. That is, how it becomes institutionalized. "Probe's" university base gave it a source of manpower and expertise—commodities *denied many nascent groups—and to a lesser extent, facilities that might otherwise have had to be bought. These, with the strong motivation of its members, constituted resources that permitted the organization to achieve quite quickly a prominence and degree of influence usually associated with much more highly organized and affluent organizations. Nevertheless, "Probe" appears to have experienced many difficulties usually faced by new issue-oriented groups. It lacked an entrée into government circles and consequently depended on the media to give it sufficient public exposure to win the recognition accorded automatically by government to any organization appearing to command widespread public support. An equally important indicator of "Probe's" status as an issue-oriented group is Chant's contention that "when seeking decisive action . . . one should approach the real centres of power: Cabinet members, provincial or federal, and other political leaders." As other papers in the collection point out, many representatives of institutional groups would disagree, arguing that political leaders are seldom able to give sustained attention to the demands of pressure groups, and that the basic fabric of policy is developed in the administrative arm.*

The roots of institutionalization can be observed in the organization's need to establish legitimacy through the preparation of exhaustive and well-researched briefs. These require considerable expenditures of time and effort on the part of professionals and cannot always be carried out with volunteer labour. As Chant points out, an organization doing work of this sort soon becomes "a modestly expensive affair and cannot for long continue its hand-to-mouth existence. Substantial and continuing financial support must be found."

It is notable that Pollution Probe has never become a national pressure group, despite the fact that environmental issues have aroused concern in every part of the country, and that the establishment of national and provincial government environmental agencies would appear to encourage the development of a federated structure of environmental pressure groups. (On the relationship between the distribution of governmental authority and the emergence of specific agency- or government- oriented pressure groups, see the articles by Kwavnick and Pross elsewhere in this volume.) It may be that Canada's environmental problems are too diverse to permit one organization to speak effectively on a national basis, but it is more likely that the reliance of Pollution Probe and similar organizations on a relatively unstable membership—drawn chiefly from the ever changing university community—has prevented the development of the permanent organizational structure needed to sustain a viable national association.

D. A. Chant has been prominent in environmental causes for a number of years. An authority on pest control and pesticides, he is Professor of Zoology at the University of Toronto.

Pollution Probe: Fighting the Polluters With Their Own Weapons*

D. A. Chant

Most Canadians are now convinced that the quality of our environment is deteriorating at an exponential rate because of population pressures and expanding technology. The day of pollution horror stories is passing rapidly as most of our society is becoming knowledgeable about the ecological crises we are facing. What must be devised now for the guidance of all who share concern about the quality of our environment, are effective action programs.

One kind of action still in its infancy is by uncommitted citizen groups that owe no allegiance to vested interests other than that of optimal living. Action from this source is needed to encourage and guide progressive governments and industries in environmental quality control, to pressure inert governments and industries into awareness and progress, and to counter lobbying and other counter-pressures from polluters who have selfish, short-term economic interests without environmental conscience.

A number of citizen anti-pollution groups are springing up across Canada. One of the most successful is Pollution Probe at the University of Toronto. Its formation and methods of operation suggest principles of action that may be useful to other groups with similar aims and to the informed reader who wonders: "What can I do?"

Pollution Probe came into being at the University of Toronto spontaneously in February 1969. Many students and staff had been alarmed for some years over the rate at which our environment is deteriorating. They had watched the cbc-tv program "Air of Death" by Larry Gosnell and Stanley Burke and approved of its message and the impact it had on concerned Canadians. Some of these students were dismayed, therefore,

* Reprinted from *Science Forum* 14, April 1970, by permission of the author and of *Science Forum: A Canadian Journal of Science and Technology*.

to learn that the Canadian Radio-Television Commission planned to investigate the program. They decided to band together to protest this investigation, both on the grounds of journalistic freedom and because the program was considered accurate and well balanced. They studied air pollution intensively, including, of course, the fluoride pollution from the Electric Reduction Company at Port Maitland and the biased and inaccurate Hall Commission Report (Report of the Committee Appointed to Inquire into and Report upon the Pollution of Air, Soil, and Water, September 1968). They invited Larry Gosnell to screen "Air of Death" at the University of Toronto and to answer questions afterwards, and the meeting had an overflow attendance. Finally, these students, still without a formal organization, wrote briefs to the CRTC protesting the inquiry and supporting the CBC. Many of them attended the three-day hearing in its entirety, and were appalled, in their innocence, at the tactics of the opposition, particularly the ERCO legal and public relations staff. They decided on the spot that there were ills in a society that permitted such moral outrages that called far more urgently for condemnation than the Vietnam war or the lack of decision-making rights of university students. And they decided to do something about these ills.

That "something" was to organize a university-based group that would, on the one hand, fight pollution and the polluters with their own weapons of publicity and government pressure, and in the courts; and on the other, seek out the basic roots of our environmental crises and change them if possible by education and even by advocating new kinds of institutional frameworks for our society as a whole.

Accordingly, in March 1969 Pollution Probe came into being as a visible entity with a name, an executive, a constitution, and most important, members from everywhere in the university—fine arts, engineering, the social and natural sciences, the humanities, administration, both staff and students. Later membership was opened to any concerned citizen for $2.00 a year, and now Pollution Probe is about 1,000 strong.

Much thought was given in those early days to aims and the most appropriate executive structure for achieving them. Probe's objectives as finally defined are broadly to seek the redress of environmental ills by activities ranging on one extreme from public education (Probe members have spoken to dozens of citizens' groups and to more than 15,000 primary and secondary students in the last six months) through information gathering and the stimulation of similar organizations at universities across Canada, to militant action programs of parades and demonstrations, and finally to the other extreme of legal action against polluters and inert government agencies.

Probe has no conventional executive. There is a board of advisers nominated by the membership, which guides but does not run the organization; it is there when wanted or needed, but otherwise does not intrude in the organization's daily affairs. It is composed of prominent dedicated people such as Marshall McLuhan, Stanley Burke, John Dales, Richard Judy, and others. In addition, Probe is organized into work teams responsible for its major activities—education, newsletter, office management, publicity, research, fund-raising, phosphate detergent pollution, SO_2 and other air pollution, legal affairs, and so on. Leaders of each team emerge not by edict or appointment but rather on the basis of dedication and interest, and most important of all in the increasingly complex and busy university milieu, availablity of time. Those with keen interest and some available time evolve as team leaders. This loosely knit, sometimes rather ephemeral group of team leaders actually functions as a sort of quasi-executive. Probe's successes to date can be credited largely to this group of 15 or 20 young people who have given its affairs their concern and much of their attention; supported, of course, in a very substantial way by the membership as a whole, who turn out by the hundreds to regular monthly meetings.

To be successful a group such as Probe must be businesslike. It must follow through effectively on administration and all its other activities, and in fact have a recognized, stable, physical presence. To ensure this, Probe became an official project of the University of Toronto, with an account administered through (but not *by*) the department of zoology, and an office in the Ramsay Wright Building. There is a full-time secretary and an office manager, and the office and adjoining work and study area are the centre of all Probe activities. The key workers, mostly undergraduate and graduate students and recent graduates, work from there and it is there that they meet to plan activities and make decisions.

Adequate finances also are essential to success. Probe has yet to mount a major fund-raising campaign but has done reasonably well with membership fees, a few individual gifts, a grant from President Bissell, and substantial subsidization from the department of zoology. It has also enjoyed truly gratifying contributions in advertising art work and layout from one firm, and free publication of educational and promotional material from the Toronto *Telegram*. More than anything else, these last two have enabled Probe to bring issues to public attention and to gain public recognition. Probe, however, is becoming a modestly expensive affair and cannot for long continue its hand-to-mouth existence. Substantial and continuing financial support must be found.

There are other characteristics of Probe to understand before discussing its accomplishments. The first is the strength it gains from the breadth of professional competence represented in its membership. There is scarcely an aspect of pollution, whether it be pesticides, urban congestion, noise, air, or water, on which one or more members are not acknowledged experts, either through personal research experience or by study and exposure. This means Probe can address itself to almost any pollution problem with confidence and authority, sure of its facts and without the vagueness that so often characterizes anti-pollution groups.

The second is the close and productive relationships that Probe has established with the communications media. The results have been so successful and important that some members of Probe have been accused of being publicity-hungry. This is unfair. Probe simply recognized the necessity of bringing pollution problems to public attention, and what more effective way is there of doing this than by using the modern, efficient methods of mass communication? The willingness, almost the eagerness, of the newspapers, radio, and TV to co-operate probably stems partly from the fact that pollution has excellent news value, but partly, I am convinced, from the fact that news reporters are not only professional communicators but also citizens. They have wives and families themselves, and they share the common concern and fear over our deteriorating environment.

Probe recognized early that effective anti-pollution action inevitably would lead to legal actions: actions to seek injunctions preventing polluting activities, and perhaps even suits to seek redress from intransigent polluters. It was fortunate in forming an association with an effective Toronto lawyer, James Karfilis, who has a well-developed environmental conscience and is willing to handle Probe's legal affairs for a retainer of one dollar per year.

Finally Probe believes that when seeking decisive action on environmental problems one should approach the real centres of power: Cabinet members, provincial or federal, and other political leaders. It is only at this level that one can rise above the inertia or outright helplessness of some arms of the civil service to bring pressure to bear, explain data and views, and seek new laws or changes in policy that will result in a cleaner environment. Probe has been fortunate in that the present Ontario and federal governments are becoming sophisticated and knowledgeable about pollution and moving in the direction of effective environmental control. Members of these governments, with few exceptions, have received Probe freely, listened to its cases and in most instances, been convinced.

In its short life Probe has embarked on several major projects. The first was a program to have DDT and other persistent organochlorine pesticides banned in Ontario. We were advised that this would take two years and even then we might not succeed. Probe's interest in DDT was activated by the author, whose personal research for 20 years has been on the principles of pest control and who is convinced that DDT and its relatives are one of the most serious long-term environmental threats now facing the world ecosystem. Initial contacts with the provincial government almost immediately resulted in a total ban on aldrin, dieldrin, and heptachlor, announced on 4 June 1969. But any restriction of DDT was refused, and this accelerated Probe's campaign. Speeches were given, meetings were held with cabinet ministers, a new minister of health and a new minister of energy and resources management were appointed and Probe compiled an up-to-date world compendium of scientific data on the physical chemistry of DDT and its effect on food chains, on avian and fish reproductive physiology, and on learning and behaviour. The Environmental Defence Fund and the Senate in the

United States provided newly released information on the carcinogenic properties of DDT in laboratory animals, and the University of Florida sent manuscripts linking high DDT residues with liver cancer and other disorders in humans. This material was incorporated into a massive brief to the premier of Ontario requesting a ban, but it was never used; in September the minister of health announced restrictions on DDT that would reduce its use in Ontario by 90%. Probe, flushed with the feeling that it had played an important role in this "ban," decided to transfer its attention to Ottawa to seek a national ban.

Accordingly in October the petition was readdressed to Prime Minister Trudeau and copies were sent to every federal minister, to every premier, to all leaders of the opposition, to every major radio and TV station, newspaper and magazine across Canada, to every university, and to all major conservation groups. Support was massive and irresistible. In November Mr. Trudeau announced nation-wide restrictions that will reduce DDT use by 90–95%.

Other action programs that achieved their aims were on the misuse of a pesticide on Toronto Island and the sewage pollution of Highland Creek in suburban Scarborough, both of which led to actions to obtain injunctions against government agencies. Both suits were withdrawn when effective anti-pollution steps were taken. Probe has also co-operated with legal actions initiated locally by conservation groups in Peterborough and Sudbury.

Probe has carried out successful programs of public education regarding litter and the gross pollution of the Don River in Metro Toronto. Moreover it is lending strong support to groups attempting to preserve the Quetico Park area as a wilderness sanctuary and to prevent the further construction of the Spadina Expressway in Toronto.

There are two current major programs. The first is aimed at Ontario Hydro, generally acknowledged to be the most serious air polluter in the Metro Toronto area. This has involved meetings with cabinet ministers and the chairman of Hydro and his advisers, climaxing in a three-day public hearing at which expert testimony was presented by all interested parties, and all sides of the question were examined by a panel of five "commissioners." The ultimate objective is to encourage Hydro to reduce or eliminate sulphur pollution by installing effective air washing devices or by changing from high to low sulphur content fuel.

The second current program is on water pollution caused by phosphate detergents. Probe has analyzed all major detergents and water conditioners sold in the Toronto area and is mounting a major campaign with two objectives: to persuade housewives to buy only low-phosphate detergents and thereby pressure the manufacturers in the marketplace; and to work with and encourage the provincial government in its inclination to ban phosphate detergents by 1972.

What principles of effective anti-pollution action have been established by Probe to date? They seem to be as follows:

1 Individuals acting alone are vitually powerless to prevent further degradation of our environment. They must band together for effective action and they must decide what particular sorts of action suit them best. Is it education, discussion, study, political pressure, demonstrations, or legal action? Or can they tolerate and support all of these and more in a single organization, such as Pollution Probe?

2 They must be shrewd tacticians. There is little point or hope of success simply to attack total environmental degradation as a vague, all-embracing concept from the beginning. They must start on a limited basis with clearly identified, highly visible local issues with which the public can readily identify before moving on to larger issues of more far-reaching importance.

3 They must be sure of their facts, and this means they must have professionally competent people within the membership—engineers, biologists, chemists, economists, political scientists, sociologists, lawyers.

4 They must work effectively with the communications media, not only by appearing in headlines and on TV but by providing background and leads and by willingly giving advice and information without regard for public credit through personal publicity.

5 They must develop educational programs by public lectures to groups of citizens, no matter how small and obscure, and to classes of students at all levels from primary schools through university. Without public awareness and broad support, environmental control will be impossible.

6 Within the limits of their collective conscience, groups must be responsible. Nothing erodes credibility more quickly than irresponsible statements or actions that cannot be supported by facts. This does not mean that dramatization has no role, perhaps even over-dramatization to overcome strong negative resistance; but there is a fine line between this and irresponsibility.

7 The group must have a physical presence in the sense of an office, a listed telephone number, and a permanent office staff. Without this, effective communication and action follow-up is impossible.

8 Finally, groups will learn quickly that the pressure they generate must be applied at the top—at the level of cabinet ministers, heads of agencies, and company presidents. It is futile and ineffective to approach anything less than the ultimate centres of decision-making.

What have we learned from Probe's activities to date? Perhaps the most striking thing is the ruthlessness and vigour with which the vested interests will fight back. This sort of backlash is seen in counter-publicity, in direct personal abuse, and in subtle innuendo among our colleagues and others in the Canadian scientific community. It is not quite proper, some suggest, for scientists and academics to get involved with public action groups, with communications media, with politicians, and with legal action. Somehow, it would seem, we are betraying our more inert brethren who would prefer to live quietly in their ivory towers behind massive walls of pseudo-objectivity, scientific "detachment", and perhaps plain fright. They "Don't want to get involved." The increase in this counter-activity, we believe, is a measure of our success to date.

Is there any justification for the view that scientists should not become involved in public controversy with timely issues such as pollution, which threaten our survival and cast serious doubts on the viability of our traditional institutional framework and social organization? I can accept the possibility that scientists in government and industry must at times be reticent and defer to official policy set by their superiors, as long as they continue to work effectively behind the scenes. But I cannot accept the same thing for scientists in universities.

Scientists in universities are independent of both government and special interest groups and are in the most advantageous position to exercise their social conscience and relate to controversial problems of the real world. I am not suggesting that a university as a whole should take a policy position on environmental problems—far from it, although the University of Toronto has given open, substantial support to Pollution Probe. Rather it is the professionals in universities who either have special competence through their research or, simply as educated citizens, have a sophisticated concern about environmental quality, who must take leadership in public action programs. To be blunt, not only do I consider this appropriate and desirable, I consider it absolutely essential. It is a major responsibility whose abdication can be read only as a lack of interest in the world around us and callous disregard for the welfare of our society as a whole.

It is necessary, however, to make a firm distinction between an individual's professional side and his active involvement in environmental issues. The principles of one can all too easily be compromised in the emotional commitment of the other. Probably it is because of this that many in the scientific community frown on those who participate in public action. Science should be rigorous and above all objective; nothing is established as truth until it has withstood the rigours of experimental analysis and repeatability. Pollution action programs, however, often depend on data obtained by inference, extrapolation, and perhaps even intuition. Usually they cannot wait for time-consuming, rigorous scientific study and analysis. Environmental problems beset us from every side and they are right-now problems; they are crises, and action right now is required for their easement.

For example, studies in a number of major cities have shown that SO_2 air pollution is harmful to plants and animals and aggravates respiratory disorders in humans. An SO_2 concentration of 0.25 parts per million for periods longer than one hour is hazardous, and 0.40 parts per million is downright dangerous. Similar studies have not been done in Toronto, to my knowledge, yet when the SO_2 concentration reaches 0.37 parts per million, as it did on Thursday 22 January 1970 we *know* that action must be taken immediately to eliminate the major sources of sulphur pollution. We do not need a local scientific study to prove this.

Moreover, our commitment to the solution of environmental problems often is emotional. It is based on knowledge of sorts, often with extrapolations into the future, but nonetheless emotional. I personally am outraged at the abuse of our environment by industries and some government agencies; but I am outraged in the part of me that is *informed citizen*, not the part that is *trained scientist*. I may say and do things that are uncomfortable to my professional standards as a scientist but are fully in keeping with my determination as an ordinary citizen to protect my environment. All of this is not easy, and some of it may well be facile rationalization. But it helps, I think, to explain how some scientists are able to get involved and it may encourage others to do so.

Scientists who can make this distinction between their various parts should adopt Pollution Probe's motto: "Do it!" Now.

4.

In her discussion of institutional pressure groups operating at the federal level, Helen Jones Dawson drew attention to the effect the federal system has on the behaviour and organization of such groups. She pointed out, in particular, how the fact of divided jurisdiction imposes certain constraints on pressure groups, forcing those with limited resources to lobby only those governments whose activities bear most directly on their concerns. Her analysis also suggested that many groups find the necessity of maintaining a federal structure parallel to the governmental structure further dissipating resources and promoting internal strain, consequently reducing their capacity to present a coherent united stand before the federal government. Finally, she noted that there are elements in the Canadian constitutional structure which can be used to advantage by pressure groups capable of exerting influence at more than one level of government.

The two following papers explore these points in greater depth. In the first, David Kwavnick assesses two hypotheses that explain how federal government relates to pressure group demands, suggesting on the one hand "that the distribution of power . . . influences the structure, cohesion and even the existence of interest groups," and on the other, that groups will attempt to influence the distribution of powers in such a way as to enhance the power of those governments with which they are most closely affiliated. In other words, pressure groups are not only affected by the federal structure of government; they themselves attempt to play a part in determining the nature of the division of powers. They are, Kwavnick points out, important informal instrumentalities of federalism capable of facilitating national integration—or of reinforcing its dissolution—and are in turn subject to exploitation by their "client" governments.

David Kwavnick is Associate Professor of Political Science at Carleton University and has written extensively on the subject of Canadian pressure groups and on French Canadian politics.

Interest Group Demands and the Federal Political System: Two Canadian Case Studies

David Kwavnick

SOME APPROACHES TO FEDERALISM

William S. Livingston, in his perceptive discussion of the sociology of federalism,[1] drew attention to the instrumentalities through which the federal nature of a society is manifested. However, as his listing of the instrumentalities of federalism indicates,[2] he is primarily concerned with the operation of the formal institutions of government. His contribution lies in the fact that he went beyond a mere legalistic description of those institutions and recognized the necessity of examining "not only the constitutional forms but also the manner in which the forms are employed . . . the way the constitution and its institutions are operated",[3] as well as the attitudes, concepts and theories underlying their operation. Livingston attempted to move away from a legalistic analysis of the formal institutions of federalism, but it was the formal institutions which nevertheless remained at the centre of his attention.

It is possible, however, that some important instrumentalities of federalism lie outside the formal structures of government; that diversities, local loyalties and other factors may be manifested through non-governmental instrumentalities. Other students of federalism, namely William H. Riker,[4] R. L. Watts,[5] Aaron Wildavsky[6] and Karl Deutsch[7] have gone beyond Livingston in attempting to deal with the extra-governmental structures underlying federal political systems. Their efforts have been appraised by Michael Stein[8] who drew attention to the consequences for a federal political system of such extra-governmental instrumentalities as political parties, pressure groups, political movements and competing elites. However, Stein's concern with pressure groups may be too restricted. After having defined federalism primarily in terms of regional ethnic-linguistic sub-cultures,[9] he states the nature of his concern with pressure groups: "In the case of pressure groups and other competitive structures, one might investigate the following: What kinds of pressure groups and political movements are formed with the specific purpose in mind of representing one of the ethnic-linguistic communities?"[10] That is, within the limits of his definition of federalism, Stein acknowledges that pressure groups established for the express purpose of influencing the operation of the federal political system may, in fact, do so. However, his concern does not extend to include the role which pressure groups may play in the operation of the federal political system—regardless of the purposes for which they were organized, or the ends which they ostensibly seek.

Pressure groups are voluntary organizations and the role of voluntary organizations as agents of socialization has been widely documented in the literature of political science and sociology. Thus, depending on the basis upon which they are organized, pressure groups may serve to further integrate a federal society or to further fragment it. That is, groups organized on a local or regional basis will tend to strengthen local awareness, local loyalties and local particularism, thus reinforcing fragmentation. On the other hand, groups organized on a national basis will tend to strengthen the national awareness of their members, to create feelings of identification with the national institutions of government, to heighten feelings of efficacy and involvement with those institutions and thus promote national integration.

But the relationship of pressure groups to the federal political system goes well beyond the actions of the former as agents of socialization. David B. Truman has drawn attention to several instances of the influence of federal political institutions upon the organization and internal cohesion of pressure groups. He notes, for example, that the American Medical Association was not formally organized until 1901, and he attributes this tardiness to the fact that in accordance with "the federal character of our political institutions, . . . the governmental means of carrying out the objectives of professional groups were in the hands of the state legislatures rather than in the domain of the national Government."[11] A similar reason is given to explain the delay in establishing a national bar association.[12] But there is no reason to assume that interest group leaders are passive observers of the federal political system; they may try to alter the federal balance or to prevent its alteration. Again, as Truman has pointed out:

> Groups that would be rather obscure or weak under a unitary arrangement may hold advantageous positions in the State governments and will be vigorous in their insistence upon the existing distribution of powers between States and nation. As the advantage of access shifts through time, moreover, groups shift from defenders to critics of the existing balance.[13]

One may add, as well, that the concern of interest group leaders with the federal distribution of powers need not end with attempts to maintain the existing distribution of powers. They may also attempt to shift powers in accordance with the maintenance and enhancement needs of their own organizations.

The purpose of this paper is to present and examine two hypotheses concerning the relationship between political federalism and the demands of interest groups. First, it is hypothesized that the distribution of power between the central and provincial governments influences the structure, cohesion and even the existence of interest groups; that is, that the strength and cohesion of interest groups will tend to mirror the strength, in their particular area of concern, of the government to which they enjoy access. Interest groups which are provincially based and which enjoy access to the provincial governments will be strong compared with nationally based groups enjoying access to the national government when the provincial governments enjoy a stronger position than the national government in the areas of concern to those interest groups, and vice versa. The examination of this hypothesis will take the form of an examination of organizations representing university students in Canada.

Second, it may be hypothesized that if the federal distribution of powers does have consequences for the strength and cohesion of the interest groups enjoying access to the different levels of government, these groups may attempt to influence the distribution of powers between those governments. That is, the struggle for status, recognition and power between a national organization and a provincial organization may cause the leaders of these organizations to attempt to influence the distribution of powers between the federal and provincial governments. This hypothesis will be examined by reference to the demands made upon the government of Canada by the Canadian Labour Congress and its Quebec-based rival, the Confederation of National Trade Unions.

ORGANIZED STUDENTS IN CANADA

The recent history of the Canadian Union of Students (CUS) and the Union Générale des Etudiants du Québec (UGEQ) provides an opportunity to examine the hypothesis that the organization and structure of a federal political system will influence the organization and structure of interest groups which seek to influence the decision-making process within that system. In addition, the recent history of CUS provides some insight into the problems which confront interest groups in federal political systems when faced with rapid shifts of power between levels of government.

The predecessor of CUS, the National Federation of Canadian University Students (NFCUS) was organized in 1926 with ten member universities. Throughout the life of NFCUS and CUS, the basis of organization was the affiliation of university unions or students' councils; there was no provision for direct membership of individual students from unaffiliated institutions. The voices which were heard within NFCUS were those of the heads of students' unions or students' councils at the affiliated institutions and their power base was election to campus office by their own student bodies. NFCUS officers were chosen from among officers of the affiliated student unions and councils and the NFCUS duties were thus a small part of the duties of busy student leaders. Such an arrangement was tolerable only if the NFCUS duties were not onerous. NFCUS was a very loose organization and it functioned primarily as a channel of communication between student leaders. With the exception of the war years, when NFCUS ceased to function, the nature of the organization did not change between 1926 and 1951.

The political conditions under which NFCUS existed prior to 1951 were marked by a virtually complete indifference to the universities on the part of the federal government. Apart from the war and post-war years' inundation of students financed by the Department of Veterans' Affairs, federal involvement in higher education was limited to the occasional research grant, usually from the Defence Research Board or the National Research Council.

In May 1951, the Royal Commission on National Development in the Arts, Letters and Sciences reported and recommended, among other things, direct federal subsidies to Canadian universities. The recommendation was that the federal contribution be made on the basis of a sum per capita of the total population, to be divided among the universities on the basis of their full-time enrollment. This recommendation was accepted almost immediately and direct federal grants to universities began in 1951. Significantly, NFCUS established its first full-time secretariat in Ottawa in 1951. The federal involvement in higher education grew steadily as the grant of just under $7 million in the 1951–52 academic year grew to more than $16 million in 1956–57, and to just under $27 million in 1963–64. As the federal involvement grew, the apparent strength and cohesion of NFCUS waxed. In 1964, NFCUS was reorganized as the Canadian Union of Students.

In 1964 the federal government went beyond simple operating grants. The Canada Student Loan Plan was introduced and the family allowance system was extended to cover students between the ages of 16 and 18. CUS publicity material of that year spoke of the necessity of maintaining a lobby in Ottawa and claimed credit for the Canada Student Loan Plan, the availability of Central Mortgage and Housing Corporation mortgage money for the construction of student residences and half-price student stand-by fares on Air Canada. But of greater importance than these achievements was the attitude of the federal government which, at the time, gave every indication of being willing to undertake still more extensive aid to higher education. It was under these circumstances that CUS launched "Operation UNIVAC" (universal accessibility) on the apparent assumption that only the federal government possessed the resources to finance such a program. CUS was at the crest of the wave.

In the autumn of 1966, by which time direct federal grants to the universities had grown to more than $70 million, disaster struck. At a federal-provincial conference in October, the federal government announced that it would henceforth abide by a strict literal interpretation of the Constitution. An immediate consequence of this policy was the withdrawal of the federal authorities from direct participation in higher education and the abandonment of any hope for new federal initiatives in that field. Although the federal government agreed to assume 50% of the current operating costs of universities, thus increasing its 1967–68 expenditures on university education to well over $200 million, no payments were to be made directly to the universities. The monies would henceforth be made available to the provincial governments, which would disburse them at their discretion. Of equal consequence for CUS was the fact that the federal government would no longer take the initiative in implementing programs of direct concern to the universities or to university students. Such programs would henceforth be the exclusive prerogative of the provincial governments.

Within one year of the fateful conference, CUS was wracked by dissension and there was talk of reorganizing into a federation of provincial student organizations. Within two years ideological disputes had come to the fore and CUS was in imminent danger of disintegration. At the annual CUS congress in September 1968, the membership roster read like the price quotations of a speculative stock during a period of hectic trading. CUS opened the congress with 40 member institutions. At the nadir there were 13 withdrawals leaving only 27 members; however there was a rally at the close and CUS came through its congress with a membership of 34. Within three years of the federal-provincial conference CUS was clearly on its last legs. In October 1969, during the referendum which resulted in the withdrawal of the University of Toronto student body, the editor of that university's student newspaper, as reported in a Canadian University Press dispatch, characterized CUS as "inherently irrelevant to the needs of today's students".[14] By November 1969, the once mighty CUS was left with less than a dozen member institutions, and on the last day of that month it formally ceased to exist.

This analysis is not intended to give the impression that disputes, ideological factionalism and personality clashes were not in evidence in CUS prior to October 1966. No general student organization would be complete without them and CUS had its full share. What is significant is that in spite of these differences, the cohesion of the organization was never seriously in question so long as there was a good and valid reason for maintaining an effective voice at Ottawa.[15] It was only when the raison d'être of this lobby disappeared that the weaknesses, which had previously been kept under control, proved fatal.

The demise of CUS did not mark the end of national student organizations in Canada. Almost immediately after it was announced, attempts were undertaken to launch another organization. Summarizing these attempts in December 1969, the Globe and Mail reported that the organization which seemed most likely to get off to a successful start was a national graduate students' union being promoted by Michael Vaughn, president of the Graduate Students' Union at the University of Toronto. Mr. Vaughn was of the opinion that a national organization was needed because graduate students had common interests such as the availability of research grants and employment opportunities for Ph.D. graduates.[16] That is, the students making the most serious effort to establish an organization at the federal level were those to whom the federal government remained as the source of potential favours.

The history of student organization in the province of Quebec is also of interest here. The universities of that province accepted the first federal grants in 1951–52 but thereafter, until 1959, were obliged to refuse them under threat of having their provincial grants cut off. Quebec's Premier, Maurice Duplessis, was acting to curb what he deemed to be a federal invasion of provincial autonomy. Following the death of Duplessis in 1959, Premier Paul Sauvé and the federal government worked out what was then a novel solution to the problem of university grants. The government of Quebec was to collect one percentage point of the federal sales tax in Quebec and apply the money to university grants. If the amount collected exceeded the Quebec universities' share of the federal grants, the excess would be refunded to the federal government; whereas if the amount collected fell short of the Quebec universities' share, the federal government would reimburse the provincial government for the difference.

When a Liberal government came to federal power, the arrangement worked out by their predecessors with respect to direct university grants was elevated to the level of high national policy under the rubric of "co-operative federalism". Under an "opting-out" formula, the government of Quebec was given fiscal equivalence for the extension of family allowances to the 16–18 year age group and the Canada Student Loans Plan. Of greater significance than these particular programs were the attitudes of the federal and provincial governments. The federal government gave every appearance of having given up the idea that it had any role to play in higher education in Quebec. The provincial government, on the other hand, was dynamic and progressive; it was committed to wholesale reform of the education system and was using the "opting-out" formula to turn Quebec into a veritable state within a state. In short, by 1964 the province of Quebec had reached, and even gone beyond, the position that all the provinces were to find themselves in after the federal-provincial conference of October 1966, and it was evident to the students of Quebec where to look for favours to higher education.

At the CUS congress in September 1964, three French-language Quebec universities withdrew to form UGEQ. Summing up the reasons for the withdrawal, a Canadian University Press dispatch said:

> There will be many theories about the reasons for the withdrawals of the three French-speaking Quebec universities. But perhaps the most concise and penetrating statement so far was

made by Jean Bazin at a congress press conference when he said, "This is not a separatist action. The feeling is simply that CUS, at present, cannot meet the needs of French-Canadian students in Quebec." . . .

The student movement in Quebec . . . has been one of the prime movers in the current reforms of Quebec's church-dominated educational system. Its interests are strictly defined by the current social, political and educational developments in the province of Quebec.[17]

That is, once the federal government had allowed the problems with which they were concerned to be defined as matters falling wholly within the sphere of the Quebec provincial government, the French-speaking students of Quebec no longer had any interest in a national organization.

This paper does not attempt to argue that the withdrawal of the three French-language Quebec universities was not influenced by French Canadian nationalism but simply that this was not the only, or even the major, consideration. French Canadian nationalism was not a new phenomenon in 1964. French Canadian students had worked within CUS and its predecessor for many years; in March 1958 both English- and French-speaking students in Quebec held a one-day strike to protest the reactionary educational policies of the Duplessis government, and in 1959 presented a joint brief to the provincial government asking that the province's universities be permitted to accept the federal grants. The existence of French Canadian nationalism had not, by itself, provided a sufficient basis for the establishment of a separate students' organization. The birth of such an organization had to await two developments: first, the advent of a provincial government dedicated to the promotion of education and the reform of the educational system, (that is, a provincial government from which favours could realistically be sought), and second, the reduction to a negligible level of the federal role in higher education in Quebec and the demise of any hope that that role might expand. By the autumn of 1964, both these conditions had been met.

Also of interest to the thesis under examination is the reaction of the English-language universities in Quebec. Although UGEQ came to be characterized by a virulent French Canadian nationalism, adopted French unilingualism and set entry qualifications which could only have been intended to humiliate any English-language institutions which might seek admission,[18] the English-language universities did eventually join. There can be no doubt, especially in the case of McGill, that the decision to seek admission to UGEQ was prompted by fears for the future of English-language education in the province and by the necessity of joining an organization having access to the government which would decide that future.[19]

The history of student organizations in Canada thus suggests that in a federal system, the distribution of powers on any particular matter between the levels of government can have profound implications for the strength, cohesion and organization of interest groups seeking to influence the formulation of government policy on that issue. In short, the pressure goes where the power is—and takes its organization with it.

ORGANIZED LABOUR IN CANADA

The competition between the Canadian Labour Congress (CLC) and the Quebec-based Confederation of National Trade Unions (CNTU), as well as the unstable state of the distribution of power between the federal and provincial governments in Canada, provide an opportunity to examine the second hypothesis; that rival groups representing the same interest but having access to different levels of government in a federal system will attempt to shift power to the level of government to which they enjoy access.

In January 1957, when federal power was at a peace-time peak, the Canadian Labour Congress presented its annual *Memorandum* to the Government of Canada. The *Memorandum* reviewed the state of federal-provincial relations and noted:

> The Canadian Labour Congress believes that increasingly closer working relationships between the Government of Canada and the governments of the provinces are necessary . . .
> Effective working relationships have been worked out in this field: in Old Age Assistance, Vocational Training and Technical Education, Apprenticeship, Hospital Grants, Rehabilitation of Disabled Persons; the latest agreements to be accomplished are in Unemployment Assistance.[20]

Co-operation in these cases had taken the form of a federal initiative supplemented by grants to encourage provincial participation in shared cost programs. The *Memorandum* continued: "The success attained should be a spur to additional efforts in this field. There are five broad areas in which we ask you to seek the co-operation of the provinces". The five areas were social security, transportation, taxation, education and labour relations. In the final area the CLC made several specific recommendations and asked "that all of these rates and conditions be made uniform throughout Canada through federal-provincial co-operation."[21] The recommendations calling for increased federal-provincial co-operation occupied four pages of the *Memorandum*, and in view of the nature of such co-operation, it is evident that the CLC was seeking a great expansion of the federal role.

In October of the same year, the CLC presented its first *Memorandum* to the newly elected Progressive Conservative government. After reviewing conditions of labour in industries under federal jurisdiction and suggesting that minimum standards be raised to at least those established by the most advanced provincial governments, the CLC noted: ". . . the Dominion should not confine itself to doing as well as the best of the provinces. It should give a lead . . . provide a spur to provincial laggards."[22]

On the subject of labour law, the CLC asked that the federal government achieve uniformity through the use of federal-provincial conferences:

> . . . bring the matter of more uniform labour legislation before a conference with the provinces. Several provincial Labour Relations Acts follow very closely the Industrial Relations and Disputes Investigation Act, and several also provide for agreements with the Government of Canada to have the Canada Labour Relations Board administer the provincial Act. It might be worth while exploring the possibility of making use of these provisions . . .[23]

And further,

> . . . do for other industries of nation-wide scope and importance what was long ago done for the grain elevators: declare the enterprises in them works for general advantage of Canada, and so bring them under the exclusive jurisdiction of Parliament. At present, in the packinghouse industry, for example, an international union bargains with each of three nation-wide companies and concludes three nation-wide agreements; but the process must be carried on under at least six different Labour Relations Acts for one firm alone . . . In such circumstances, a legal nation-wide strike becomes a problem in higher mathematics; and strikes are sometimes necessary and ought not to be hamstrung by legal technicalities.[24]

Another field in which the CLC has consistently sought an expansion of federal authority has been that of highway transportation. In the *Memorandum* of January 1957, the CLC said: "Water, rail and air services are within the federal jurisdiction. Interprovincial and international highway transportation is also federal. The legislation which transfers this responsibility to the provinces should be repealed."[25] This request has been repeated regularly.[26]

Finally, the CLC has asked that substantial amendments be made to the British North America Act to empower Parliament to legislate on matters which fall within the exclusive legislative jurisdiction of the provincial legislatures. Thus, on the ratification of International Labour Organization (ILO) Conventions, the CLC urged the government to ratify those which fall within federal jurisdiction and then turned its attention to the others:

> Even as to those Conventions which are wholly or partly within provincial jurisidiction the Government need not simply forward them to the Lieutenant-Governors for such action as their advisors may see fit. It can use its powers of persuasion upon provincial governments. It can bring the matter up at the next Dominion-provincial Conference. It can seek to have the British North America Act amended to give Parliament power to implement I.L.O. Conventions.[27]

In all of these instances the CLC, a national organization enjoying access at the federal level, was urging the federal government to expand the areas of its legislative competence—either by acting to occupy those areas, or by means of declarations under the provisions of Section 92:10 of the British North America (BNA) Act, or finally, by securing amendments to the BNA Act itself.

In those policy areas which are of concern to them, interest groups seek to strengthen the level of government to which they have access. They are then able to make demands upon that government which are realistic in the sense that it lies within the power of that government to meet the demands. The result of having access to a government which, either through external circumstances or through self-imposed abstention, is unable to meet a group's demands is evident from the history of the Canadian Union of Students. The relationship between the relative power of the federal government vis-à-vis the provincial governments and the ability of the Canadian Labour Congress to make realistic demands upon the federal government is illustrated by the experience of the CLC in the field of education.

In January 1957, the CLC *Memorandum* to the government dealt with education in a section entitled "Dominion-Provincial Relations", the implicit assumption being that education was no longer to be regarded as an exclusively provincial function but as a proper subject for co-operation between the two levels of government. This assumption was made explicit in the text, which noted: "If the needs of a growing population requiring more and more education and training in an expanding economy are to be met adequately, the Government of Canada will have to share the responsibility with the provinces . . ."[28]

The *Memorandum* of October 1957 devoted twice as much space to education as had that of the previous January, and the proposals were based upon the assumption that "education has national aspects and the national Government and Parliament must provide for them."[29] The *Memorandum* then went on to point out the specific areas in which the federal government might aid education:

> The Congress . . . believes that this whole question requires the fullest and freest discussion. It therefore proposes that the national Government call a Dominion-provincial Conference on Education, which could:
> (a) find out exactly what the needs are, for buildings, facilities and teachers;
> (b) find out just how much the municipalities and the provinces can do to meet the needs, and how much national aid is necessary, and recommend on what basis it should be provided;
> (c) consider the extension of teacher training programmes and recommend policies which will attract more men and women of the necessary calibre to the teaching profession.[30]

The next *Memorandum*, presented to the government in January 1959, went even further and urged that the federal government undertake programs of its own in education. Specifically, it recommended:

(1) . . . financial assistance to the provinces for a high standard of education at all levels from grade school to university without regard to residence;

(2) Convene a Dominion-provincial conference on education;

(3) Introduce and assist in the financing of a wide program of scholarships for qualified students who otherwise may not be able to complete their education;

(4) Establish advanced technical institutes in all major industrial centres;

(5) Institute an extension of teacher-training programs, and establish policies, including adequate salary schedules for qualified personnel, which will attract more men and women of the necessary calibre to the teaching profession and

(6) Undertake a school construction program with federal assistance to provide for sufficient classrooms.[31]

The *Memorandum* presented in January of 1960 repeated these demands. By February 1961 the *Memorandum* spoke only of federal grants to equalize educational opportunity and the CLC was obliged to note that "we are well aware of the entrenched rights of the provinces on the subject of education and we are not suggesting that these be tampered with."[32] As federal power waned and provincial power waxed, the demands which the CLC could realistically make upon the federal government in the field of education decreased. After March 1962, the CLC's annual presentations to the government of Canada were, with two minor exceptions,[33] devoid of any mention of education.

The declining power of the federal government meant that the federally based CLC could no longer make realistic demands upon that government in the field of education. The provincially based Confederation of National Trade Unions sought to hasten the federal evacuation of this field:

> What about the projects of aid to education? Education is one field where Provincial jurisdiction is most evident. Yet it appears that in a single year, the Central Government has spent nearly $500 million dollars on education . . . The real question is not whether or not we approve of education but much more the fact that Federal grants to education disturb the power relationship between the Federal and Provincial Governments.[34]

Another area in which the CLC and the CNTU have competed, each on behalf of their own level of government, is medical care insurance. In January 1957, the CLC told the federal government that a "comprehensive programme should be initiated on a nation-wide basis either by the Government of Canada or jointly in co-operation with the provinces as a complete health insurance plan. . . . We strongly urge the Government of Canada to proceed now with the establishment of a comprehensive nation-wide health insurance plan."[35] In October of the same year, the CLC again looked to the federal government to initiate a medical care plan and provide the provincial governments with the necessary leadership: "Constitutionally, health insurance is a provincial responsibility ... but the initiative must come from the national Government. The bulk of the cost must be borne by the national Government. The general framework must be set up by the national Government."[36]

Between 1957 and 1965 the relative strengths of the federal and provincial governments altered drastically and the *Memorandum* of March 1965 reflected this fact:

> We support the Report of the Royal Commission [on Health Services] and we are pleased to observe that it enjoys the support of other major Canadian institutions. We cannot urge you too strongly to do all that is in the power of your Government to make the Health Charter a reality. We realize that in terms of jurisdiction the initiative lies with the provinces.[37]

The *Memorandum* merely recorded the fact that between 1957 and 1965 the initiative had passed from the federal government to the provincial governments. At the same time, the ability to apply pressure to government on such matters had passed from organizations enjoying access at the federal level, such as the CLC, to organizations enjoying access at the provincial level, such as the CNTU. The CNTU, in its brief to the federal government, said:

> As workers we are very much interested in certain aspects of the legislative programme of your Government. Foremost in our view is the announcement of a medicare programme and of better allowances for workers who will undergo professional training. But in both cases we do not believe that the Federal Government enjoys the required jurisdiction.[38]

Similarly, in the area of social welfare legislation, the CLC has consistently urged the federal government to expand its activities in this field. On the other hand, in its brief of February 1969, the CNTU said: "tout la sécurité sociale devrait être de compétence provinciale ... les domaines qui ont été concédés par voie d'amendements constitutionnels doivent être rapatriés aux provinces."[39]

In general, the CNTU has attempted to weaken the federal government in order to strengthen the provincial governments, the Quebec government in particular. The CLC, on the other hand, has striven mightily to restore or preserve the authority of the federal government and to cajole it into regaining the initiative. At the 1964 CLC convention, President Jodoin told the delegates: "It is time for those of us who believe in a strong and a united Canada to speak out. It is typical of some destructive minorities that they talk with loud voices. We must not let ourselves be fooled by this. It is time to put these narrowminded pursuers of selfish objectives in their place."[40] In its next *Memorandum*, submitted in March 1965, the CLC devoted more than two pages to a discussion of what it believed to be one of the causes of the declining power of the federal government,—the declining prestige of Parliament. The aim of the CLC leadership was summed up in the statement:" We wish to see it [Parliament] strong, effective and commanding the respect of the people."[41] The next *Memorandum*, submitted in February 1966, contained a four-page section entitled "A United Canada" which described the provincial assault upon federal power, drew a dark picture of the consequences of allowing that assault to succeed and said:

> We have never suggested nor do we do so now that Canada should be transformed into a unitary state. But we do subscribe to the proposition that certain and very important powers and obligations rest with the federal Government and that these must be exercised boldly and imaginatively in the interests of the Canadian people as a whole regardless of where they live, what language they speak and whatever their cultural or ethnic background may be . . . We call on you as the Government of Canada to use those powers which are legitimately yours and the exercise of which is essential for the well-being of Canada.[42]

It is unlikely that either the CLC or the CNTU were involved in plots, the former to weaken the provincial governments and the latter to weaken the federal government. However, both organizations, by the very dynamics of the situation in which they found themselves, and as a result of their organizational needs, were obliged to attempt to alter the inter-governmental balance of power. To the extent that they contributed to such an alteration, the competition for power and influence between nationally based and locally based organizations was reflected in the distribution of power between the two levels of government.

CONCLUSIONS AND POLICY IMPLICATIONS

This paper has presented two case studies dealing with the relationship between federalism and interest groups. The first study examined the effects of shifts in power from one level of government to another upon the cohesion of an interest group. It was seen that the weakening of a particular level of government relative to the other level will weaken or destroy the organizations dependent upon the former while strengthening those dependent upon the latter.

The second study examined the demands made by federally and provincially based interest groups during a period when the distribution of power between the two levels of government was in a state of flux. It was found that the leadership of both groups made demands which, if adopted, would have resulted in the strengthening of "their" level of government. The federally based organization made demands which would have had the effect of strengthening the federal government vis-à-vis the provincial governments, while the provincially based organization made demands which would have had the effect of strengthening the provincial governments vis-à-vis the federal government.

Before proceeding to an evaluation of these findings, it is necessary to point out certain facts concerning interest groups and their activities. Foremost is the fact that interest groups do not merely aggregate and present the demands of their members. Those demands may be impossible to attain and interest group leaders must show results of some kind if they are to preserve their organizations and their positions within them. In fact, many of the demands emanating from interest groups are initiated by the interest group leaders themselves and must then be "sold" to the membership and to the general public. In "selling" those demands, the interest group leaders create the climate of opinion which legitimizes the action of government, should it decide to meet the demands.

Thus, to the extent that interest groups, like other voluntary organizations, are agents of socialization serving to orient their members and the general public toward the level of government to which their demands are directed, it would appear that both the centralization and the disintegration of a federal political system, once begun and other factors remaining unchanged, are self-sustaining processes. That is, strong governments give rise to strong interest groups which can realistically make demands whose satisfaction would necessitate an expansion of the role of the government upon which the demands are made. The making and the "selling" of these demands helps to legitimize that expansion. If the demands are met, the resultant expansion of that government level's role and relative power further strengthens the position of the interest groups dependent upon it and enables them to make further demands, and so on.

It is unlikely that the leaders of the CLC or the CNTU understood fully the nature of the relationship between the relative strength of governments in a federal system and the relative strength of the organizations dependent upon them. There is, however, some evidence to indicate that the leaders of the CNTU had at least an intuitive understanding of the nature of that relationship, and there is no evidence for supposing that the leadership of the CLC was not equally perceptive. A joint brief submitted to the Quebec Legislative Assembly's Committee on the Constitution by the CNTU and other Quebec provincial labour and farm organizations noted:

> L'accroissement progressif de la compétence relative du pouvoir provincial, par effet des réalités nouvelles auxquelles pouvaient s'appliquer ces pouvoirs, nous a pour ainsi dire été révélé par l'exercice effectif et accéléré de quelques-uns d'entre eux. Par le fait même, le Québec a pris davantage conscience de ses aspirations comme pouvoir politique et inversement le fédéral a pris davantage conscience de son recul.
>
> Le syndicalisme . . . exerce sur le pouvoir provincial une pression qui incite davantage ce dernier à occuper le champ de sa compétence, travaillant ainsi à l'augmentation du poids politique de la province.
>
> Le Québec actuel ne serait pas ce qu'il est, comme entité avec laquelle il faut compter, s'il n'y avait pas eu cet apport.[43]

In general, it may be concluded that at either level in a federal political system, government and the organizations dependent upon government (such as interest groups) tend to mirror each other with respect to their strength and cohesion relative to that of government and organizations at the other level. That is, as one level of government grows stronger relative to the other level, organizations dependent upon it will tend to gain in strength and cohesion relative to the organizations speaking on behalf of the same interest but dependent on the other level of government. Similarly, strong and cohesive organizations tend to strengthen the level of government upon which they are dependent. Furthermore, it would appear that these points are understood, if not fully and explicitly then at least intuitively, by interest group leaders who face rivals claiming to speak on behalf of the same interest but who operate at another level within the federal political system.

A further conclusion is that when the balance of power between the federal and local governments is in a state of flux, interest group leaders at both levels will, as a matter of organizational preservation and enhancement, make demands which, if acted upon, would strengthen their level of government vis-à-vis the other level.

Finally, a wider implication is that the form of government known as political federalism does not exist in a vacuum apart from the social, economic and other realities of the society in which it is located. Federal political institutions are an important determinant in shaping other institutions and organizations in society, and it is therefore logical to expect that the operation of the federal political institutions will become a subject of contention among the leaders of these other organizations and institutions. As a result, other institutions, such as interest groups and private organizations in general, attempt to influence the operation and evolution of the federal political institutions.

The major policy implication to be drawn from these conclusions is that one means by which a government in a federal political system may strengthen itself vis-à-vis government at the other level would be to encourage the development of as broad a range as possible of strong and cohesive private organizations dependent upon it.[44]

NOTES

1. W. S. Livingston, *Federalism and Constitutional Change*, (Oxford University Press, 1956), p. 1–15.

2. *Ibid.*, p. 10–11.

3. *Ibid.*, p. 6–7.

4. William H. Riker, *Federalism: Origin, Operation, Significance*, (Boston: Little Brown & Co., 1964).

5. R. L. Watts, *New Federations: Experiments in the Commonwealth*, (Oxford University Press, 1966).

6. Aaron Wildavsky, *American Federalism in Perspective*, (Boston: Little, Brown & Co., 1967).

7. Karl Deutsch, *Political Community and the North Atlantic Area*, (Princeton University Press, 1957).

8. Michael Stein, "Federal Political Systems and Federal Societies", *World Politics*, XX (1967-68), p. 721–747.

9. *Ibid.*, p. 729.

10. *Ibid.*, p. 739.

11. David B. Truman, *The Governmental Process: Political Interests and Public Opinion*, (New York: Alfred A. Knopf Inc., 1951), p. 94.

12. *Ibid.*, p. 95.

13. *Ibid.*, p. 323.

14. *The Sheaf*, University of Saskatchewan, October 28, 1969, p. 1.

15. The withdrawal of the Quebec universities, which does not detract from the validity of this statement, is discussed below.

16. *The Globe and Mail*, (Toronto) December 8, 1969, p. 10.

17. Canadian University Press Dispatch, Sept. 1964, cited in *The Sheaf*, Oct. 21, 1964, p. 5.

18. See the *McGill Daily*, January 11, 1967, p. 1 and January 18, 1967, p. 1.

19. At the time of the first McGill referendum on UGEQ membership, an article by Victor Rabinovitch, *McGill Daily Supplement*, October 14, 1966, page 3, noted:
    . . . as its many contacts with the Government aptly show, UGEQ is the only body representative of Quebec students today.
    . . . UGEQ is fully recognized by the Government, by other organizations, by the press and by the public, as being a real 'general union of Quebec students'.
    UGEQ sits on several Government committees in its representative capacity, and is replacing the older, university based committees of which McGill was a member. The Student Consultative Committee to the Government Student Aid Service, for example, has largely fallen into disuse. It was UGEQ that convinced the Government to prepare a long-range scheme aimed at eliminating tuition fees. And it is UGEQ that has been submitting briefs on the recommendations of the Parent Commission and the organization of schools. Despite all this, McGill is not a member. On the other hand, decisions are being made in the name of all Quebec students, but McGill has no voice in creating those decisions.
    At the time of the second McGill referendum Jim McCoubrey, Students' Society President said, "I think we can do a lot within UGEQ to stress the rights of the English minority". *McGill Daily*, February 9, 1967, page 1.

20. Canadian Labour Congress, *Memorandum to the Government of Canada*, January 23, 1957, p. 17. (The annual memoranda submitted to the Government of Canada will henceforth be cited as *Memorandum* followed by the month and year of presentation.)

21. *Ibid.*, p. 18–19.

22. *Memorandum, October 1957*, p. 18–19.

23. *Ibid.*, p. 19.

24. *Ibid.*, p. 19–20.

25. *Memorandum, January 1957*, p. 19.

26. *Memorandum, October 1957*, p. 32; *Memorandum, January 1959*, p. 43; *Memorandum, January 1960*, p. 43; *Memorandum, February 1961*, p. 27; *Memorandum, March 1962*, p. 33.

27. *Memorandum, October 1957*, p. 11.

28. *Memorandum, January 1957*, p. 20–21.

29. *Memorandum, October 1957*, p. 34.

30. *Ibid.*, p. 34–5.

31. *Memorandum, January 1959*, p. 45.

32. *Memorandum, February 1961*, p. 24.

33. *Memorandum, February 1966*, p. 28, in a section entitled "War on Poverty", the Congress suggests that enhancement of educational opportunity be one

of the objectives of the "war"; *Memorandum, February 1968*, p. 30 in a section entitled "Bilingualism and Biculturalism" the Congress supports the provision of educational facilities in both official languages.

34. *Memorandum Submitted by the Confederation of National Trade Unions to the Federal Cabinet* (February 16, 1966), p. 21.

35. *Memorandum, January 1957*, p. 14.

36. *Memorandum, October 1957*, p. 16.

37. *Memorandum, March 1965*, p. 19–20.

38. *Memorandum Submitted by the Confederation of National Trade Unions to the Federal Cabinet,* (February 16, 1966), p. 19–20.

39. *Mémoire de la Confédération des syndicats nationaux au Gouvernement du Canada,* (le 18 février 1969), p. 19–20.

40. *Fifth Constitutional Convention of the Canadian Labour Congress, April 20-24, 1964. Report of Proceedings.,* (Ottawa, 1964), p. 2.

41. *Memorandum, March 1965*, p. 7.

42. *Memorandum, February 1966*, p. 10–11.

43. *Mémoire de la Confédération des syndicats nationaux, de la Fédération des travailleurs du Québec et de l'Union catholique des cultivateurs soumis au Comité de la Constitution de l'Assemblée législative du Québec,* (Avril 1966), p. 8.
   This brief, while rejecting separatism, recommended a vast expansion of provincial powers: joint federal-provincial regulation of broadcasting, monetary and fiscal policies; exclusive provincial jurisdiction over all forms of social security and the return to the provinces of those aspects of social security ceded to the federal government by constitutional amendment and the right of provinces to enter into international cultural agreements.

44. It follows from this that the action of one level of government in ceding jurisdiction over a particular class of matters to the other level of government makes the interest group concerned with that class of matters entirely dependent upon that other level of government. Furthermore, since complete jurisdiction will now be concentrated in one government, that interest group will tend to be strong and cohesive.
   In the case of activities which are not subject to government regulation, or whose practitioners do not look to government for favours, the enactment of regulatory legislation will tend to strengthen the cohesiveness of such organizations as may exist in that field, or force the creation of organizations if none exist. Moreover, the enactment of such regulatory legislation would result in the creation of dependence on the part of the group's leaders upon the government which enacted it.

5.

While some pressure groups have had to adapt their structures and procedures to the Canadian federal system, others have used the system's division of powers to their own advantage. Few have had more success in this endeavour than the mining and oil interests, as M. W. Bucovetsky demonstrates in this discussion of their role in the recent tax reform debate. These industries, having considerable economic and institutional power, dominate specific regions and political constituencies. Regional pressure coupled with economic might created an "inexorable pressure" that provincial leaders could not resist. They in turn persuaded Ottawa to abandon important elements of its proposed tax reforms.

At the time of the debate, the mining industry had long been recognized as one of Canada's principal resource industries, "mineral privilege had become well entrenched in Canadian tax practice", and the industry had established such close institutional ties with government that representatives of the mineral industry formed a recognized component of the annual conference of ministers of mines. The industry representatives constituted highly developed institutional pressure groups in most Canadian jurisdictions. This examination of their performance in the tax reform debate offers an opportunity to observe the basis of their power and the techniques available to them in challenging proposed changes in government policy.

Although a public discussion of mineral tax policy was an unfamiliar experience to the industry, its representatives moved quickly to use the media and other forms of political communication to alert its constituency to the threat posed by first the Carter and later the Benson tax reform proposals. Deriving particular strength from the fact that its geographic dispersal gives it considerable influence with provincial governments, the mining industry was able to persuade provincial leaders to exert pressure on the federal government in a generally successful attempt to moderate the effects of reform. This demonstration of the power sources of certain types of pressure groups in the Canadian federal system is the most striking feature of Professor Bucovetsky's discussion, but it also underlines the advantage institutional pressure groups enjoy in being able to afford the support of expert research in preparing briefs to public forums, such as parliamentary committees, which generally do not have the capacity to challenge the assertions of specialists on complex questions. Similarly, the study lends weight to the claim of economic nationalists that institutional groups dominated by multinational corporations are motivated as much by the desire to influence the policies of other governments, and particularly that of the United States, as by considerations related primarily to the Canadian scene.

Professor Bucovetsky's analysis also sheds light on the "withinput–input" problem, more fully defined in a subsequent chapter. While evidence supports the view that close relations exist between institutional groups and administrative units facilitating mutual accommodation, his study points out the fact that because bureaucracy is not monolithic, the objectives of one agency—in this case the Department of Finance—may be thwarted by alliances between other agencies, such as the federal and provincial mines and energy departments, and the affected interest groups. The complexity of the political communications process is thus considerably enhanced. A final aspect of the discussion is its suggestion that the openness of the tax reform debate has to some extent changed the basic conditions of policy-making in the tax field and has caused at least some institutional groups to adopt new and more public techniques of political communication. Such moves in the direction of a more open system of political decision-making are discussed more fully elsewhere in this volume, in Aucoin's review of the effects of recent changes in the policy-making process.

M. W. Bucovetsky is Associate Professor of Economics in the Department of Political Economy, University of Toronto.

The Mining Industry and the Great Tax Reform Debate*

M. W. Bucovetsky

In December 1971 Parliament passed Bill C-259, an Act to amend the Income Tax Act, and so culminated a ten-year sequence of study, proposal and debate. However, the reformed Canadian tax structure that emerged from the lengthy process is hardly the monument to equity and economic efficiency envisaged in the Royal Commission Report that set the reforms in motion.[1] The tortuous retreat from the Royal Commission's lofty design was characterized by the exercise of intense political pressure on the part of interests whose established tax privileges were threatened. It offers an instructive lesson in the interaction of economic and political spheres, particularly in a federal state. None of the proposed reforms were more bitterly attacked than those related to mineral taxation. Hostility to explicitly mineral-centred proposals that were ventured at all stages of the tax reform debate acted as a catalyst in dismembering many recommendations of more general applicability. The mineral taxation issue assumed a key role in marshalling articulate opposition to a fundamentally altered tax structure. Opposition by the mineral industry itself is hardly surprising; the industry had a great deal at stake. Of greater interest is the industry's demonstrated capacity to make its opposition effective.

The purpose of this essay is to chronicle and perhaps explain the degree of success achieved by the mining industry in influencing the decade of Canadian tax reform. In a wider context, it is concerned with the persistence of so-called "tax aids" to particular industries.[2] Toward this end we shall outline the former method of federal mineral taxation, review the stages of Canadian tax reform, indicate the reaction to those stages, and sketch some apparent consequences. Our concern will be mainly with the federal income tax. However, the central role played

* While the author accepts full responsibility for the errors of fact or interpretation, he acknowledges the valuable comments of Richard M. Bird on an earlier draft of this paper. He is also grateful to the editor of this volume for many helpful suggestions.

by the provinces in the tax reform battle requires that we first look at an additional tax liability on the mining industry in the form of unique provincial taxes levied on mining income.

THE PROVINCIAL MINING TAXES

All of the provinces, except Prince Edward Island, have a distinctive source of revenue in their mineral industries.[3] Mineral levies predate the income tax and, indeed, date from before Confederation.[4] The rationale for such charges is that they are fees paid for the privilege of private exploitation of a natural resource originally in the public domain. They are regarded as "a means of securing for the Province a share of the economic rent for the use of its resources."[5] The form that mineral resource revenue may take varies from province to province and sometimes from mineral to mineral. The levy may be a separate tax on mining profit, a tax on mineral acreage, a tax on the assessed value of mineral deposits, and/or royalties on the value of minerals produced. Royalties on production from Crown land (and proceeds of the auctioned right of entry to the Crown-owned deposit) are a very important source of revenue to the western provinces, based on their oil and natural gas, and potash deposits. However, where the provinces have permanently alienated their mineral rights on Crown lands, a levy on gross output is regarded as an indirect tax and therefore outside the provinces' constitutional competence. Since the usual early form of land tenure did involve outright grants, the chief means by which the provinces have "shared in the economic rent" on the solid minerals has been a special tax levied on mining profits.

There is considerable variation among the provinces both in defining mining profit and in the rates applied. All of the provinces intend the profit taxed to be exclusive of processing profits beyond the mill or concentrator. Rates of tax may be either flat or graduated percentages. With minor exceptions, 1973 rates ran in the range of 10% to 15%.[6] The history of the mining taxes shows a tendency for rates to rise irregularly over time; it seems that no one province dare get seriously out of line, but that incremental innovation by one is emulated by the others.

In principle, the federal Income Tax Act has treated these provincial taxes as royalties deductible from income otherwise subject to the corporation tax. In practice, deductibility has been less than complete.[7] Nonetheless, the greater proportion of mining taxes have, in fact, been a permitted charge against the income upon which corporation tax is paid.[8]

We should observe that the provinces also levy their own general corporate income taxes on all corporation income earned in the province with rates from 10% to 13%. The federal government accommodates the latter taxes by an "abatement" of ten percentage points of profit, deductible from the corporation tax which it would otherwise levy itself. Until the recent federal tax reform, the basis of the provincial taxes, including provision for distinctive treatment of mineral income, was identical to that of the federal corporation tax.

Before leaving matters of provincial jurisdiction, mention should be made of a proposal to revise the mine profit tax in one province. Simultaneously with the appointment of the federal Royal Commission on Taxation, four provinces named expert committees or Royal Commissions to review their own tax systems.[9] The Report of one of these, the Ontario Committee (Smith Committee), scrutinized the existing provincial taxation of mine profits and made proposals for its drastic re-design.[10] The main recommendation of the Smith Committee in this area was that the single-tier tax on mine profits be replaced by a two-tier tax. The first stage, a benefit principle Mine Services Tax, was to yield the province an amount equal to the transfer payments made to mining municipalities. The second stage, the Mine Profits Tax, was meant to appropriate a share of the scarcity rents accruing to owners of highly profitable mines. The counter-attack that followed was scarcely less acrimonious than that which six months earlier had greeted the federal Royal Commission Report. The Ontario government referred the Smith Report for Study and amendment to a Select Committee of the Legislature.[11] The Select Committee rejected the two-tier system; when the Mining Tax Act was amended in 1969, the most notable change was an increase from the existing graduated tax, that ranged between 6% and 12%, to a single flat rate of 15%.[12]

THE INCOME TAX ON MINING, PRIOR TO 1972

Four notable types of special provision were used to implement tax aids to the extractive industries under the former federal Income Tax Act. The first of these had the effect of accelerating the timing of deductions related to essentially long-term capital investments, by qualifying corporations. A corporation whose principal business was in the mineral field, broadly defined, was allowed to treat as current expenses for purposes of determining taxable income all costs of Canadian mineral exploration and development, excluding land costs and treatment plants.[13]

On the other hand, discrimination was implied against an individual who explored or a corporation that did not qualify as to principal business. To those taxpayers, the right to write off exploration and development costs was, in effect, confined to the cost of ventures that turned out successfully and after success was attained.

Mining structures not subject to the "expensing" provisions were recoverable against future taxable income on a reducing balance schedule, like that for other industries, but depreciation rates for the extractive industries permitted a more rapid cost recovery than elsewhere.

The second distinctive provision was the outright exemption from income tax of the first three years' profit from a new mine.[14]

The third group of tax aids were the percentage allowances, commonly termed "depletion", which further reduced the base on which tax was calculated. In the general case, this meant that after taking all permitted deductions, a mineral operator was allowed to reduce his taxable income by a further 33⅓%.[15] "Non-operators" (i.e. royalty holders), with an interest in mineral profits, were allowed a 25% deduction from gross mineral income. Shareholders in mining corporations were allowed a further personal depletion allowance of 10% to 20% against mineral-source dividends.

The fourth special provision was that income received by prospectors and their financial backers (grubstakers) from the sale of mineral properties was excluded from income subjected to tax.

There is no doubt that these provisions, taken together, considerably lightened the relative burden of income-related taxes on the extractive industries, even allowing for the additional provincial mine profit tax. However, it is difficult to be precise about the magnitude of the tax favour. Published data do not lend themselves to simple application of the economist's concept of gross and net return. And the mining industry is correct in complaining that some recent attempts to measure the result of the tax aids understate the effective rate of tax on the industry.[16] Nonetheless, the orders of magnitude can be illustrated in the following numbers, for the 1969 taxation year. In these calculations, taxes paid are computed as the sum of remitted federal and provincial corporation taxes and provincial mining and logging taxes.[17] Operating profit is net book profit with mining and logging taxes and book provision for income tax added back, and non-taxable dividends received subtracted. The percentage ratio of taxes paid to operating profit for the aggregate extractive sector, including vertically integrated companies classified to smelting and refining, and petroleum and coal products, was 17.71%. The similar percentage ratio for the aggregate non-extractive remainder of the corporate sector was 42.18%.[18] If royalties paid by petroleum producers are regarded as a form of taxation, the effective tax rate for the extractive sector rises to 20.46%. The conclusion is inescapable that the effective tax burden on mineral corporations is not more than half that on non-mineral corporations.

These data are necessarily highly aggregative. It may be observed that the benefits of the mineral tax provisions are unevenly dispensed. Such provisions as the expensing of exploration and development costs favour the existing vertically integrated operator with a processing plant in existence. For the beginning explorer, their benefit lies in the promise of a higher relative pay-off in an uncertain future; they make no direct contribution to the exigency of investment finance. It may then be argued that the tax provisions promoted concentration of ownership in the mineral industries. The Royal Commission on Taxation calculated that in 1964 five mining companies and three petroleum companies accounted for 85% of the total depletion claimed.[19] Also in 1964, four mining companies accounted for over three-quarters of the income exempted under the three-year provision.[20]

For major Canadian mines it appears that the amount of profit exempted from taxation in the initial three years has been as large as (or larger than) the total capital cost of the venture.[21] And this route to capital recovery is in addition to the rapid write-off of exploration and development, favourable depreciation rates on plant, and an effective tax rate reduced by the ⅓ percentage allowance.

The history of mineral tax aids and the reasons stated for their being granted are subjects too lengthy to be detailed here.[22] The oldest of the Canadian tax aids, the depletion allowance, was introduced with the inception of the income tax. At the time, depletion itself and allowances for depreciation were on a less generous scale and represented far less duplication of tax favour than did their historical outgrowth. The depletion allowance derived in concept, if not in precise form, from a United States precedent. The three-year exemption was first introduced in 1936 primarily as a depression-inspired spur to gold mining; gold was perhaps the only commodity with a ready sale on world markets. The write-off of exploration and development was introduced during World War II as an incentive toward finding needed mineral deposits. Whatever its original reason, each provision became a permanent part of the taxing statute and grew in dimension over time.

Mineral privilege had become well entrenched in Canadian tax practice. There is no doubt that this meant considerable prosperity to a number of mineral companies. However, until the appointment of the Royal Commission on Taxation, there was very little serious discussion of the ends, and almost none of the means, of mineral tax policy.

THE CARTER REPORT AND ITS AFTERMATH

The Royal Commission on Taxation (Carter Commission) was appointed by the Diefenbaker government in September 1962, ". . . to make recommendations for improvements in the tax laws and their administration. . . ."[23] The Commission received about three hundred briefs, held extensive hearings and commissioned over thirty research studies. In the light of the present narrative, it should be noted that spokesmen for the mineral industries were given every opportunity to make their case. The Commission's Report was made public by the Liberal government in late February 1967.

We are concerned here with the Commission's recommendations for the tax treatment of the extractive industries. But these must be viewed as only one application of a coherent tax design. Starting with a strong predilection for the criteria of equity and neutrality, the Commission, by inexorable logic, developed a blueprint for a rational tax system whose main features would be:

a) Prime emphasis on a progressive personal income tax applied to an "income" comprehensively defined to include virtually all accretions to wealth.
b) Full integration of the personal and corporation income tax to eliminate all anomalies from the coexistence of the two taxes.
c) Elimination or mitigation of other anomalies in such matters as fluctuating earnings, deductibility of business expenses, and loss carry-forward.

In the specific area of mineral taxation, the Commission could see little reason for tax preferment other than the risks inherent in new exploration ventures. Nonetheless, it did not recommend complete removal of the tax aids.[24] It did advise that percentage depletion, be it to operators, non-operators, or shareholders, should end immediately, and that the three-year tax exempt period for new mines should be phased out within five years. It saw more merit in the immediate write-off of exploration costs, which should apply equally to all taxpayers. The write-off provisions, it said, should be somewhat broadened to include the cost of depreciable assets used in exploration projects. On the other hand, the immediate write-off of development costs should be phased out in from five to ten years, and thereafter receive depreciation treatment. Land costs should also be capitalized and amortized for tax purposes.

A novel proposal, made by the Commission, was that, to encourage exploration, people who bought newly-issued mineral shares should be able to match their cost against taxable personal income to the extent that the proceeds were used for exploration and development. The prospectors' and grubstakers' exemption would be ended and replaced by generous write-off provisions for prospecting expenses.

The Commission's revenue estimates show that mining firms would incur more than twice the tax liability under its proposals as compared with the existing system, and oil and gas firms about 40% more.[25] However, over 80% of these increases would be borne by fifteen large mining and oil companies.[26]

Reaction to the Carter proposals was intense. Such general recommendations as the comprehensive income tax base including full taxation of capital gains, the family tax unit, and integration of the corporation and personal income taxes raised considerable furor. Nonetheless, it is probable that as much public comment was drawn by the proposals made for the extractive industries as by any of the recommendations of more universal application and greater potential impact. Certainly in no other area was public comment as one-sided (i.e. hostile to the Report) and, apparently, as well-organized.

The author has been able to find only two "industry" sources whose comment on the Report was sanguine. One of these was by the United Steelworkers of America, the pre-eminent union in the mining industry.[27] The other was apparently an unguarded comment by the vice-president of a large then-developing mine property who avowed that the proposals would make little practical difference in the decision whether or not to develop. Prompted by his president, the indiscreet VP recanted a week later.[28]

What appears to have been an orchestrated campaign of alarm took shape about a month after the Report came out.[29] Portents of economic enervation resulting from the Report's mineral tax proposals were sounded in increasing number at annual shareholder meetings and in newspaper accounts. The *Globe and Mail* of Toronto, whose masthead proclamation "Canada's National Newspaper" is not entirely hyperbole, published a sequence of news stories, reports of addresses, and signed comments whose message was that uncertainty engendered by the Report was already responsible for the loss of millions of dollars in capital spending by the mineral industries, with much more to come if the government did not disavow the Report.[30] The campaign by head-line reached its culmination on April 29, 1967, when the front page of the *Globe and Mail* carried a three-inch banner proclaiming "$90 million program. Noranda shelves plans, blames Carter Report."[31] The story beneath was of the Noranda mining group's announced suspension of development of two British Columbia copper mines, one of them a $60 million project of Brenda Mines Ltd., at Penticton.

Ross Thatcher, the Premier of Saskatchewan, joined the fray. A sum-mary of an address he delivered in London, Ontario, on April 26th, said:

> (He) criticized certain recommendations of the Carter report as an "overt and blatant" proposal to remove several of the investment incentives left to industry. "Personally, I believe that those recom-mendations made by the Carter commission which would remove existing incentives to the oil and mining industry are ill-advised and short-sighted." At least two potash complexes in Saskat-chewan were holding up construction plans while waiting for a government statement of intentions regarding the report, Mr. Thatcher said.[32]

The message of a mounting "capital strike" in mining was getting through to the federal government. On May 2nd the *Globe and Mail* reported that the Minister of Finance was preparing a statement that would reassure investors in the mining industry, at least until govern-ment's own review of the Carter proposals was completed.[33]

Nine days later the Minister delivered a placative response in the form of the following short-term undertakings:

a) that in the event that the three-year exemption for new mines were withdrawn, such withdrawal would not apply to income earned before January 1, 1974.

b) that in the event that the prospectors' and grubstakers' exemption were withdrawn, such withdrawal would not apply to amounts received before January 1, 1969 related to properties acquired before January 1, 1968.[34]

The industry was somewhat reassured and the Minister was suitably rewarded for moving in the right direction. The day after his message, Noranda announced that it would proceed with the $60 million Brenda project after all. But this was not the end of the campaign; indeed it was only the beginning. At a Canadian Tax Foundation conference in April, Mr. Sharp had issued a general invitation for interested parties to submit briefs to him in reaction to the Report.[35] The mineral in-dustries took full advantage of the opportunity; by the September 30th

95

deadline, over 100 protesting submissions were made to the Minister by the oil industry alone.[36] The industries continued to be vigorously supported by provincial premiers, at that stage mainly those of the western provinces. On June 22nd, the three prairie Premiers, acting in concert, sent a telegram to Prime Minister Pearson expressing "grave concern at federal government haste in implementing parts of the Carter Royal Commission Report on Taxation."[37] Of six objections raised in the telegram five were of a general nature and one was related explicitly to resource taxation. In Parliament the next day, Mr. Pearson confessed ignorance as to why the Premiers thought the government would hastily implement the Report. "There are no grounds for such fear," said the Prime Minister.[38]

Members of Parliament gave enthusiastic support to the well-harmonized effort. Speaking in the budget debate of the following October, Mr. Deachman, the Member for Vancouver Quadra and a member of the government caucus, made an impassioned plea on behalf of the mining industry, quoting liberally from the industry's briefs to the Minister and from newspaper stories.[39] He warned Mr. Sharp that a short-term guarantee was not enough, that he must declare that the depletion allowance and the three-year tax holiday would not be seriously upset.

Not everyone was persuaded by the public relations campaign. In the Ontario Legislative Assembly, Mr. Sopha, the member for Sudbury, disparagingly described the reaction of the International Nickel Company to the provincial and federal tax commission reports:

> It only took them one thin volume to criticize the recommendations of the Smith Committee, but they very kindly delivered to me a copy of their criticism of the Carter commission. I thought somebody had brought me a case of beer. That is the size of the box it took to deliver the three very thick volumes which led me immediately to conclude that there must be merit in the Carter commission, since it took them so many pages to criticize it.[40]

By February of 1968 the worst seemed to be over. The president of the Mining Association of Canada was able to report to his membership that at a meeting with Mr. Sharp, the Minister had indicated to the Association that "we had made our point" on the Carter recommendations.[41] Even earlier, in his "mini-budget" presentation to Parliament on November 30, 1967, Mr. Sharp signalled the demise of the pristine Carter reforms. He gave four reasons: the difficulty of predicting the effects of a Carter tax structure, its divergence from the systems of other countries, its inadequate provision for incentive to saving and growth,[42] and, of most relevance to the present subject, ". . . a widespread concern over the regional impact of the commissioners' proposals, particularly those related to the mining and petroleum industries."[43]

Nonetheless, the Carter Report had raised too many fundamental issues of principle to be buried without a trace. Even the *Globe and*

Mail published an editorial advocating that the government "salvage the Carter virtues."[44] The government was committed to producing its own tax design; it was apparent that in that design the extractive industries would not emerge unscathed.

THE BENSON WHITE PAPER

The government's own tax design took the form of a White Paper tabled in Parliament by the new Minister of Finance, Edgar Benson, on November 7, 1969.[45] Usually, under the Canadian parliamentary system, tax policy changes are first revealed in a formal budget presentation which represents a government commitment from which retreat is difficult. In the present case, however, the government's views on tax reform were deliberately tentative; the White Paper was said to express the thrust of government thinking, to which it was, nonetheless, not irrevocably committed. The procedure thus provided freedom for alteration or strategic retreat.

As a tax reform blueprint, the White Paper lacked the consistency and comprehensiveness of the Royal Commission's analysis and recommendations. Yet the influences of the Royal Commission Report are unmistakable. Moves toward a more comprehensive definition of taxable income and elimination of anomalies were accompanied by a partial integration of the personal and corporation income taxes. In the specific area of mineral taxation, it accepted the "risks of exploration" and "regional development" arguments for tax aids.[46] The scheme devised was an imaginative compromise aimed at converting mineral tax preference into an unequivocal incentive to explore. The proposals in this area, while considerably less severe than those of the Royal Commission, nonetheless implied a heavier burden of income tax on mineral revenues than had the existing tax structure.[47]

To begin with, the White Paper recommended repeal of non-operators' depletion, shareholders' depletion, and the prospectors' and grubstakers' exemption. On the other hand, it favoured extension of the principle of rapid write-off. The White Paper would have continued the right to expense full costs of Canadian exploration and development against all income from mineral properties. A new provision would allow similar costs to be recovered as depreciation, against income from any source, if the taxpayer did not have sufficient mineral income. Costs of mining land would be added to the expensible items. Although the three-year exemption for new mines would end on December 31, 1973, the rapid write-off privilege would now be applied to the entire plant cost of a new mine.[48]

An innovation was the suggestion that operators' depletion be converted into a genuine incentive, viz. into a 133⅓% allowance for exploratory and development expenditures on new mines. The means of effecting this excess write-off would be to retain the form of the old operators' allowance. However, one-third of mineral income after all other eligible deductions would now become a taxpayer's maximum allowance in a year. His actual allowance would depend on his spending on exploration, development, and capital assets of new mines, excluding the costs of mineral rights in land. Each $3 of such expenditure would "earn" him $1 in depletion.[49]

The White Paper procedure was designed to evoke public reaction. The government had declared its willingness "to change any proposals that are in the White Paper if [it] can be convinced."[50] It need hardly have been a surprise that those who stood to lose and had the means to make their objections heard would do so. Yet, the government seems scarcely to have been prepared for the vehemence of the reaction. A forum was provided for the debate by means of hearings on the White Paper conducted by the House of Commons Standing Committee on Finance, Trade, and Economic Affairs and by the Senate Committee on Banking, Trade and Commerce. Because of the arrayed vested interests, the Committees' inadequate and temporary staffs, and the very novelty of the Committee procedure, the debate turned out to be rather one-sided.[51]

In the Committee hearings and outside, the publicists focused on many issues with widespread emotional appeal, such as the proposals regarding capital gains, integration, and elimination of the dual rate of corporation income tax. However, opposition to these proposals of broad application was rivalled if not surpassed by pressure exerted to change the projected treatment of the mineral industries. Of the 214 witness groups appearing before the Commons Committee conducting hearings on the White Paper, 43, or about 20%, can be judged to have been primarily interested in overturning the mineral tax proposals. This count is apart from other groups for whom this objective was important but not paramount. The provincial governments played an active role in the campaign, not least against the mineral provisions. The Senate Committee, at the conclusion of its hearings, remarked: "It is significant that in the briefs published by the various provinces in recent months, the two items in the White Paper that were most strenuously objected to were integration and the proposed treatment of mining and oil and gas industries".[52]

The provincial authorities of central Canada, who had been less visibly disturbed by the Carter proposals than their western colleagues, now assumed a leadership role. The government of Ontario went so far as to publish its own design for federal tax reform.[53] The Ontario document lauded the contribution to the Canadian economy made by the mining industry and then pointedly drew attention to the fact that

> Jurisdiction over natural resources in Canada was given exclusively to the provinces under the British North America Act. In Ontario, a mining tax was imposed on the profits attributable to the removal of natural resources ten years before any income tax was imposed by the federal government. This fact has been completely ignored by the white paper.
> We urge the federal government, therefore, to recognize the

right of the provinces to tax profits derived from the exploitation of their natural resources, and to leave them taxing room for this purpose.[54]

The Premier of Quebec, Robert Bourassa, expressed himself in rather similar vein.[55]

A reading of industry briefs to the committees leaves the impression that the tactics of the mining industry proper involved a more defensive stance than did those of the oil and gas producers. The oil and gas industry had less to lose under the White Paper. Although it is not necessarily true of each individual company, the petroleum industry as a whole had been spending an amount on exploration and development that would have amply "earned" its current level of depletion.[56] Nonetheless, the oil and gas industry rose to the attack. Having withstood the most repugnant of the Carter Commission recommendations, it now argued that existing concessions were insufficient:

> The existing provisions have not been sufficiently attractive to encourage many Canadians to invest in the petroleum industry because the incentives have not been adequate to produce a satisfactory rate of return to the industry.
> Depletion should be calculated at 20% of gross production income limited to $33\frac{1}{3}$% of exploration and development expenditures including the cost of mineral rights.[57]

This particular scheme would likely eliminate all income tax from petroleum companies. The call for a gross depletion allowance, on the American model, recurs in many of the briefs. Gross depletion is more lucrative to the industry because the amount of the allowance is not reduced by other permitted tax deductions as is the case with the net allowance.[58]

The loss of tax advantage implied by the White Paper was more severe in mining proper. Having more to lose, the mining industry seemed prepared to concede some of its existing tax advantages if it might retain the more significant ones. Among the briefs that deal with mining, those that express a willingness to compromise focused on four main propositions:

1. Willingness to concede an upper limit to the three-year exemption. As an example, "the amount of exempt income permitted could be limited to the lesser of the income earned in a three-year period or the amount of the investment in the project."[59]
2. Recommendation that the basis for earned depletion be broadened to include expenditures on processing plant beyond the milling stage, and on mine expansion after commencement of production.
3. Recommendation that in addition to "earned" depletion there be an automatic "unearned" allowance (at a reduced rate of, say, 15-20%).
4. Recommendation that more explicit account be taken of the concurrent provincial taxes on mining profit.

One or more of the above propositions figure in most of the mining briefs. The last three were endorsed by the Canadian Bar Association.[60] An effort seems to have been made to co-ordinate the protests and to make them conciliatory. The federal government would have great difficulty gainsaying a campaign that was both massive and temperate.

The leadership of the provinces is unmistakable in this consensus of "responsible" opposition. The province of Ontario, in particular, appears to have taken the lead in apparently accepting the reform spirit of the White Paper while compromising its essential thrust. All four of the propositions listed above were approved by Ontario.[61] The last three propositions also figured in a statement made by the Premier of Quebec to a meeting of Ministers of Finance.[62] In the event, as detailed below, Mr. Benson subsequently amended his White Paper to accommodate the second and fourth of the propositions we have noted.

THE WHITE PAPER REVISIONS OF AUGUST 1970

The first visible crack in the White Paper structure appeared in late August 1970, even before the completion of reports by the parliamentary committees. An earlier Minister of Finance had first signalled his abandonment of the Carter Report's recommendations with an announcement on mineral policy; now Mr. Benson heralded the dismemberment of the White Paper with a major revision to the proposals that applied to the mining industry. The means by which the modifications were detailed is itself of interest because their announcement took the unusual form of a letter sent by him to provincial finance ministers and treasurers.[63] The three amendments to the White Paper that he offered were these:

1. Expenditures which qualified to "earn" depletion would be enlarged to include costs of new facilities located in Canada to process mineral ores to the "prime metal stage" or its equivalent.[64]
2. "Certain expenditures connected with major expansions of a mine" would qualify for "earning" depletion. The announcement did not spell out the definition of a "major expansion", although it is understood that, at that stage, routine modernization of equipment would not have qualified.[65]
3. When the new basis for taxing mines became fully effective, the provincial abatement against federal corporation income tax would be increased by 15 percentage points (from 10), for mining profits only. This provision has the effect of decreasing the effective rate of the federal corporate income tax on mining companies from 40% to 25% of taxed profit. The former deductibility of provincial mining taxes from the income subjected to the corporation income tax would be replaced by this more generous tax credit.

The significance of these revisions may be gauged by an estimate that the new offer removed almost two-thirds of the tax increase on the extractive industries implied in the original White Paper proposals.[66]

The main force motivating the Minister's capitulation was undoubtedly the influence of the provinces. Three weeks before his announcement, Mr. Benson had acknowledged inexorable pressure from the provinces for mitigation of the mineral tax provisions:

> There have been serious representations from most of the provinces with respect to taxes on the extractive industry and the effects on them. We will have to take these into consideration along with the Committee report before we ultimately make our decision.[67]

However, Mr. Benson's timetable was sped up by concurrent pressure on the Premiers on the part of the industry. One Premier who had particular reason to twist Mr. Benson's arm was the harried Premier of Quebec, Mr. Bourassa, who had to make good a pre-election promise of 100,000 new jobs for Quebec. The Premier was quite candid in explaining his support for revision of the White Paper provisions for mineral taxation:

> Several expansion plans, entailing in total several hundred million dollars, have been postponed or—so we are told—are likely never to materialize because of the implications of tax reform. . . .
>
> Quebec cannot afford to lose promising investments in this fashion.[68]

Ironically, Mr. Bourassa's employment problems were compounded by the federal government's short-term stabilization policies. Mr. Benson's department, obsessed with the fear of inflation, was pursuing a relentlessly contractionary fiscal policy in 1969 and 1970.[69] Federal government policy thus contributed to the bargaining strength of the large mining firms. Faced with the immediate threat of curtailed mine expansion, Mr. Bourassa presumably conveyed his sense of urgency to Ottawa. This urgency, and the reason that Mr. Benson's concession took the form of a letter to his provincial colleagues, can be understood in the light of two announcements that followed hard on the Minister's letter. Nine days later it was reported that Quebec Cartier Mining would start immediately on the second phase of developing its Mount Wright iron deposits in Quebec.[70] A further six days later, Iron Ore Co. of Canada also announced a major increase in capacity in Quebec and Labrador.[71] A pertinent comment appeared in a construction trade journal:

> The revisions are particularly favourable to the iron ore mining companies. Because of their large capital investment requirements for surface plant, they stand to benefit most from the broadened definition of earned depletion.[72]

Industry gratification with Mr. Benson's letter was tempered with some nervousness. This stemmed from the fear that hard-pressed provincial treasuries would find it difficult to resist the temptation to reoccupy the tax room opened up by the federal abatement. It was reported at the 1971 meeting of the Mining Association of Canada that, in the view of John L. Bonus, the organization's managing director, the industry had reason to be concerned that Ottawa's new position failed to guarantee a tax rate that in the long run "would be sufficient for the industry to pursue its growth."[73] Recent developments, discussed below, lend some substance to this possibility.

THE FINALE OF TAX REFORM

The Senate Committee Report on the White Paper appeared in September 1970, and that of the Commons Committee the following month.[74] In the main, and particularly in the area of mineral taxation, the Commons Committee was more sympathetic toward the White Paper's viewpoint. The Senate Committee in this as in most areas was reluctant to effect any change. Both advocated further retreat from the White Paper proposals affecting the extractive industries. The Mining Association derived some comfort from both, seeing in them "substantial opposition" to the White Paper proposals, though the association's managing director expressed some reservations about each. The Senate Committee, Bonus felt, had overstated some points and thus lost credibility whilst the Commons report was "less favourable" to the mining interests, even though it represented an improvement—from the industry's point of view—over the White Paper and Carter proposals.[75]

When the actual tax reform legislation was finally unveiled in Mr. Benson's budget presentation of June 18, 1971, it was profoundly different from the White Paper and the Carter design. The end product was "a reformed tax system which looks in some key aspects more like the present American system than the Royal Commission blueprint."[76] In terms of the usual equity standards, some modest gains were made in such matters as partial taxation of capital gains. On the other hand the changes made, together with final abandonment of any attempt to integrate the corporation and personal income taxes, represent a slight reduction in economic efficiency and growth incentive.[77]

So far as mineral taxation is concerned, the last act of the tax reform drama was anti-climactic. Erosion was well advanced after the events of the previous August. The reform Act itself contained more of the same. The following list covers only provisions in the new Act that modify or extend those already mentioned above in connection with the original White Paper and the revision of August 1970.[78]

1. Foreign exploration and development expenses may now be claimed for tax purposes. The annual claim is the greater of total foreign mineral income or 10% of the unclaimed balance.
2. The right to write-off plant costs on an accelerated basis, as rapidly as a taxpayer's income permits, was extended to include all assets related to a new mine including a refinery and townsite facilities.
3. Accelerated depreciation was also extended (but on a slightly more limited basis) to cover assets related to the expansion of an existing mine where the capacity is increased by at least 25%.

4. The old automatic percentage allowance will continue through 1976. For 1977 and later years, depletion will have to be "earned". However, a new technicality ensures that it will be many years before the "earning" constraint becomes operative. Income from any property, whether owned on the date the White Paper appeared or not, will enjoy depletion to the end of 1976. On the other hand eligible expenditures made from the White Paper date to December 31, 1976 will build up a bank of earned depletion that may be claimed in 1977 and subsequent years.[79]

5. Expenditures eligible to "earn" depletion were extended to include all the assets mentioned above under items 2. and 3., excepting townsite facilities.

6. Rentals and royalties received from mineral properties will be counted as production income for the purpose of defining the maximum depletion allowance that may be claimed.

7. Although prospectors' and grubstakers' income is no longer exempt, when they exchange properties for company shares they will be taxed on the sale of the shares at preferred capital gains rates.

The next following annual budget, presented by Mr. Benson's successor, John Turner, on May 8, 1972, contained further significant concessions to the extractive industries beyond those in the tax reform Act:

I propose that the class of expenditures which earn depletion be extended to include all equipment acquired after tonight for the purpose of processing in Canada mineral ores after extraction and up to the prime metal stage. This will include all processing, whether or not related to a new mine or a major expansion, as well as custom processing. Furthermore, I propose that all of the income from such processing operations be considered as income against which depletion may be claimed and in respect of which the 15 per cent provincial abatement will apply.[80]

Mention must be made also of the revised Ontario Corporations Tax Act of 1972.[81] A major concern throughout the federal tax reform process was that the tax system which emerged must preserve the advantages of the existing system under which provincial governments levied income taxes on the same basis as the national government. It was this concern that gave the provinces a substantial veto power over federal tax design. As Mr. Mahoney, the Parliamentary Secretary to Mr. Benson, put it after the introduction of the federal reform Act,

One of the major objectives of tax reform is provincial acceptability. We do not want a tax jungle in Canada, we want a tax system that the provinces can and will use.[82]

Passage of the federal Act was followed by accommodative legislation on the part of the provinces. The one exception concerns those portions of the Ontario Corporations Tax Act covering the mining industry. Ontario chose to retain in its Act all the provisions of the expired federal Act including the three-year exemption, automatic depletion allowance, and prospectors' and grubstakers' exemption. This decision will involve the Ontario government in considerable administrative complexity and expense, for example, in determining eligibility for the three-year exemption, a task formerly undertaken by the federal civil service. An opposition member of the Legislature, Mr. Cassidy, points out that an Ontario mining company must now keep three sets of books in order to get maximum advantage from both the Ontario and the federal statutes.[83]

The response to this kind of criticism by the Ontario Treasurer, Mr. MacNaughton, is interesting because it gives a clue to the thrust of the reformed federal Act:

> The federal rules would give reduced taxes to large corporations which can earn maximum depletion, but would increase taxes on smaller mines.[84]

A similar view was recently expressed by a consulting geologist:

> We have been through the ordeal of tax reform that has removed a number of incentives both to companies and to individuals, and will tend to favour the larger integrated companies because of the earned depletion concept.[85]

They might have added that accelerated depreciation also especially favours massive, capital intensive projects. To the small, independent, high-grade mine, the three-year exemption was of greater benefit than is accelerated depreciation. The 15% abatement of corporation tax, assuming that the provinces do not increase their mine profit taxes, represents a far larger tax saving than did the previous deductibility of mine profit taxes paid; but in either case the potential benefit depends on the mine's having taxable profit. Moreover, the more "processing" in which a mineral firm engages, the more valuable does the abatement become.[86] On all the available evidence, the new Act is likely to impose no greater tax burden on the extractive industries as a whole than did the previous Act. As we noted, the Carter Commission had demonstrated that the old tax aids were of disproportionate benefit to the major companies. The advantages conferred by the new Act are biased even more heavily in favour of large, vertically integrated and growing companies. Tax reform is likely to accelerate the trend toward concentration of ownership in the mineral industry.

THE MINERAL CONSTITUENCY

The foregoing narrative illustrates the considerable success achieved by the extractive industries in blunting and, indeed, reversing the thrust of tax reform in Canada. But the leverage exerted by the mineral industries was much more than a passing phenomenon, although it did draw considerable potency from the coincidence of high unemployment with the culmination of the debate. In the longer view it is apparent that institutional and political factors have always been more important in framing and retaining mineral tax policies than have economic considerations.

To the extent that implicit ends were understood in Canadian mineral tax policy prior to the Carter investigation, their rationale had a physiocratic ring. Underlying much of the folklore of mineral policy, in respect of tax matters and non-tax matters alike, is a sense of the uniqueness of the extractive industries in utilizing a gift of providence. This orientation can lead to a narrowly conservationist view, but more often leads to conclusions hospitable to fostering exploratory spending and hence mineral discovery regardless of the real cost in terms of opportunities forgone. It is but a short jump from that position to an over-riding concern with the prosperity of the extractive industries.[87]

Obviously, there has been an international demonstration effect at work. We noted earlier that emulation of the United States pattern was an important element in introducing mineral tax aids into the Canadian tax structure. "Incentives available in other countries" remained a pivotal consideration to the end of the tax reform debate.[88] Conversely, it may be speculated that the vehemence of industry reaction, particularly that of the major international oil companies to the Carter proposals, stemmed not so much from their assessment of what the Canadian government was likely to do, but rather from the proposal's indications to the U.S. government of what might be done.[89]

As with any government program, the element of simple inertia is an important factor in explaining the persistence, if not the origin, of mineral tax preferment. It is frequently observed that annual budgeting is incremental, not comprehensive. As a result, old expenditure programs rarely die.[90] If inertia characterizes budgetary outlays, it is even more relevant to "tax expenditures", on which an accounting is rarely presented, and which are not subject to periodic review. From the standpoint of tax rationality, the main positive benefit of the tax reform debate was that just such a review of Canadian tax aids was provided. For the first time, the defenders of the existing arrangements had to acknowledge that, justified or not, there is such a thing as subsidy by way of tax preferment.

But the most important single element that explains the potency of the extractive industries in obtaining and defending a tax favoured position in Canada stems from their geographic localization. The mining and petroleum industries can bring intense political pressure to bear because mining shapes so many regionally distinct communities. Where mining exists, it tends to dominate. At the same time, the federal character of the constitution, the national diffusion of the industry, and its common viewpoint on federal tax policy increase the number of political pressure points on which local influences can be brought to bear.[91]

It is a corollary of the economic theory of democracy that "government is bound to be more attentive to producers than consumers when it creates policy."[92] Yet, as Olson points out, "the business community in the aggregate is . . . not uniquely effective as a pressure group."[93] Smaller and more cohesive business groupings are more likely to obtain special favours in matters like taxes and tariffs, because their focus is concentrated and because there are no directly opposed pressure groups with countervailing interests. Where producer interests are concentrated in particular areas, they are even more able to bring their influence to bear on legislation.[94]

In a recent article Stigler speculates on the kinds of industries that are likely to undertake the costs and enjoy the benefits of influence in the political market place. Three of the characteristics he mentions appear to be relevant to the mineral industries in Canada: large size, geographical concentration (most particularly concentration in sparsely settled political subdivisions), and concentration in the sense of dominance by a few large firms.[95]

A further consideration is that localized industries are able to mobilize regional opinion beyond even the purely economic interest of the region. At the base of the political influence of the mining and petroleum industries is their success in identifying their own prosperity with the prestige of particular regions, generally the less-developed regions of Canada.[96] In turn, regional prestige may be viewed "as a kind of collective good that is consumed by the residents."[97]

> The smaller and more isolated (in the sense of less interaction and information flows) the geographic unit with which we are concerned, the more likely it is that there will be relative homogeneity of values within the unit. Residents of such communities will tend to be 'loyal' to their community, that is, to be willing to act in pursuit of such collective goods as group status. When these loyalties exist, all members of a group can gain potentially from collective action that adds to the prestige or self-respect of the group—as politicians are well aware.[98]

Local prestige is bound to be a more relevant political consideration at the provincial level than at the federal, particularly so with regard to federal tax concessions. National tax concessions render costs nationally, and benefits, not least in terms of collective prestige, locally. It is little wonder that the tax reform proposals disturbed a hornet's nest of intensely perceived local loyalties; the proposals, in short, produced symptoms of "geographic alienation". In the view of Premier Thatcher of Saskatchewan, the Carter mineral taxation proposals "very clearly discriminate against Western Canada."[99] Even after most of the threatening clouds had passed, Mr. Ritchie, the Member for Dauphin Manitoba, said in the parliamentary discussion of the 1971 tax reform Act, "The government has made a calculated effort to discriminate against communities on the periphery of the country in order to build up a central manufacturing industry."[100] The increasingly articulated "separatism" of western Canada no doubt owes a great deal to the hostility fostered by the tax reform proposals.

It is not only political representation that has come to reflect the concentrated impact of the mining industry's views; those views are also reflected in the federal and provincial departments with jurisdiction over mining.[101] The symbiotic relationship between government agencies and their clientele is a well-known administrative phenomenon.[102] In particular, the effective functioning and growth of a government bureau depends on its having a strong goal consensus. The more homogeneous the bureau's clientele and the more clearly defined the clientele's interests, the more it will be to the bureau's own advantage to adopt goals that are harmonious.[103]

One Canadian institution which is able to mutually reinforce the collective influence of the mining industry, the provincial Cabinets, and the provincial and federal bureaucracies in the interests of the mining industry is the Mines Ministers Conference. The annual conference is itself a hybrid group, made up of provincial Ministers and officials, industry representatives and federal observers.[104] Six continuing sub-committees (one on taxation) of officials and industry representatives carry out background work which forms the basis on which representations are made to Ottawa by the Ministers who thus present "a common front on behalf of their respective jurisdictions."[105]

Until the appearance of the Carter Report, the mining industry apparently felt its position to be sufficiently secure so as not to require the exercise of the more obvious arts of public persuasion. In rising to the Carter and Benson challenges, that omission has been rectified. The tax reform proposals impelled an accelerating flow of printed and broadcast institutional advertising from individual firms and from the industry, a flow that has not yet abated. The trauma of tax reform has made the industry public relations-conscious. Eight months after the Royal Commission Report appeared, the advertising trade press reported that the International Nickel Company was launching a print advertising campaign expected to cost $750 thousand a year "to broaden knowledge of its activities."[106] For some years before, Inco had been sponsoring radio newscasts with a "public service" rather than a merchandising message. However, until 1967 it was the only mining company on the annual list of the "top 100" national radio advertisers. In 1967, Inco was joined among the top 100 by Dominion Foundries and Steel, and in 1969 by Cominco.[107] Of the mining companies' trade association, the advertising trade press had this to say, after the appearance of the White Paper:

> The Canadian mining industry is using radio for the first time—in a campaign to broaden its public image. . . .
> . . . from now until the end of May the Mining Association of Canada is spending $100,000. on 32 stations in 10 cities from Victoria, B.C. to Quebec City.

> It is using five 60-second commercials run in rotation in prime time, plugging the theme: "Canada counts on mining." . . .
>
> In the past, its ad campaigns have been aimed primarily at opinion leaders.[108]

Despite the apparent success of the campaign, the mining industry seems somewhat apprehensive. The experience of having to defend what it had come to regard as great eternal verities has left the industry shaken. The financial press reported that, in the wake of tax reform, the "industry is far from happy."[109] More recently, the outgoing president of the Mining Association of Canada pinpointed the malaise.

> The problem arises in determining what constitutes an incentive taxation system. At the moment the federal Government and some provincial governments have a different conception than ours on this issue.[110]

There are, indeed, indications at the present time that this apprehension is not without foundation.

SEQUEL

For the extractive industries perhaps the most enduring consequence of tax reform is that they are more strongly than ever confirmed as the clients of the provinces. In addition, the tax reform debates shook loose a good many implicit and unexamined propositions with regard to mineral taxation, a factor that may prove critically important in the light of the provinces' increasing revenue requirements.[111] Were it not for the reluctance of any one province to get out of step with the others for fear of punitive reaction, it is likely that by now the provinces would have moved to increase their revenue from mining.

The possibility of provincial moves in this direction is reinforced by the election of New Democratic Party governments in three of the four western provinces between June 1969 and August 1972. To date of writing, however, the most notable increase of provincial mineral exactions, since the federal tax reform, has not involved the mine profits tax. Rather, it has concerned extension of the royalty concept applied to oil and natural gas production. The lead here was taken by the province of Alberta. With something over 75% of total Canadian crude oil production and about 85% of total Canadian proved reserves, and fully aware of the gathering energy crisis, Alberta was in a position to take unilateral action.[112] A new annual tax on all crude oil reserves in the province, with an option for "voluntary" payment of higher royalties on Crown-land production, was initially expected to raise an additional $70 million in revenue for the province in 1973.[113]

A more ominous development for the mining industry is the report on natural resource policy by Eric Kierans, commissioned by the province of Manitoba.[114] Mr. Kierans advocates that the province ultimately take over the exploration, mining and milling functions from the private sector. As an interim measure, he calls for a heavy property tax on reserves held under Crown-lease, and replacement of the province's 15% tax on mining profit by a 15% tax on the gross value of mine output. Although he is aware of the reluctance of a single province to initiate draconian action, he thinks that it could do so without inviting disaster.[115] While it seems unlikely that Manitoba will implement his full recommendations in the foreseeable future,[116] the Kierans report, along with rising provincial oil revenues, emphasizes that the future tax burden on the mining industry will depend more on the provinces than on Ottawa. The probability of rising provincial mining taxes is enhanced by the impending vacuum to be opened up by the federal corporation tax abatement.

By way of summary, this paper has been concerned with pressure exercised by and on behalf of the mineral industries in relation to Canada's decade of tax reform. We noted that not only were the reform proposals in respect to mineral taxation considerably blunted, but that the mineral taxation issue assumed a catalytic role in compromising the broader objectives of tax reform. In explaining the success of the mineral industries in coercing the federal government, we pointed particularly to their ability to mobilize regional opinion. Provincial governments were the main instrument through which regional displeasure was manifested at the national level. In the upshot, the major companies may well have made net gains, in the short term, from the tax changes and collateral events. We also observed, however, that this large measure of success carried an implicit price, and that explicit payment may yet be exacted. In particular, the industry is confirmed as a dependency of the provinces. Furthermore, the tax reform debate put a great many unexamined premises of mineral tax policy under scrutiny. In the aftermath, the position of the industry is more vulnerable to government action than it was in the past.

NOTES

1. Royal Commission on Taxation, *Report*, Volumes 1–6, (Ottawa: Queen's Printer, 1967).

2. The term "tax aids" is the one that now seems to be preferred in the Public Finance literature for describing implicit public grants through preferential taxation. See G. G. Rudney, "Implicit Public Grants Under the Tax System: Some Implications of Federal Tax Aids Accounting", in K. E. Boulding and M. Pfaff, eds., *Redistribution to the Rich and Poor*, (Belmont, Calif.: Wadsworth, 1972), pp. 175–81.

3. The federal government levies analogous taxes on mineral revenues in the Territories. See E. C. Hodgson, *Digest of Mineral Laws of Canada*, Mineral Report 13, Dept. of Energy, Mines and Resources (Ottawa: Queen's Printer, 1967), pp. 24–8.

4. For a summary history of these taxes, see The Ontario Committee on Taxation, *Report*, Vol. 3, pp. 303–5, (Toronto: Queen's Printer, Aug. 30, 1967).

5. *Ibid.*, p. 314.

6. The present paper deals only with events that occurred to the middle of 1973. Since then, under the spur of commodity price inflation, quite dramatic in-

creases and innovations in provincial mining taxes have been enacted or officially forecast. These developments have confirmed the prognosis of the present paper rather more rapidly that foreseen. For a summary of the provincial mining tax changes to mid-1974, see R. D. Brown, "The Fight Over Resource Profits", *Canadian Tax Journal*, Vol. XXII, July–August 1974, pp. 315–37.

7. For a full discussion of this problem see D. Y. Timbrell, *Taxation of the Mining Industry in Canada*, Study No. 9 of the Royal Commission on Taxation, (Ottawa: Queen's Printer, 1967), pp. 67–9 and 139–42. The Royal Commission on Taxation recommended removal of the existing anomalies affecting deduction of provincial mining taxes. (*Report, op. cit.*, Vol. 4, p. 350).

8. Evidence is cited in M. W. Bucovetsky, "Tax Reform in Canada: A Case Study of the Mining Industry", Unpublished Ph.D. dissertation, University of Toronto, 1971, pp. 21–2.

9. Ontario, Quebec, Saskatchewan, and Alberta.

10. The Ontario Committee on Taxation, *Report*, Volumes 1–3, Toronto: Queen's Printer, Aug. 30, 1967). The sections relevant to mining taxation are found in Vol. 2, pp. 171–90, and esp. Vol. 3, pp. 303–49.

11. *Taxation in Ontario, A Program for Reform*, The Report of the Select Committee of the Legislature on the Report of the Ontario Committee on Taxation, Toronto, Sept. 16, 1968. The sections relevant to mining are found at pp. 255–71.

12. Bill 111, 2nd Session, 28th Legislature, Ontario, 18 Eliz. II, *An Act to amend the Mining Tax Act*.

13. The general statement in the text, above, is incomplete with regard to land costs (more correctly, capital sums spent for the right to exploit a potential mineral deposit). In fact, so far as these rights concern oil and gas, they have been expensible since 1962. For the solid minerals, lump sum payments for land could not be charged off against taxable income but their amount has not been significant.

14. The exemption applied to income derived in Canada from the proceeds of a mine through the "prime metal stage", (e.g. to the stage of refined nickel or pig iron,) so long as the output remained the property of the exempted corporation. This obviously favoured the large, vertically integrated corporation. Moreover, the amount of income exempted from tax was not reduced by the simultaneous write-off of pre-production costs against a company's other mineral income. It should also be noted that the three-year exemption did not apply to oil or gas wells.

15. Again, the allowance applied to income from Canadian treatment up to the "prime metal stage". Special rules for computing depletion applied, under the old Act, to gold mines and coal mines. Sand pits and quarries were allowed simply to amortize their actual cost over their productive lives.

16. Press release by the Mining Association of Canada, *The Globe and Mail*, Toronto, June 15, 1971.

17. Data are derived from *Corporation Financial Statistics*, 1969, and *Corporation Taxation Statistics*, 1969, Statistics Canada.

18. Since some firms receiving mineral tax aids are classified to industries that we have called "non-extractive" and conversely some "mining" firms (e.g. quarries and drilling contractors) do not receive such aids, the figures quoted understate the relative advantage of mine-tax-treatment. Calculations for other recent years show quite similar results.

19. *Report, op. cit.*, Vol. 4, p. 365.

20. *Loc. cit.* This would be out of a rough estimated total of about 25 to 30 mines that would have had exempt income in that year.

21. From the brief of the International Nickel Company of Canada to the parliamentary Committees that considered the government White Paper on Taxation, it may be deduced that the company's total exploration spending plus its cost of new mine development and plant, during the 1960s, was about $210 million and that its total exempted profit was approximately $225 million in the same period. See *Minutes of Proceedings and Evidence*, Standing House of Commons

Committee on Finance, Trade and Economic Affairs (hereafter cited as *Commons Committee*), No. 64, June 16, 1970, pp. 75 and 86. The same company, during that period, appears to have claimed depletion of about twice the amount of its tax exempt profit (*loc. cit.*). Pine Point Mines (controlled by Cominco) "recovered" its invested capital out of the exempt profit of a single year's operation. (*Commons Committee*, No. 88, July 30, 1970, p. 190).

22. The history of the provisions is detailed in Timbrell, *op. cit., passim.* For further discussion of the implied rationale, see Bucovetsky, *op. cit.,* pp. 177–228.

23. *Report, op. cit.,* Vol. 1, p. v.

24. *Ibid,* Vol. 4, pp. 373–5.

25. *Ibid,* Vol. 6, p. 96.

26. *Ibid,* Vol. 6, pp. 96 & 121.

27. *Information,* United Steelworkers of America, Vol. 15, June 1967, pp. 10–19.

28. See *The Globe and Mail,* Toronto, Aug. 30, 1967, and Sept. 6, 1967.

29. The speed and breadth with which the campaign against the Carter proposals was mounted is illustrated in a very illuminating interview with the director of a provincial Chamber of Mines, quoted by Presthus. See Robert Presthus, *Elite Accommodation in Canadian Politics,* (Toronto: Macmillan, 1973), pp. 148–52.

30. A few headlines give the tenor of the campaign. Apr. 5, 1967: "Carter report one reason Asbestos Corp. halts mine job." Apr. 7, 1967: "Tar sands project is threatened by Carter plan, developer says." Apr. 28, 1967: "Alarm in mining, but no one's giving up yet." A careful reading of the stories indicates that despite inferences in the headlines, even if the curtailment of investment plans were taken at its face value, rising costs or declining demand may have been a more relevant consideration.

31. *The Globe and Mail,* Toronto, Apr. 29, 1967.

32. *Canadian News Facts,* May 8, 1967, p. 67.

33. *The Globe and Mail,* Toronto, May 2, 1967.

34. *House of Commons Debates,* May 11, 1967, p. 111.

35. *Report of Proceedings of the 19th Tax Conference,* Toronto, Canadian Tax Foundation, 1967, p. 473.

36. *The Globe and Mail,* Toronto, Sept. 26, 1967.

37. *Canadian News Facts,* July 3, 1967, p. 98.

38. *House of Commons Debates,* June 23, 1967, p. 1874.

39. *Ibid.,* Oct. 6, 1967, pp. 2882–86.

40. *Ontario Legislative Assembly Debates,* July 17, 1968, p. 5854.

41. *The Globe and Mail,* Toronto, Feb. 22, 1968.

42. This is a contention that might be disputed by many economists. See, for example, A. R. Dobell and T. A. Wilson, "Overall Effects of the Proposed Tax Reforms: Savings, Investment and the Balance of Payments," Working Paper Series No. 6806. (Toronto: Institute for the Quantitative Analysis of Social and Economic Policy, University of Toronto, 1968).

43. *House of Commons Debates,* Nov. 30, 1967, p. 4906.

44. *The Globe and Mail,* Toronto, Dec. 2, 1967.

45. Hon. E. J. Benson, *Proposals for Tax Reform,* (Ottawa: Queen's Printer, Nov. 7, 1969). (Cited hereafter as *White Paper*).

46. *Ibid.,* p. 64.

47. *Ibid.,* ss. 5.23 to 5.45 (pp. 64–66).

48. It should be commented that in the subsequent discussion, qualitative and quantitative, little mention was ever made of this *new* tax aid, accelerated depreciation of the entire capital cost of a mine.

49. The right to earned depletion could be carried forward indefinitely until it could be claimed.

50. Evidence of Hon. E. J. Benson, *Commons Committee*, Jan. 15, 1970, p. 9. Although White Papers are not a new Canadian phenomenon, the device was used in a novel fashion in the tax reform procedure. Earlier White Papers merely presented information or outlined government policy; this document was specifically intended to elicit public debate and criticism of a tentative government policy. See A. D. Doerr, "The Role of White Papers," in G. Bruce Doern and Peter Aucoin, *The Structures of Policy-Making in Canada*, (Toronto: Macmillan, 1971), pp. 179–204.

51. For a fuller critique of the "White Paper procedure" as the proposed tax reforms filtered through the committees, see M. W. Bucovetsky and R. M. Bird, "Tax Reform in Canada: A Progress Report", *National Tax Journal*, Vol. XXV, No. 1, (March 1972), pp. 15–41, and J. G. Head, "Canadian Tax Reform and Participatory Democracy", *Finanzarchiv*, Vol. 31, No. 1, 1972, pp. 48–68.

52. *Report on the White Paper Proposals for Tax Reform*, Standing Committee on Banking, Trade and Commerce, Ottawa, Sept. 1970, p. 39. Reproduced with permission of the Senate of Canada.

53. Charles MacNaughton, *Ontario Proposals for Tax Reform in Canada*, Dept. of Treasury and Economics, (Toronto: Queen's Printer, June, 1970).

54. *Ibid.*, p. 36.

55. "Statement of the Premier of Quebec to the Federal–Provincial Conference of Ministers of Finance, Winnipeg, June 5–6, 1970"; printed in *Commons Committee*, No. 90, Aug. 4, 1970, pp. 126–49.

56. See Bucovetsky, dissertation, *op. cit.*, Appx. B, pp. 297–304.

57. Brief of Hudson's Bay Oil and Gas Company Limited, *Commons Committee*, No. 50, June 2, 1970, p. 189.

58. However, unlike the scheme quoted above, the United States gross depletion has some revenue safeguard in that the gross allowance is limited to 50% of net income. The oil industry has harped upon the gross depletion theme before a good many government bodies. It succeeded in convincing one enquiry, the Royal Commission on Canada's Economic Prospects (Gordon Commission). See that commission's *Final Report*, (Ottawa: Queen's Printer, Nov. 1957), pp. 130–1, and 494–7.

59. Letter from H. M. Griffith, President, The Steel Company of Canada Limited, to the Standing House of Commons Committee on Finance, Trade and Economic Affairs, June 8, 1970, reprinted in *Proceedings*, Standing Senate Committee on Banking, Trade and Commerce (hereafter cited as *Senate Committee*), No. 39, Sept. 15, 1970, p. 13. See also Cominco brief, *Commons Committee*, No. 88, July 30, 1970, p. 41, and Noranda hearings, *Senate Committee*, No. 6, Jan. 29, 1970, p. 15. The last citation makes it plain that this "concession" would be additional to 100% write-off of capital costs.

60. *Commons Committee*, No. 46, May 21, 1970, pp. 150–52.

61. MacNaughton Proposals, *op. cit.*, p. 37. Alternatively, the Ontario treasurer proposed that the existing arrangements be retained but with a kind of "excess profits tax" on highly profitable mines.

62. Statement of the Premier of Quebec, *op. cit.*, pp. 137–8.

63. Reported by Department of Finance, News Release No. 70–105, Ottawa, Aug. 26, 1970.

64. For example, to the stage of pig iron ingots in steelmaking.

65. R. D. Brown, "Round Three for the Taxation of Mining Income", *Canadian Tax Journal*, Vol. XVIII, 1970, p. 375.

66. Estimate derived from figures quoted in J. Bossons, "An Economic Overview of the Tax Reform Legislation", *Report of Proceedings of the Twenty-Third Tax Conference*, (Toronto: Canadian Tax Foundation, 1972), p. 49.

67. *Commons Committee*, No. 91, Aug. 5, 1970, p. 16.

68. Statement of the Premier of Quebec, *op. cit.*, p. 137.

69. A useful review of the federal government's stabilization objectives and actions during this period is given in W. I. Gillespie, "The Federal Budget as Plan, 1968—1972", *Canadian Tax Journal*, Vol. XXI, Jan.–Feb. 1973, pp. 64–84.

70. *The Globe and Mail*, Toronto, Sept. 5, 1970.

71. *Ibid*, Sept. 11, 1970.

72. *Heavy Construction News*, Sept. 7, 1970, p. 5.

73. *The Globe and Mail*, Toronto, Feb. 25, 1971.

74. *Report on the White Paper Proposals for Tax Reform*, Standing Senate Committee on Banking, Trade and Commerce, Ottawa, Sept. 1970; *Eighteenth Report Respecting the White Paper on Tax Reform*, Standing House of Commons Committee on Finance, Trade and Economic Affairs, Ottawa, Queen's Printer, Oct. 1970.

75. *The Globe and Mail*, Toronto, Oct. 23, 1970.

76. Bucovetsky and Bird, *op. cit.*, p. 16.

77. For further detail, see *ibid.*, pp. 40–1.

78. *Canadian Income Tax Act*, Chap. 63, S.C. 1970–71. A summary of the new Act, although one that is not completely accurate is: Hon. E. J. Benson, *Summary of 1971 Tax Reform Legislation*, Ottawa, June 1971.

79. On the other side of the ledger, the additional abatement from corporation tax of 15% of mineral profits, announced in August 1970, would also not take effect until 1977.

80. *Budget Speech*, delivered by the Hon. John N. Turner, Minister of Finance in the House of Commons, Mon., May 8, 1972, Finance Department Release, p. 8.

81. Bill 215, 2nd Sesion, 29th Legislature, Ontario, 21 Eliz. II, *The Corporations Tax Act*, 1972.

82. *House of Commons Debates*, June 25, 1971, p. 7333.

83. *Legislature of Ontario Debates*, Dec. 12, 1972, p. 5558.

84. *Ibid.*, p. 5578.

85. W. P. Hammond, quoted in *The Globe and Mail*, Toronto, March 13, 1973.

86. The provincial mine profit taxes, hence the amount by which taxable corporation profit of mining companies was formerly reducible, apply only to "the value of the ore at the pit's mouth" (or more correctly to the net profit therefrom). The new abatement is, in effect, a corporation tax *credit*; moreover, it applies to "taxable production profits from mineral resources", a much broader concept.

87. For further elaboration, see Bucovetsky, dissertation, *op. cit.*, pp. 191–95.

88. See the defence of the tax reforms in the 1971 budget debate by J. J. Greene, Minister of Energy, Mines and Resources, *House of Commons Debates*, June 23, 1971, p. 7312.

89. For amplification, see G. D. Quirin, "Economic Consequences on the Primary Mineral Industries of the Adoption of the Recommendations of the Royal Commission on Taxation", Working Paper Series No. 6804, Institute for the Quantitative Analysis of Social and Economic Policy, University of Toronto, 1968, pp. 4–5.

90. See Aaron Wildavsky, *The Politics of the Budgetary Process*, (Boston: Little, Brown & Co., 1964), esp. pp. 13–16. See also R. M. Bird, *The Growth of Government Spending in Canada*, (Toronto, Canadian Tax Foundation: 1970), pp. 132–35.

91. In this respect the influence of the mining industry is not dissimilar to that of agriculture, on which see H. J. Dawson, "Relations Between Farm Organizations and the Civil Service in Canada and Great Britain", *Canadian Public Administration*, Vol. 10, 1967, pp. 450–70. The mining industry, however, is both better financed and more homogeneous than are the farm groups.

92. Anthony Downs, *An Economic Theory of Democracy*, (New York: Harper, 1957), p. 255. See also A. Breton, "The Economics of Nationalism", *Journal of Political Economy*, Vol. 72, 1964, pp. 376–86, and Breton, "A Theory of Demand for Public Goods", *Canadian Journal of Economics and Political Science*, Vol. 32, 1966, pp. 445–67.

93. Mancur Olson, *The Logic of Collective Action*, (Cambridge, Mass.: Harvard University Press, 1971), p. 147.

94. See also H. G. Johnson, "The Economic Approach to Social Questions", *Economica*, N.S., Vol. 35, Feb. 1968, p. 11.

95. See G. J. Stigler, "The Theory of Economic Regulation", *Bell Journal of Economics and Management Service*, Vol. 2, No. 1, Spring 1971, pp. 3–21.

96. J. Bossons, "The Value of a Comprehensive Tax Base as a Tax Reform Goal",

Journal of Law and Economics, Vol. 13, Oct. 1970, p. 330. The importance attached by the mining industry to disseminating its message on the Carter report in the "backwoods" regions of Canada is evidenced in Presthus' interview with the director of a provincial Chamber of Mines. See Presthus, *op. cit.*, p. 149.

97. R. M. Bird and D. G. Hartle, "The Demand for Local Political Autonomy: An Individualistic Theory", *Conflict Resolution*, Vol. XV, No. 4, 1972, p. 454.

98. R. M. Bird and D. G. Hartle, "The Design of Governments", in Bird and J. G. Head (eds.), *Modern Fiscal Issues, Essays in Honour of Carl S. Shoup*, Toronto, © University of Toronto Press, 1972, p. 53.

99. *The Globe and Mail*, Toronto, June 15, 1967.

100. *House of Commons Debates*, Oct. 22, 1971, p. 8962.

101. A good instance is the brief to the parliamentary Committees by a group of geologists, some from the federal and provincial governments and others from the industry, the Solid Earth Science Study Group of the Science Council of Canada. *Commons Committee*, No. 48, May 28, 1970, pp. 249–91.

102. On this, see Anthony Downs, *Inside Bureaucracy*, (Boston: Little, Brown & Co., 1967), Chap. 19. Also see Wildavsky, *op. cit.*, pp. 66–7, and Presthus, *op. cit.*, pp. 211–24.

103. In this regard, it is interesting to note a minor furor in Parliament and the press over the appointment of a mining executive as Deputy Minister of the federal Department of Energy, Mines and Resources. See *House of Commons Debates*, May 11, 1970, p. 6792, and Vaughan Lyon, "The Danger of Conflicting Loyalties", *The Globe and Mail*, Toronto, July 2, 1970.

104. See Institute of Intergovernmental Relations, Queen's University, *Report, Intergovernmental Liaison on Fiscal and Economic Matters*, (Ottawa: Queen's Printer, 1969), p. 117, & Appx. D, and Edgar Gallant, "The Machinery of Federal Provincial Relations", *Canadian Public Administration*, Vol. 8, 1965, p. 521. There are, to be sure, numerous other forums in Canada that bring together government officials and private interest groups. The references cited single out the Mines Ministers Conference as being unique in the sense of its official status, its continuity and its influence.

105. *Ontario Department of Mines Review, 1969*, (Toronto: Queen's Printer, 1970), p. 98.

106. *Advertising Age*, Vol. 38, Oct. 30, 1967, p. 46.

107. *Canadian Broadcaster*, and *Broadcasting*, various issues.

108. *Marketing*, March 16, 1970, p. 6.

109. *Financial Times of Canada*, March 1, 1971, p. 15.

110. *The Globe and Mail*, Toronto, Feb. 15, 1973.

111. The provincial revenue "bind" and the federal government's increasing reluctance to vacate direct tax sources for the provinces' occupancy is witnessed by the inconclusive battles fought in the Tax Structure Committee and at meetings of the Ministers of Finance. As an instance of mounting provincial frustration, see "Fiscal Policy Management and Tax Sharing Reform," Statement by the Hon. John White, Treasurer of Ontario, to the Meeting of the Ministers of Finance at Ottawa, Jan. 18–19, 1973, p. 17.

112. British Columbia followed the Alberta lead, in 1973, by increasing its royalty percentages on both oil and natural gas.

113. This revenue estimate was based on the price of oil at the time the scheme was announced. With price increases that took place since then, the yield in 1973 should be greater by half than the original estimate, despite the federal ceiling imposed on oil prices in the fall of 1973. Late in that year Alberta declared that this scheme would be scrapped in 1974 to be replaced by even more lucrative levies.

114. Eric Kierans, *Report on Natural Resources Policy in Manitoba*, prepared for the Secretariat for the Planning and Priorities Committee of Cabinet, Government of Manitoba, Feb., 1973.

115. *Ibid.*, p. 41.

116. The government has directed the report to an interdepartmental task force for study. (*The Globe and Mail*, Toronto, Feb. 28, 1973.)

6.

Donald Barry's study of the Biafra issue provides us with an opportunity to compare the behaviour of issue-oriented groups with that of institutional groups. It confirms the view that issue-oriented groups, having few commitments to long-term organizational goals, and consequently being unimpeded by a need to preserve continuing access to government officials, resort to public methods of persuasion far more readily than do institutional groups. It adds, as well, some interesting data on the interrelations between issue-oriented and institutional groups, suggesting that institutional groups—through ad hoc alliances and the informal secondment of personnel—may encourage issue-oriented groups to use public persuasion where behind-the-scenes efforts have failed. In view of the benefits that institutional groups can derive from such alliances—particularly where there is broad agreement on ends and where concerted action would considerably widen the means of persuasion open to all groups—it is somewhat surprising that their existence is not more widely reported and commented upon. The fact that it is not may simply reflect poor observation of the Canadian political scene, or it may suggest that differences in organizational structure impose impenetrable barriers to communication and co-operation. This conclusion is supported by Barry's observation that the pro-Biafra issue-oriented groups failed to appreciate the inability of the institutional groups to lead public opinion. The leaders of the issue-oriented groups had no organizational need to maintain working relations with government, and consequently felt no hesitation in arousing public hostility to Canada's official position. The established groups not only had to safeguard their capacity to work with Canadian and other governments, but had absorbed an appreciation of the rationale for government policy.

Integral to the success of the pro-Biafra groups was the co-operation of Parliament and the media, and the general support of public opinion. Barry's study shows that while Parliament and the media responded to *the issue, with Parliament in particular placing the government under considerable pressure, the lack of general support from the public convinced the government that it did not have to substantially modify its position. In the end, despite intense activity on the part of all pressure groups, the advice of the administrative arm, chiefly the Department of External Affairs, was followed. This is a striking contrast with Bucovetsky's description of the success experienced by the mining industry in opposing proposed changes in federal tax policy. It emphasizes the advantages that accrue to pressure groups from the possession of regional power bases, from identification with an issue that is of immediate concern to large segments of the general public, and from longstanding and mutually supportive relations between pressure groups and specific centres of governmental power. The Biafra groups—institutional and issue-oriented—had some organizational links with government, and the institutional groups claimed large congregations, but their chief source of strength lay in their capacity to create a public issue. The issue itself—unlike that embraced by Pollution Probe—did not attract the kind of support needed to modify government policy.*

Donald Barry is currently completing doctoral studies in Canadian–American relations at Johns Hopkins University.

Interest Groups and the Foreign Policy Process: The Case of Biafra*

Donald Barry

Foreign policy issues have seldom caused widespread debate in Canada. Usually the general public has been indifferent to international events that have not had an immediate and obvious bearing on Canadian domestic affairs.[1] The "attentive public"—that segment of the public which takes a continuing interest in foreign affairs—has remained small in number, and the range of its active participation in these issues has been limited. Interest group involvement in this area has been termed "erratic" and focused on a limited range of subjects such as tariffs, immigration, and the concerns of ethnic minority groups.[2] Moreover, as one author has put it, their pressures have "seemed mild . . . even by Canadian standards of interest group activity on issues of domestic politics."[3] In consequence, government officials often have been permitted to develop Canadian foreign policy relatively free of the domestic constraints that could be imposed by large interested publics.

The case of the Nigerian civil war, however, formed an important exception to this pattern of behaviour. The civil war, and especially the plight of the secessionist state of Biafra, became one of the main political issues in Canada during 1968, dominating the attention of the public, Parliament, and the media. One unidentified Cabinet Minister described it as "the most voluble Canadian foreign policy issue in anyone's memory."[4]

The Biafra episode illustrates the important role which interest groups can play in bringing a subject to the attention of the public, thereby creating a major political issue. In fact, the prominence it received largely resulted from the activities of interest groups which sought, in a variety of private and public ways, to influence Canada's policy toward the war. This paper will examine these activities in an effort to extend our

* I would like to thank Denis Stairs and A. Paul Pross for their helpful comments on an earlier version of this article. Responsibility for its content, however, is my own.

117

knowledge of several aspects of the processes of policy formation in Canada.

Our chief purpose will be to consider the behaviour of institutional interest groups and issue-oriented interest groups and the relationships that exist between them. In addition, this essay will attempt to show how the behaviour of specific interest groups reflects their views or perceptions of the part they play in the making of public policy, and, in turn, how these perceptions determine the ways in which they will try to influence government officials.

The study also allows us to make some observations about the processes of Canadian government. First, the episode saw Parliament play a highly significant role in creating and sustaining a political issue. Generally students of interest group behaviour in Canada have attached little importance to Parliament as a forum for influencing government policy. Yet, the Biafran example suggests that this role of Parliament can sometimes be a crucial one. Secondly, this essay argues that the bureaucracy had a primary role in the making of the government's Biafra policy. It takes issue with those authors who have suggested that the issue revealed the ascendent position which the Office of the Prime Minister (PMO) had attained as a source of policy initiation and advice at the expense of the bureaucracy and the Department of External Affairs in particular,[5] which they claim, was the result of changes made in the executive structure by Prime Minister Trudeau in 1968.

The time period covered extends from June 1967, when the Biafra interest groups became active, to December 1968. Although Canadian interest in the issue did not cease until the end of the conflict in January 1970, the shorter time span has been chosen partly to reduce the study to manageable proportions and partly because the pattern of interest group behaviour had completed its first cycle by the end of this period. By December 1968, the initial impetus had clearly gone from the issue and public interest in it did not reawaken until the summer of 1969.

THE CANADIAN RESPONSE TO BIAFRA: AN OVERVIEW

The civil war in Nigeria began in July 1967, after Colonel Odumegwu Ojukwu had proclaimed the state of Biafra (formerly the eastern region of the country) and declared its secession from the Nigerian federation. The declaration capped a period of increasing political turbulence in the African nation. Although Nigeria was a sister member of the Commonwealth, her relations with Canada had not been intimate. So it was not surprising that initially the conflict created little interest in Canada. Media reports about it were sporadic. The reaction in Parliament was similar. In 1967 only eight questions concerning the issue were asked of the Pearson government.

This attitude of indifference continued during the early months of 1968. The Canadian Committee for the Relief of Biafran Refugees, formed in Toronto by a group of former Canadian University Service Overseas (CUSO) volunteers who had worked in Nigeria, Biafran students in Canada, and other concerned individuals attested to this in an appeal for funds in March. "A war," the committee said, "has been going on in Nigeria for the best part of a year now. We don't hear much about it; Nigeria is a long way away."[6] Its appeal raised only $4,300. The conflict was remote from Canada and it was overshadowed by domestic political events; first, by the campaign for the leadership of the national Liberal Party, then by the subsequent general election in June. It was not until July, with the appearance of the first reports of mal-nutrition and starvation among large numbers of the beleaguered Biafran population, that public concern was aroused.

Interest groups had begun their attempts to influence the government's policy much earlier, however. Officials of the Presbyterian Church in Canada, closely informed of developments in Nigeria and Biafra through their missionary activities there, had begun contacting officials of the Department of External Affairs in June, 1967, shortly before the conflict began.[7] Later Biafran students and returned CUSO volunteers had sought increased Canadian involvement in peace-making and relief assistance. But their efforts had produced few results.

In July 1968, pictures and films of starving Biafran children began to appear in the newspapers and on television newscasts. The press began to criticize the government's policy and the interest groups began to carry their efforts into the public forum. Publicly the government's initial reaction to the developing criticism of its policy appeared to be one of amused surprise. Prime Minister Trudeau, when asked by a newsman about the possibility of sending Canadian aid to the war's victims reportedly replied, "You have the funniest questions. We haven't considered this as a government . . . I think we should send aid to all needy people but we can't send it to everyone and I'd have to see what our priorities are prior to the Biafra people."[8]

Early in July a group of Church and relief organizations formed the Nigeria/Biafra Relief Fund of Canada[9] and launched a national campaign for funds to be distributed among international agencies furnishing relief assistance in Nigeria "and the eastern region known as Biafra." In response to requests from the Fund's member agencies, the Secretary of State for External Affairs, Mitchell Sharp, announced that the government had decided to make a substantial contribution of food aid, later disclosed as $500,000, "for the provision of emergency supplies . . . for relief in that area of Nigeria affected by hostilities."[10] He also said that Canada would be prepared to assist in the airlifting of supplies if it proved practical and was approved by the Nigerian and Biafran authorities.[11]

But the Prime Minister's remark, together with the disclosure that Canada's first shipment of food and medical supplies would be sent to Lagos, Nigeria and not to Biafra,[12] where estimates of death by starvation were as high as 6,000 a day, increased the attacks on the government's policy. The press began to urge the government to hasten the flow of emergency aid to Biafra, to request countries supplying arms to the combatants to end the shipments,[13] and to attempt to secure a cease-fire.

In September, the government announced that it had accepted the Nigerian Federal Military Government's (FMG) invitation to send a Canadian observer, together with those from Britain, Sweden, the United Nations, and the Organization of African Unity (OAU), to visit the areas of military operations in Nigeria and to observe the conduct of federal troops. The government had been reluctant to accept the invitation, but did so following Nigerian assurances that the observer group would be guaranteed free movement within the territory and would be able to make impartial observations and reports.[14]

When the opening session of the new Parliament began, the Progressive Conservative and New Democratic parties mounted a sustained attack on the government's Biafra policy. Provided with a constant flow of information from the interest groups, they directed a barrage of questions at the new government during the fall months. Together, the interest groups, the media, and the parliamentarians made four main demands of the government. They urged it to: 1) attempt to secure a cease-fire and a negotiated settlement through the United Nations; 2) request arms-supplying nations to halt their shipments to both parties; 3) ask the Nigerian government to permit relief flights into Biafra; 4) speed the flow of aid to Biafra by providing relief assistance and aircraft.

The government agreed to make a second contribution of $500,000 in food aid for distribution in Nigerian-held territory,[15] but it argued that it could not undertake unauthorized relief flights to Biafra. Mr. Trudeau stated, "We cannot intervene short of committing an act of war against Nigeria and intervening in the internal affairs of that country."[16] Mr. Sharp did agree, though, that the government would bring the humanitarian aspects of the question before the United Nations if the OAU (then considering the issue) did not do so. However, he said later that Canada could not obtain the support of other member delegations to raise the matter there.[17] On September 30, despite its earlier announcement that aircraft would not be provided except with the prior approval of the relevant authorities, the government stated that it was prepared to provide a Canadian Armed Forces Hercules aircraft for relief operations in federal Nigeria.[18] The FMG accepted the offer on October 7.

In spite of this action, criticism of the government's policy persisted. The interest groups, the opposition parties, and the media continued to demand that Canada bring the issue before the United Nations and find ways of channeling relief supplies to Biafra. Public interest reached its peak following the 36-hour visit to Biafra (October 1 to 3) of two Members of Parliament, Andrew Brewin (NDP, Greenwood) and David MacDonald (PC, Egmont). The two had been invited there by Presbyterian Church officials to observe the situation at first hand. Their reports of massive starvation in Biafra, and their request for a Canadian initiative at the United Nations and a large scale relief action brought renewed pressure on the government. Direct news reports from Biafra by Charles Taylor of *The Globe and Mail*,[19] who had accompanied Brewin and MacDonald on their visit, and Ontario MPP Stephen Lewis, in the *Toronto Daily Star*,[20] together with those of CBC and CTV news teams helped to sustain the issue's momentum.

On October 7, the House of Commons unanimously approved Conservative Opposition Leader Stanfield's motion to set up immediately its Standing Committee on External Affairs and National Defence to consider the Nigeria-Biafra question.[21] The next day Mr. Trudeau announced that Mr. Sharp had secured an agreement from the Nigerian Commissioner for External Affairs, Dr. Okoi Arikpo, that Canadian Armed Forces Hercules aircraft with their service crews and equipment be permitted to fly relief supplies into both federally held and Biafran territories, under the aegis of the International Committee of the Red Cross (ICRC). The first Hercules destined for relief flights in the federally occupied area arrived in Lagos on October 14, but after it arrived the FMG refused to allow it to operate, ostensibly because the airstrips involved were in poor repair and could not withstand repeated landings of an aircraft of its size. A second Hercules was sent to the island of Fernando Po, off the coast of Nigeria, from where it was to fly its missions to Biafra. After encountering some delays in securing clearance from the newly independent state of Fernando Po, the plane began its mercy flights on the night of October 30. (At that time all of the relief flights were taking place at night.)

By now, however, the government had an opportunity to assess the extent of public support for the interest groups' position, and had discovered that, despite the publicity the issue generated and the criticism of the government voiced by the interest groups, the parliamentarians, and the media, the general public's reaction appeared to be largely a passive one. During the early stages of the debate, public opinion appeared to the government to be on the side of the critics. That the pressure and criticism were effective was shown by its initial responses. The government's position during this period was primarily a reactive one. But by late October its perception of the public's reaction had changed and it became less responsive to the demands. The limited success of the relevant fund-raising appeals and the small number of representations received by Members of Parliament were specifically cited in interviews with government officials as evidence of the low level of public interest in the issue. At the same time the National Gallup Poll report[22] indicated that the government's popularity had continued to rise during the autumn months of 1968. As the government now perceived the issue, the level of public support for the interest groups' demands was not sufficient to warrant further action on its part. It shifted ground accordingly and, on October 21, Mr. Trudeau began a strong counter-attack. Arguing that "there has been a lack of reality in a lot of the criticism of the Canadian public on this,"[23] he used an escalating series of analogies and warnings comparing, for example, Canadian involvement with that of the United States in Vietnam in support of his government's non-intervention policy.[24]

On November 4, Mr. Trudeau told Parliament that his personal representative, Professor Ivan Head, who had just returned from a visit to Nigeria, had obtained an agreement from the Nigerian leader, General Gowan, which would guarantee the safety of Red Cross daylight flights to Uli, the only remaining Biafran airstrip, from either Lagos or Fernando Po.* The Prime Minister noted that:

> General Gowan has placed a single condition on this guarantee, one which I regard and which I am sure all Canadians will regard as eminently reasonable. It is that Colonel Ojukwu, (head of the Biafran regime) will undertake not to employ the Uli airstrip during daylight hours for arms flights. In this regard it should be borne in mind that such an understanding would in no respect reduce the present level of arms shipments to the rebels. Uli airstrip is not now being (used) for any purpose during daylight hours . . . I therefore now address a public and urgent appeal to Colonel Ojukwu to seize this opportunity to open up his airstrip to daylight relief flights and so permit the Red Cross to increase substantially food shipments to those civilians in the rebel areas needing help.[25]

Two days later the ICRC cancelled all of its flights to Biafra after a night-time Nigerian air attack on Uli airstrip. Although it resumed its flights shortly thereafter, the Canadian Hercules remained grounded because the Nigerian authorities refused to continue to assure the safety of night flights to the airport. When questioned about this in Parliament, Mr. Trudeau said that because "it is during the night that all the arms are getting in . . . we can only assume that (the Biafran authorities) have an interest in intermingling arms and relief flights in order that there may be confusion."[26] On December 11, without Biafran assurances that Uli would not be used for daylight arms flights, the Hercules was withdrawn from Fernando Po.

We have little knowledge of the circumstances of the day–night relief flight controversy. It was commonly supposed, as Mr. Trudeau argued, that the Briafrans were attempting to mix arms and relief flights at night. But, unknown to the press and the public, and apparently to Mr. Trudeau, Uli was being used by arms-carrying aircraft regularly during the day. We can speculate that Gowan's proposal was intended to put a halt to these flights.

After the Gowan offer, and Biafra's failure to accept his conditions, criticism of the government eased sharply. Newspapers which had strongly disapproved of government policy reversed their positions. The Biafran authorities began to draw the bulk of newspaper criticism.

By November 26, when the House of Commons held a special debate to consider the Standing Committee's report on the Nigeria-Biafra question, public interest in the issue had diminished noticeably. The principal development of the debate was Mr. Sharp's announcement

---

* The daylight flight offer, however, was not the main purpose but only a by-product of Professor Head's visit to Nigeria.

that Canada would provide a further $1.6 million for relief in Nigeria and Biafra. A Conservative–New Democratic Party motion which asked the government to request that countries supplying arms to the belligerents end the shipments, and to bring the issue to the United Nations was defeated easily in the ensuing vote as the House divided along party lines. By December, Biafra had ceased to be a significant issue in Canadian politics.

THE BIAFRA CASE: THE POLICY ACTORS

Elsewhere in this collection of essays, A. P. Pross has reviewed the Canadian literature concerned with interest group studies and has presented an analytic approach which distinguishes between issue-oriented and institutional groups. In the following pages we shall use this approach to examine the Biafra episode, first, to determine whether the actions of the Biafra interest groups conform to the generally observed patterns of behaviour identified in the literature, and second, to discover whether we can make some new observations about interest group behaviour on the basis of this study.

THE INTEREST GROUPS

Both institutional interest groups and issue-oriented interest groups were involved in the Biafra issue. The most important of the institutional groups were the Presbyterian Church in Canada, which was concerned because of its extensive missionary work in Nigeria; the Canadian Red Cross Society, which became involved through the ICRC, its parent body; and the Church and relief organizations which formed the Nigeria/Biafra Relief Fund of Canada. None of these groups existed for the sole purpose of influencing government decisions. Rather their participation was an outgrowth of their broader organizational roles. The issue-oriented groups were formed for the specific purpose of altering the Canadian government's Biafra policy. The most important of these groups were the Canadian Committee for the Relief of Biafran Refugees, which later evolved into the Canadian Union for the Rights of Biafra; Biafran students' groups; and the Aid to Biafran–Nigerian Children Committee of Canada.

The Institutional Groups:

THE PRESBYTERIAN CHURCH IN CANADA   Because of its large-scale missionary activity in Nigeria, the Presbyterian Church was the Canadian organization most immediately affected by the civil war. Its involvement there began in 1954 when it entered the country on a co-operative basis with the Church of Scotland. Its early work was concentrated in the eastern region, which subsequently became Biafra; but in 1963 it moved into the western area, establishing a congregation at Lagos. The Church's missionary work brought its officials into direct contact with Nigerian political authorities and citizens. Dr. E. H. Johnson, who had been its General Secretary for Overseas Missions since 1954, travelled widely in Nigeria and was acquainted with a number of its prominent politicians including Dr. Okoi Arikpo, Nigerian Commissioner for External Affairs, and Dr. Francis Ibiam, senior advisor to the Military Governor of Biafra, both of whom were leading Presbyterian elders. Through its missionary work the Church also developed high level contacts with the Department of External Affairs in Ottawa.

In the case of Biafra, its objectives were both political and humanitarian. It actively sought to have the Canadian and other governments (including the Nigerian and Biafran authorities) and international organizations attempt to achieve a negotiated settlement of the war. It also wanted the Canadian government to play a more extensive role in the relief effort.

THE CANADIAN RED CROSS SOCIETY   The Canadian Red Cross became involved in the issue at the request of the ICRC. As an international relief assistance organization, it wanted the Canadian government to increase its relief aid to provide aircraft for participation in ICRC-sponsored airlifts to Biafra. The ICRC was the only international assistance organization which operated with the approval of the FMG. It also acted as the principal channel of communication, on relief matters, between the Canadian government and the Nigerian and Biafran authorities.

THE NIGERIA/BIAFRA RELIEF FUND OF CANADA   The Nigeria/Biafra Relief Fund grew out of a meeting of representatives of the Canadian Catholic Organization for Development and Peace, the Canadian Red Cross Society, the Canadian Council of Churches, the Presbyterian Church in Canada, and Oxfam of Canada which had been called to discuss the situation in Nigeria-Biafra in early July 1968. Its objective was to provide humanitarian assistance to Nigeria-Biafra and it launched a national appeal for funds for this purpose in August 1968. It also maintained an informal liaison with the Canadian government. Although the Fund was set up for a specific short-term purpose, it has been included as an institutional group because all of its members were established organizations.

The Issue-Oriented Groups:

CANADIAN COMMITTEE FOR THE RELIEF OF BIAFRAN REFUGEES/CANADIAN UNION FOR THE RIGHTS OF BIAFRA   The Committee, which became the Canadian Union for the Rights of Biafra (CURB) in September 1968, began as a humanitarian organization which sponsored an appeal for Biafran relief funds in March of the same year. Its membership, aside from a nucleus of less than ten persons, was fluid. It consisted mainly of returned CUSO volunteers and other concerned persons who had served in Nigeria or, more generally, in Africa. As events unfolded the group's activities became increasingly politicized, and it was the most important of the issue-oriented groups. CURB placed its primary stress on the political aspects of the issue, urging that the Canadian government help achieve a political settlement of the conflict and seek an end to foreign arms shipments as a necessary prelude to effective relief assistance.

BIAFRAN STUDENTS   On the whole, Biafran students did not play a large role in the issue. The most important of the groups was located in Toronto and consisted of about ten persons. Its most significant liaison for political purposes was with the Canadian Union for the Rights of Biafra. Its main objectives were similar to those of CURB.

AID TO BIAFRAN-NIGERIAN CHILDREN COMMITTEE OF CANADA   This group was formed in Toronto in September 1968 by Mr. and Mrs. Gordon A. Purdy. Its membership was small. Initially it concentrated on the humanitarian aspects of the issue, but like the other groups, its orientation became increasingly political during the fall.

Analysis of Interest Group Behaviour:

Conceptually the pattern of the interest groups' behaviour can be divided into two general phases. During the first phase (June 1967 to June 1968), those interest groups which were active concentrated their attention mainly on senior government officials. But this approach had only limited success. Accordingly, during the period from July to December 1968, a variety of private and public approaches were used by the interest groups in their efforts to alter Canada's Biafra policy. The following chart outlines their initiatives. The subsequent comments will analyse their behaviour in a more detailed way.[27]

Institutional Groups   The distinguishing characteristic of the behaviour of the institutional interest groups in the Biafran example was the rather cautious role they played in attempting to influence the government's policy. For the most part, they confined themselves to private approaches to the Secretary of State for External Affairs and his departmental officials. Neither the Red Cross nor the Nigeria/Biafra Relief Fund deviated from this course throughout the period. Although the Presbyterian Church did take a more public stand, its main approach was to concentrate its efforts directly on the relevant government officials. As we have seen, a turning point in its actions occurred in August 1968 after Dr. Johnson, following his second visit to Biafra, had unsuccessfully conferred with Mr. Sharp and his advisors. After that, the Church did adopt a more public position, but it was careful not to follow a course that would have jeopardized access to the government.[28]

The circumscribed approach adopted by the institutional groups reflects their understanding of the role they play in the policy-making process. As long-term goal-seeking organizations, institutional interest groups have established regular patterns of communication with, and high level access to, government officials. To the extent that such access is recognized and accepted by government decision-makers, the groups do have a certain "legitimacy" within the policy process. They will attempt to maintain that status perhaps because of their own

Table 2   *INSTITUTIONAL INTEREST GROUPS*

	Presbyterian Church	*Canadian Red Cross Society*	*Nigeria/Biafra Relief Fund*
June 1967	Church officials made their first approaches to senior officials of the Department of External Affairs (DEA).		
Aug. 1967			
Oct. 1967	Throughout the fall and winter, officials were in regular contact with the DEA. They also held several meetings with Paul Martin, then Secretary of State for External Affairs. In November, they tried unsuccessfully to arrange meetings between DEA officials and visiting Biafran envoys.		
Jan. 1968	Dr. E. H. Johnson made a fact-finding tour in Nigeria and Biafra. He held talks with authorities on both sides, including General Gowan and Colonel Ojukwu. He reported his findings to British, Canadian, and US governments, and UN and Commonwealth officials.		
Feb. 1968	Officials tried to interest MPs and the media in the issue.		
March 1968	Dr. Johnson gave evidence to the Parliamentary Standing Committee on External Affairs. Again without success, officials tried to arrange meetings between Biafran envoys and DEA officials.		

| Table 2, continued | ISSUE-ORIENTED INTEREST GROUPS | |
CCRBR/ CURB	Biafran Students	Aid to Biafran– Nigerian Children Committee
		Telegrams sent to Prime Minister Pearson, Opposition leader Diefenbaker and T. C. Douglas (NDP). They received no replies.
A group of returned CUSO volunteers sent letters asking for Canadian initiatives to several major newspapers.		
The Canadian Committee for the Relief of Biafran Refugees was formed. In March it launched an appeal for relief funds.	Several Biafran students joined CCRBR.	
	The students arranged a press conference in Toronto for Biafran envoys who visited the city at their request.	

	Presbyterian Church	Canadian Red Cross Society	Nigeria/Biafra Relief Fund
May 1968		At the request of the ICRC, the Society asked the External Aid Office to contribute to the latter's relief program in Nigeria-Biafra. It also asked the Canadian government to request Nigeria to lift its blockade of Biafra so that relief efforts could be successful. The government agreed to both requests.	
June 1968	The Church's General Assembly passed resolutions encouraging more active Canadian mediation efforts.		
July 1968			The Fund was established and some of its agencies met with Mr. Sharp, the new Secretary of State for External Affairs to discuss possible areas of Canadian involvement in peace-making and relief. The Fund launched a public, non-political appeal for funds for Nigerian-Biafran relief.
Aug. 1968	Dr. Johnson made a second visit to Biafra. He later met with Mr. Sharp and officials of his department. Arguing that the conflict would be a prolonged one, he tried to persuade the government to propose a cease-fire and to increase its relief contributions. The officials tried to discourage him, arguing that a Nigerian victory was imminent. The Church then began a more active public effort to influence the government. It increased its contacts with the media and encouraged MPs to raise the issue at the approaching session of Parliament.	The Society's National Commissioner, Major-General A. E. Wrinch asked the government to provide Hercules aircraft for the proposed ICRC airlift to Biafra. Because Nigeria had not given its formal approval, the government declined the request.	

By September, organizational contacts among the interest groups had been establishe

CCRBR/ CURB	Biafran Students	Aid to Biafran– Nigerian Children Committee
	Several members of the group, together with Biafran students held a public demonstration in Ottawa, aimed at the Soviet and British missions. Some representatives also met with DEA officials.	Representatives met with Mr. Sharp's Parliamentary Secretary and presented a brief which was highly critical of Canadian policy.

Table 2, continued   *INSTITUTIONAL INTEREST GROUPS*

Presbyterian Church	*Canadian Red Cross Society*	*Nigeria/Biafra Relief Fund*
Sept. 1968 Officials arranged for the visit to Biafra of two MPs – Andrew Brewin and David MacDonald. They also arranged to have Charles Taylor of the *Globe and Mail* to accompany them. The Church also became a major source of information for the opposition parties in Parliament.	The Red Cross acted as the official channel of communication on relief matters between the Canadian government and Nigerian and Biafran authorities. It was in constant contact with DEA and Mr. Sharp throughout.	The fund maintained an informal liaison with DEA through the Red Cross. As a result of its private requests, the government agreed to distribute part of its initial shipment of relief supplies at Fernando Po from where it could be sent to Biafra. The shipment was originally intended to be sent only to Lagos.
Oct. 1968 At Dr. Johnson's suggestion, Mr. Stanfield moved that Parliament set up its Standing Committee on External Affairs and National Defence to investigate the issue. On October 15, Dr. Johnson testified before the Committee. Despite these public actions, the Church's main approach remained its contacts with DEA.	Under ICR sponsorship, Canadian Hercules were provided for relief flights to Nigeria and Biafra. The Red Cross used no public approaches to influence government policy.	

organizational requirements (Kwavnick suggests that such recognition may give their organizations additional status and strengthen the position of their leaderships within them[29]), but also because access is a capability for exerting influence. It does not necessarily follow that such groups have a significant influence on all or many policy decisions. It does mean that because they must continue to deal with the government in future situations, stepping outside their usual lines of communication with government officials could jeopardize the groups' status within the policy process, remove a potential channel for influence, or impair their future activities. Thus, unless they consider an issue to be of sufficient importance to them, institutional groups will confine themselves to private efforts to influence government policy. We can illustrate this by referring to the groups that we are considering here.

It was because it did not wish to jeopardize its position as an impartial international assistance organization that the Red Cross avoided public approaches in its attempts to obtain Hercules aircraft for relief flights to Biafra. Its restraint was also dictated by the fact that the Red Cross was the only organization which had the approval of the Nigerian government to co-ordinate relief actions in Nigeria and Biafra, a role which permitted it to serve as the channel of communication in relief matters between the Canadian government and the Nigerian and Biafran authorities. Similarly, several of the member agencies of the Nigeria/Biafra Relief Fund thought that their impartiality and their future operations would be jeopardized if the Fund made any concerted attempts to influence the government.[30] The clearest example is that of the Presbyterian Church. Its officials believed that the best prospects for the resolution of the conflict lay with those governments and organizations which were concerned with the problem and they wanted to maintain their access to them. Throughout the war, Dr. Johnson remained in contact with the Commonwealth Secretariat, government officials in Canada, Britain, and the United States, the United Nations, Nigerian and Biafran authorities, and the relief agencies supplying assistance to the stricken areas.[31] Church officials had access to the Biafran sector and they regarded their function partly as providing the Canadian government with information which was otherwise not easily available.[32] Furthermore, throughout the conflict the Church had more of its missionaries in Lagos than in Biafra. Active public involvement on its part, especially in emphasizing the plight of the Biafrans, would have damaged its officials' lines of communication to the relevant decision-makers, including the Nigerian authorities. It might also have endangered its missionary activities in Nigeria and in other developing countries, because it could have been charged by sensitive nations with interfering in the internal affairs of a sovereign state.

Issue-Oriented Groups   Like the institutional groups, the issue-oriented interest groups made a number of private approaches to the government. But their behaviour differed from that of the former for they relied increasingly on public initiatives to try to influence its policy. Their greater use of public actions developed after they realized that both their own private initiatives and those of the institutional groups were insufficient to alter government policy.[33] These actions were attempts to create public support for their demands thereby enhancing their prospects of influencing the government.

The more public behaviour of the issue-oriented groups can also be explained in terms of their perceptions of their role in the policy-making process. Issue-oriented interest groups are short-term goal-seeking organizations which attempt to influence government policy on a single specific issue. Unlike institutional groups they do not have to be concerned about their continuing relationship with a government, for the nature of their organizations and goals deprives the latter of any countervailing leverage in the future. Hence, they have greater freedom in their choice of approaches to influence government policy. In addition, the example of the Biafran students suggests that some issue-oriented groups might undertake public initiatives more readily because they do not have easy access to government officials.

INTEREST GROUP INTERACTION

The Biafran experience suggests that institutional interest groups with established access to a government sometimes have the least effect upon its policy. On the other hand, those groups which used approaches normally regarded as cumbersome and inefficient most effectively embarrassed the government and achieved a temporary modification of policy. This suggests that, in some cases, issue-oriented interest groups can influence government decisions more effectively than institutional interest groups. What occurs in such cases is that institutional groups, after their private approaches have failed, cannot attempt to create public support for their objectives because they risk future reprisals from government. This limitation does not apply to issue-oriented groups because they do not take the same risks. It is apparent, however, that the extent to which public approaches can be successful depends upon the amount of support which the interest groups can mobilize for their demands.

When an institutional interest group is reluctant to act publicly to influence policy for fear of jeopardizing its relationship with a government, it may encourage issue-oriented groups in their attempts to arouse mass support. Therefore, issue-oriented groups can offer a way of diverting dissatisfaction within institutional groups maintaining, at the same time, the latters' legitimacy within the policy process and perhaps making their own approaches more effective. Thus, to some extent, the strategy by which Presbyterian Church officials and other institutional groups concentrated their actions directly on senior government decision-makers while the Canadian Union for the Rights of Biafra and the Aid to Biafran-Nigerian Children Committee focused their attention on the public was a deliberate one. During the fall of 1968 the groups met regularly with each other to discuss their activities.[34] But ultimately CURB and the institutional groups began to disagree on their approaches and the contacts between them became less frequent. CURB became critical of the institutional groups because they did not utilize their positions of leadership to create public support for their demands. As one CURB member later put it, "The Churches and relief groups really put down any attempt to do political work. They played a numbers game with starvation figures and tonnage figures. That gave Trudeau an easy way out—he just threw the issue back to the people, telling them to give more money."[35] At the same time, Presbyterian Church officials considered CURB's public demonstrations too militant, and damaging to their own efforts.

THE MEDIA, PARLIAMENT AND THE GENERAL PUBLIC

The media, Parliament and the general public played major roles in the Biafra issue in Canadian politics in the autumn of 1968. They constituted important targets for the interest groups in their efforts to influence the government. Conversely, the government's perceptions of their various reactions largely determined the course of Canada's Biafra policy. The significance of these three actors can be illustrated by tracing the process by which Biafra became a prominent political issue.

The interest groups had begun by concentrating their efforts directly on government officials. But this approach had brought them only limited success. They then began trying to influence government policy in additional ways with the institutional groups concentrating primarily on government decision-makers and the issue-oriented groups adopting a more public course. Media interest in the issue began to develop in the summer of 1968. But Biafra did not become a major political issue in Canada until it became an important one in Parliament. The interest groups acted through the parliamentarians. Media interest crystallized because the issue was such an important one in the House of Commons. Continued criticism in Parliament, interest group activity, and the media's coverage of both (as well as its own demands) were, in turn, fed back to the government, which then recognized the issue's political importance and responded to many of the demands. But this approach was successful only as long as the government saw that the interest groups' demands were reflective of the general public's view. After that perception changed, the interest groups' subsequent actions lost political effect.

We can only understand this process of dynamic interaction, however, if we extrapolate from our general discussion the roles played by each of the individual actors.

The Media

The media was an important actor in the Biafra issue in several ways. First, by reporting the issue, the media reflected the intense interest which the question had generated as a political debate. In turn, it contributed to sustaining that debate. Secondly, interest groups used the media directly as an additional means of pressuring the government. Thirdly, it acted in its own right as an influential critic of government policy.

Media interest in the issue developed rather slowly at first. Some interest groups, primarily the Presbyterian Church,[36] tried to draw its attention to the conflict at an early stage, but extensive coverage did not begin until the summer of 1968. In July pictures of starving Biafran children began appearing in the press and on television, and the issue became a subject of increasing editorial criticism.[37] Two major factors account for the strong media interest which subsequently developed. First, news of the conflict, and particularly of the situation in Biafra, did not appear in Canada until about the same time as it became prominent in the world press. This was largely a reflection of the media's dependence on foreign news agencies such as Associated Press, Reuters, and United Press International for much foreign news coverage. Secondly, the issue arose in Canada when there were few important news developments in the country.[38] Media interest was heightened by the interest groups' activities and the fact that the new government's initial clumsy response to the problem occasioned some of the first public disillusionment with Mr. Trudeau. One prominent newsman cited two points at which the issue's importance was intensified. The first was when Mr. Trudeau was asked in the summer about the prospect of sending Canadian aid to Biafra. His careless replies ("You have the funniest questions." and "Where's Biafra?") gave the subject additional news value and also increased the criticism aimed at him. The second was when the Prime Minister faced Parliament in early September. Opposition Leader Stanfield made the Biafra issue his first question at the initial House of Commons question period. Mr. Trudeau directed the question to Mr. Sharp who did not handle it well. Because the opposition parties gave the issue a high priority and because the government's replies were not very effective, it became a major news item.[39]

At the same time, the interest groups (particularly the Presbyterian Church and CURB) had established influential contacts among the Toronto press and the CBC and CTV television networks and were providing them with information about the conflict and their own activities. Through their press connections, for example, Presbyterian Church officials arranged to have Charles Taylor of the *Globe and Mail* accompany Andrew Brewin and David MacDonald on their visit to Biafra.[40] Events such as the Brewin–MacDonald visit gave the issue additional momentum. For instance, subsequent visits made to Biafra by CBC news teams were direct consequences of the two parliamentarians' reports.[41]

The main government targets of the editorial criticism in the press were Mr. Sharp and the Department of External Affairs. In particular, the *Globe and Mail*, aware of its readership among high-level government officials, carried on an open debate with Mr. Sharp and his Departmental advisors.[42] Government officials later indicated that press coverage, editorials, and especially television had significant effects upon them.

Initially, media interest in the issue developed because reports of widespread starvation in Biafra had aroused humanitarian concern.[43] The impact of the political aspects of the question was sharpened by the adeptness with which the Biafrans explained their case. By contrast the Nigerian case was poorly presented.[44] The media's interest, however, was most stimulated by Canadian involvement in the issue—the activities of the interest groups, the debates in Parliament, and the government's response.

Parliament

Parliament's part in the Biafran controversy was of primary importance, for its concentration on the issue largely awakened and sustained public interest in the question. During the autumn months of 1968 especially, it was the major focal point of the interaction among the interest groups, the media, the public and the government.

Like that of the media, Parliament's interest in the issue did not crystallize at an early stage. The interest groups, primarily the Presbyterian Church, made some attempts to involve Members of Parliament in the subject in the spring of 1968. The public impact of these actions was not immediately evident, but they did create a number of contacts for the interest groups and they established a nucleus of Conservative and NDP MPs around which subsequent interest group activities could be centered.

The issue was the subject of the first question asked of the government in the 28th Parliament in September. The opposition parties used their traditional weapon, the question period, to good advantage. Informed by the interest groups, primarily the Presbyterian Church and the Canadian Union for the Rights of Biafra,[45] they directed nearly 250 questions at the government during the autumn.[46] The Conservative Party's decision to concentrate on the issue, made by Mr. Stanfield and his advisors late in July,[47] was probably influenced by the interest group overtures made to them directly and through concerned MPs as well as by the developing public interest in the question.

In the House of Commons the Conservative and New Democratic parties executed a contrapuntal attack upon the government. A select group of informed opposition Members almost systematically exploited the weaknesses of the government's position. They concentrated their questions on Mr. Sharp, the recently appointed Secretary of State for External Affairs. The strategy, highlighted by the dramatic visit to Biafra of Andrew Brewin and David MacDonald, was effective. *The Gold and Mail* reported that the Minister "often seemed rattled when questioned about Biafra"[48] and under the barrage of criticism the government responded to many of their demands.

Acting on the suggestion of Presbyterian Church officials, Opposition

Leader Stanfield moved, on October 7, that Parliament immediately constitute its Standing Committee on External Affairs and National Defence to consider the Nigeria-Biafra question.[49] The Standing Committee became an additional forum for the interest groups. Major-General A. E. Wrinch, of the Canadian Red Cross, was invited to testify on October 8. Dr. E. H. Johnson gave evidence on October 15. Keith Bezanson, whose presentation the Canadian Union for the Rights of Biafra had helped to prepare, appeared before the Committee on October 17. Persons who had recently visited Biafra including Andrew Brewin, David MacDonald, Charles Taylor, and Stephen Lewis also testified. Mr. Sharp and officials of the Department of External Affairs put forward the government's case.[50]

Although the Committee did not have a direct policy-making role it did provide a means for examining the question. More significantly, perhaps, it was an additional focal point through which the interest groups' demands and the observations of those who had been to Biafra could be refracted into the decision-making process. Moreover, because the Committee's deliberations were widely reported in the media, it generated a means of further pressuring the government and sharpening its perception of the issue as a politically significant one.

Both the intensity and the duration of the criticism of its policy took the government by surprise. One senior official said that there was "almost incredulity" that it continued for so long and with such strength. The officials indicated that while the media's attacks had a clear impact throughout this period, the most effective pressure on the government came from the opposition.[51]

Thus the centrality of Parliament's position in the Biafra episode should not be underestimated. Not only did the government perceive it to be the most influential critic of its policy, but also it was through Parliament that Biafra became a major public issue. Because of parliamentary concern the intense media interest developed. The issue reasserted the validity of R. MacGregor Dawson's view that the question period is "one of the most formidable devices which the opposition has at its disposal" for it allows it to bring "the acts of government out into full publicity and threatens at all times to submit the most obscure happenings to a sudden and unexpected scrutiny."[52] Parliament is the central forum where a government must defend its policies, and through the House of Commons, both the government and the opposition have equal access to the public which ultimately controls a government. The Biafra debate supports Hockin's view that even though Parliament is dominated by disciplined parties it is "still a theatre for political upheavals and for erosions of party and personal reputations . . . failure in Parliament has a way of being transmitted to the public at large."[53]

Public Opinion

Ultimately, the attitude of the general public toward the Biafra issue was singularly important. The government's conclusion that the public was generally indifferent to events in Biafra perhaps more than any other factor undermined the political effectiveness of the interest groups.

The nature and sequence of the government's perceptions of the issue's political significance show the importance of the public's role. The context within which such a process takes place is one in which government officials receive messages from a number of sources on a foreign policy matter that is not functionally related to any well-defined Canadian interest. The problem for the officials then becomes one of determining what these communications mean in political terms. In the Biafran case, their perceptions fell into three stages. The government began by assuming that the issue was not a politically sensitive one. Mr. Trudeau's somewhat careless replies to questions concerning it during the summer, and officials' admissions of surprise at the extent of the criticism of government policy support this claim. By September, however, government perception of the issue's political importance had changed. The extensive opposition to its policy generated by the interest groups, the parliamentarians and the media, forced the government to view the issue as a politically sensitive one, and it responded to the demands. But finally, by mid-October, caucus surveys revealed that the number of representations being received by MPs was generally small. This, together with the limited success of the relevant fund-raising appeals, was specifically cited in interviews with government officials as evidence of the public's passivity.[54] After this had become apparent to the government, it decided that its first position had been the correct one, and in the words of one official, that the safe position was to "ride it out."

The precise reaction of the public to the issue is difficult to gauge for there were no public opinion polls taken on the subject. Moreover, in Canada we do not have any systematic analysis of what a strong public reaction in the foreign policy field actually is. But comments made to the author by several Members of Parliament show that they thought public interest to be generally low, suggesting that the general public had only limited concern in a matter that was of no obvious consequence to itself. A Quebec MP noted that the subject "seems of rather no interest to my electors." An Ontario Member wrote "There was really no interest whatsoever. People feel we have enough trouble at home." In the judgment of a second Ontario MP, "While the people of (constituency) are naturally concerned about the Nigerian-Biafran problem; they are vitally interested in the unusual high cost of living and the many difficulties that are the result." A British Columbia MP reported that to his surprise "the issue was largely ignored despite the amount of comment in Press, TV, and radio."[55]

The number of representations sent to Members of Parliament on the subject generally corroborate this assessment. They are shown in the following figures. Figure 1 shows that 65.3 per cent of the MPs responding to a questionnaire on the subject (75 of 115 MPs) received less than 10 communications on the question. Seventy-one per cent of them (49 of 69 MPs) indicated that the flow of messages did not exceed or was less than the average number of representations on any issue. (Figure 2).

Figure 1

Question: How many representations (i.e. letters, telegrams, telephone calls, briefs) did you receive on this issue? (A close approximation is sufficient).

MEMBERS OF PARLIAMENT (TOTAL)

	5000	500	300-400	151-200	101-150	76-100	51-75	26-50	11-25	01-10	0	Replies	Total Replies	Total MPs
Nfld.	0	0	0	0	0	0	0	0	1	1	2	4	4	7
N.S.	0	0	0	1	0	0	0	0	0	2	2	5	6	11
P.E.I.	0	0	0	1	0	0	0	0	0	1	1	3	3	4
N.B.	0	0	0	0	0	0	0	0	0	1	3	4	4	10
Que.	1	0	0	0	0	0	0	0	2	11	7	21	21	74
Ont.	0	1	1	0	2	0	3	3	11	16	6	43	44	88
Man.	0	0	0	0	0	0	0	1	0	1	4	6	6	13
Sask.	0	0	1	0	0	0	0	0	1	0	3	5	6	13
Alta.	0	0	0	2	0	0	0	1	4	3	2	12	13	19
B.C.	0	0	0	0	0	0	0	0	3	7	0	10	10	23
NWT. / Yuk.	0	0	0	0	0	0	0	0	0	1	1	2	2	2
Total No.	1	1	2	4	2	0	3	5	22	44	31	115	119	264
%*	.9	.9	1.7	3.5	1.7	0	2.6	4.4	19.1	38.3	27			

* Calculated on the basis of 262 questionnaires sent to Members of Parliament.

Figure 2

Question: To what extent (if any) did this exceed your normal flow of representations?

	100%	75%	50%	25%	Less than 25%	No Change	Less than Normal	Replies	Total Replies
Nfld.	0	0	0	0	0	0	0	0	4
N.S.	0	1	0	0	0	0	0	1	6
P.E.I.	0	1	0	0	0	0	0	1	3
N.B.	0	0	0	0	0	0	0	0	4
Que.	0	0	0	2	1	9	0	12	21
Ont.	3	0	2	2	0	20	5	32	44
Man.	0	0	0	0	0	1	0	1	6
Sask.	1	0	0	1	0	1	0	3	6
Alta.	1	2	2	1	0	3	1	10	13
B.C.	0	0	0	0	0	6	1	7	10
NWT.									
Yuk.	0	0	0	0	0	1	1	2	2
Total									
No.	5	4	4	6	1	41	8	69	119
%	7.3	5.8	5.8	8.7	1.5	59.4	11.6		

The Prime Minister received many more communications. Officials reported that between January 1, 1968 and mid-May 1969, over 5000 messages were sent to his office. This number was surpassed only by those relating to the issues of Canadian diplomatic representation to the Vatican and the abortion aspects of the Criminal Code amendments. But most of the Biafra messages were of the organized variety and parliamentarians usually do not give such communications any significant consideration.[56]

The evidence indicates that government officials, in acquiring their perceptions of public opinion on foreign policy issues, do regard the media as important. The impact of editorials, press coverage, and especially television was said by officials to have had important effects upon the government. But it is also evident that they consider communications to MPs an important index of public opinion. Perhaps such communications, in the long run, are more significant than media reaction.

THE POLICY-MAKERS

Two conflicting interpretations have been advanced about the role played by executive agencies in the making of Canada's Biafra policy. On the one hand Andrew Brewin and David MacDonald argue that the government's policy was largely determined by the Department of External Affairs[57] and that, moreover, the Department was not prepared to change its traditional outlook. They suggest that "the basic reason for Ottawa's refusal to take the Biafran affair to the United Nations has been much more the adherence to a style and attitude in international affairs that has become characteristic of Canada. There is an attitude of caution, an attitude of weighing the views of our allies rather than the merits of the issue."[58]

On the other hand, some authors have argued that the Biafra issue illustrated the extent to which the Office of the Prime Minister had replaced the bureaucracy as a source of policy initiation and advice. William A. Matheson writes, "An outstanding example of a shift in influence was the decision to send Professor Ivan Head, one of Mr. Trudeau's personal assistants, rather than an official of the Department of External Affairs to negotiate with the Nigerian government regarding relief flights into Biafra."[59] Journalist Walter Stewart agrees. He says, "A much more normal course would have been to send an official from the External Affairs Department; but Head was not sent as the representative of Her Majesty's Government in Canada; he was the Prime Minister's personal representative, the equivalent of an American president's private emissary."[60] Our purpose is not to make general statements about the larger question which these authors raise but rather to discuss the Biafra case. However, the view of Biafra taken here does not support their claims.

The Trudeau government, which was a new administration in the process of establishing itself, relied essentially on the advice of its

Department of External Affairs advisors in making its Biafra policy.[61] The Department took the view that the interest groups' demands were impractical and that Canada should not become involved in an external issue in which it could have little effect. Interest group representatives said that they found members of the government willing to consider their views, but that those of External Affairs were more persuasive. Andrew Brewin and David MacDonald reported a somewhat similar experience.[62] The Department was the main point of contact with the relevant governments and organizations which were concerned with the problem. It was also the focus of the interest groups' actions. The agreement resulting in the provision of Canadian Hercules crafts for emergency flights to Nigeria and Biafra was made by Mr. Sharp and his departmental officials. Moreover, it is clear that Professor Head's mission to Nigeria did not signal a change in policy, because thereafter the government continued to follow what appeared to be the prevailing view of the Department of External Affairs.

Essentially, Matheson and Stewart base their case on Professor Head's Nigeria mission. But this is not an accurate interpretation. Furthermore, the relief flight question was only a by-product of his visit. His mission resulted from the fact that throughout the autumn months the Nigerian press had given prominent coverage to the Canadian debate about the Biafra issue. The press was reflecting, in a simplistic way, the concern being expressed by the media and in Parliament. Canada's High Commission in Nigeria found that the Nigerian authorities were interpreting these views as being the government's outlook. Despite the reassurances of the Canadian diplomats, Canadian-Nigerian relations had reached a point of strain at which it was necessary to reinforce the representations made by External Affairs officials. Professor Head's visit had three purposes: first, to assure General Gowan that Canada supported a unified Nigeria; secondly, to tell the Nigerian authorities that Canada desired a non-military solution of the conflict; and, thirdly, to make a fresh appraisal of the problem.

It was during Professor Head's discussions with General Gowan that the subject of daylight flights to Biafra arose. General Gowan had first made the offer to Colonel Ojukwu through Red Cross officials about two weeks before Head's visit. The Biafran regime had refused the offer, but neither the proposal nor its refusal had been made public. When the offer was brought to Canada's attention, Mr. Trudeau immediately publicized it.[63]

But Canada's involvement in the offer, and the circumstances surrounding General Gowan's proposal suggest that the government was not well informed about it. The view prevailed among government officials that Biafra had refused to guarantee that Uli airstrip would not be used for arms flights during daylight hours because its leaders wanted to bring in arms shipments through a screen of relief flights at night. But in reality, arms-carrying aircraft were eluding the unsophisticated Nigerian ground and radar control and using the airstrip regularly during the day. Thus, it seems that General Gowan's offer was not as magnanimous as it appeared. Apparently it was aimed at halting the daylight arms flights to Biafra. That Uli was being used during daylight hours was doubtless known to many. Yet, either the government chose to ignore this, or more likely, it did not know about it, for it seems improbable that the government would otherwise have participated in the proposal.[64]

It is apparent, however, that Canada's ability to follow a political course other than the one it adopted in the Biafra case was restricted by the policies of other nations. Further, though government officials denied it, the question of Quebec separatism probably had some effect on Canada's policy. For example, Mr. Sharp drew attention to the Gabon-Quebec parallel when defending the government's position.[65] But the effect of the Quebec situation was probably to strengthen and rigidify a policy that would have been adopted for other reasons in any case.[66] In his testimony to the Standing Committee on External Affairs and National Defence, Mr. Sharp drew attention to the principle of non-interference in the internal affairs of other states. He said, "Non-interference and territorial integrity are issues of manifestly great importance to the newly formed states of Africa . . . It would be a grave move for any non-African state and particularly a white non-African state, to take steps that could be interpreted as intervention."[67]

It seems clear that an attempt to raise the issue at the United Nations would not have been successful. Speaking in the House of Commons on November 26, Mr. Trudeau acknowledged that "world concern for the promotion and protection of basic rights has enabled the assembly effectively to overcome past objections that even the mere discussions of these rights constituted a form of intervention. However, in this particular instance there was no general desire to have the item discussed at the United Nations."[68] Canadian diplomats had tried to obtain support from member delegations to raise the issue at the United Nations but they could not secure positive responses from their heads of missions. France, the Soviet Union and the United States were all unwilling to have the subject discussed.[69]

It is more difficult to discuss the question of government assistance to organizations which were sending emergency aid to Biafra. It can be noted, however, that other nations, particularly the Scandinavian countries, West Germany, and the United States all provided assistance through these agencies without incurring obvious political reprisals from Nigeria. Moreover, in January 1970, the Canadian government itself agreed to make funds available to Canairelief for its emergency operations in Biafra, although the conflict ended shortly thereafter and the funds were not provided.

CONCLUSION

The Biafra case study has permitted us to examine the dynamics of the generation and development of a major political issue. This analysis

143

has focused primarily on the behaviour of institutional interest groups and issue-oriented interest groups. It has also drawn attention to other aspects of the processes of Canadian government; namely, the important part played by Parliament in focusing public attention on a political issue, and some facets of the making of Canada's Biafra policy.

We have argued that the cautious behaviour of the institutional groups resulted from the fact that they are long-term goal-seeking organizations. The pursuit of such goals may require the development of private methods of communication with government officials and the acceptance of the constraints that such relationships impose. But issue-oriented groups, which pursue short-term goals, are not bound by these constraints. Thus, they have greater latitude in their choice of strategies to influence government policy. Moreover, we can suggest that such groups might undertake public initiatives more readily because often they do not have large constituencies of public support upon which they can draw, nor in some cases, do they have easy access to government officials. Creating public support for their demands, therefore, is one of the main ways by which they can bring added pressure on a government. An interesting consequence follows from this conclusion: in cases where institutional groups cannot use public approaches, issue-oriented groups may be able to influence government policy more effectively. But it is apparent that the degree of success of public initiatives depends upon the amount of support which the interest groups can generate for their demands. Finally, we have suggested that the strategies of institutional groups and those of issue-oriented groups may be complementary, for institutional groups may encourage issue-oriented groups to undertake public initiatives while they concentrate their attention on senior government decision-makers. This allows them to preserve their access to a government and perhaps to enhance their own efforts.

Our conclusions about Parliament's part in the issue differ from those generalizations about its influence on government policy found in the existing literature. Its role in influencing policy and making Biafra a major public issue was of critical importance. It may be argued that the Biafran example was a deviation from what usually happens to political issues in Canada, because a spontaneous public movement appears to have emerged. But the movement was not spontaneous. Parliament did much to create and sustain it. On the other hand, we can suggest that Parliament's role was a crucial one in this situation because the Biafran issue was a highly visible one, capable of attracting public attention and response. It was the interaction, then, of parliamentary criticism, media and general public reaction which influenced the government's policy. Nevertheless, the point remains that Parliament's role in this whole process was an important one. At the very least this study suggests that closer examination should be given to how parliamentary and public criticism interact to influence government policies.

Lastly, this study has argued that the bureaucracy had a major part in the making of the government's Biafra policy. Contrary to the interpretation of Matheson and Stewart which suggested that the issue showed the growing ascendence of the Office of the Prime Minister in the policy-making process, it has been argued here that its role was of secondary importance. Perhaps obliquely, the essay suggests that recent theses about the rise of "presidential" or "prime ministerial" government in Canada are in need of further empirical research.

NOTES

1. James Eayrs, "The Foreign Policy of Canada," J. E. Black and K. W. Thompson, eds., *Foreign Policies in a World of Change*, (New York: Harper & Row, 1963), p. 680. R. Barry Farrell, *The Making of Canadian Foreign Policy*, (Scarborough: Prentice-Hall of Canada, Ltd., 1969), p. 75.

2. Farrell, *op. cit.* p. 75.

3. *Ibid.*

4. Quoted in *Time* Magazine, November 15, 1968, p. 19.

5. See William A. Matheson, "The Cabinet and the Canadian Bureaucracy," W. D. K. Kernaghan and A. M. Willms, eds., *Public Administration in Canada*, 2nd. edition, (Toronto: Methuen Publications, 1971), pp. 339-348. Walter Stewart, "The 30 Men Trudeau Trusts," *Maclean's Magazine*, October, 1969, p. 43, and also *Shrug: Trudeau in Power*, (Toronto: New Press, 1971).

6. Canadian Committee for the Relief of Biafran Refugees, *Campaign Appeal Statement*, March 4, 1968.

7. Rev. Walter F. McLean, *Interview*, June 4, 1970.

8. Quoted in J. L. Granatstein, "External Affairs and Defence," *Canadian Annual Review*, 1968, Toronto, 1969, p. 260, and James Eayrs, *Montreal Star*, September 16, 1968.

9. Its membership consisted of the Canadian Catholic Organization for Development and Peace, the Canadian Red Cross Society, the Canadian Council of Churches, the Presbyterian Church in Canada, and Oxfam of Canada.

10. Canada, Office of the Prime Minister, *Press Release*, July 31, 1968.

11. Report of the Canadian Red Cross Society, *Involvement in the Nigerian civil war*, November 20, 1968.

12. *The Globe and Mail*, August 2, 1968.

13. The countries referred to were Britain and the Soviet Union which were providing arms to the federal side, and France which was furnishing arms to Biafra. The editorials reasoned that if the shipments were ended the belligerents, deprived of their armaments, would be forced to negotiate a settlement of the war.

14. Mr. Trudeau in House of Commons, *Debates*, October 7, 1968, p. 843. (Hereafter referred to as *Debates*)

15. Canada, Department of External Affairs, *Press Release*, No. 31, Sept. 18, 1968.

16. *Debates*, September 27, 1968, p. 500.

17. *Ibid.*, September 20, 1968, p. 264 (The OAU had decided not to bring the issue before the United Nations and requested other countries not to intervene in the question.)

18. Canada, Department of External Affairs, *Press Release*, No. 33, Sept. 30, 1968.

19. *The Globe and Mail*, October, 5, 7, 9, 10, 11, 12, 14, 1968.

20. *The Star* (Toronto), October 9, 10, 11, 12, 14, 1968.

21. The Standing Committee began its sessions on October 8 and held 24 meetings to consider the issue. It submitted its report to Parliament on November 6.

22. Canadian Institute of Public Opinion, *Gallup Report*, November 20, 1968.

23. Quoted in *The Globe and Mail*, October 22, 1968.

24. Although the government's position did not go unchallenged (see, for example, Denis Smith, "Biafra, A Case against Trudeau's view", *The Globe and Mail*, October 30, 1968) its critics became less and less effective both in influencing public concern and in modifying government policy.

25. *Debates*, November 4, 1968, p. 2345.

26. *Ibid.*, November 18, 1968, p. 2844.

27. For a detailed account of the interest groups' actions see my *Interest Groups in the Canadian Foreign Policy Formulation Process: The Case of Biafra*, unpublished M.A. thesis, Dalhousie University, 1971, chapter 3.

28. Dr. E. H. Johnson, *Interview*, September 23, 1969.

29. Kwavnick (1970).

30. *Confidential Interview*, September, 1969.

31. Dr. E. H. Johnson, in *Minutes of Proceedings and Evidence*, House of Commons Standing Committee on External Affairs and National Defence, October 15, 1968, p. 194.

32. Dr. E. H. Johnson, *Interview*, September 23, 1969.

33. Grant Wanzel, *Interview*, August 15, 1969.

34. Gary Webster, *Interview*, August 26, 1969.

35. Grant Wanzel, quoted in *The Globe and Mail*, November 28, 1972.

36. Dr. E. H. Johnson, in *Minutes, op. cit.*, October 15, 1968, pp. 206, 217.

37. For a description of press comment see Barry, *op. cit.*, Chapter 4.

38. *Confidential Interview*, June, 1969, also Peter Worthington, *Interview*, September 23, 1969.

39. *Ibid.*

40. Dr. E. H. Johnson, *Interview*, September 23, 1969.

41. Tim Ralfe, *Interview*, June 24, 1969.

42. *Confidential Interview*, June, 1970.

43. Peter Worthington, *Interview*, September 23, 1969.

44. *Ibid.*

45. Andrew Brewin, *Interview*, June 16, 1969; Gordon Fairweather, *Interview*, June 8, 1970.

46. September—60 questions; October—135; November—42; December—12.

47. Gordon Fairweather, *Interview*, June 8, 1970.

48. *The Globe and Mail*, September 28, 1968.

49. Dr. E. H. Johnson, *Interview*, September 23, 1969.

50. For an account of witnesses and Committee deliberations see House of Commons, Standing Committee on External Affairs and National Defence, *Minutes of Proceedings and Evidence*, October 8, 1968, pp. 1–544.

51. *Confidential Interviews.*

52. R. MacGregor Dawson, *The Government of Canada*, 5th edition, revised by Norman Ward, (Toronto: University of Toronto Press, 1970), p. 369.

53. Thomas A. Hockin, "The Prime Minister and Political Leadership: An Introduction to Some Restraints and Imperatives," Hockin, ed., *Apex of Power*, (Scarborough: Prentice-Hall, 1971), p. 10.

54. *Confidential Interviews*, June, 1969.

55. Confidential letters to the author (these comments were appended to questionnaires sent to Members of Parliament by the author in June, 1969, for the purpose of gauging the flow of Biafra representations to them during the fall of 1968.)

56. See, for example, the transcript of Prime Minister Trudeau's press conference, Ottawa, October 15, 1969. The subject arose in the context of representations concerning Canada's diplomatic recognition of the Vatican. (The above figures do not include communications which were received by the Secretary of State for External Affairs. This statistic was not made available to the author.)

57. Andrew Brewin and David MacDonald, *Canada and the Biafran Tragedy*, (Toronto: James Lewis and Samuel, 1970), pp. 31–33.

58. *Ibid.*, p. 135.

59. William A. Matheson, *op. cit.*, p. 347.

60. Walter Stewart, *Shrug: Trudeau in Power*, p. 177.

61. This interpretation is based on a series of interviews conducted by the author with officials in the office of the Prime Minister, the Department of External Affairs, the Liberal Party, Members of Parliament, and interest group representatives, in June and September, 1969.

62. Brewin and MacDonald, *op. cit.*, pp. 30–33.

63. *Confidential Interview*, June, 1969.

64. *Confidential Interview*, August, 1969 (Brewin and MacDonald also allude to this, although they are less than categorical on the point. See *Canada and the Biafran Tragedy*, p. 88.)

65. *Minutes, op. cit.*, October 10, p. 144.

66. *Confidential Interview*, September, 1969.

67. *Minutes, op. cit.*, October 10, p. 122.

68. *Debates*, November 26, 1968, p. 3195.

69. *Confidential Interview*, September, 1969.

7.

One of the most commonly noted facets of pressure group–government relations in Canada is the great importance institutional groups attach to their contacts with the public service. Because of administrative secrecy enshrouding much of this communication and because of its essentially informal character, useful evidence concerning the nature of the relationship has been difficult to obtain. For this reason, the following account of a policy debate within the Ontario provincial government has been included, despite the fact that it is somewhat dated.

The case study tends to confirm several hypotheses that have emerged in recent years concerning the role of the bureaucracy in Canadian policy formation, and particularly its dominant role in relation to pressure groups. It also picks up themes that recur in other contributions to this volume. Notably it considers, in a different context, Kwavnick's hypothesis that pressure groups try to influence the distribution of government power so as to maximize their own ability to influence decisions of concern to them. Similarly, the case study illustrates the manner in which shifts in government policy and reorganization of relevant agencies contribute to the emergence of pressure groups, determine the nature of relations between group and agency, and partially define the pattern of group behaviour. Finally, the study attempts to elucidate the manner in which the organizational drives of both agencies and groups interact in the processes of policy deliberation.

A. Paul Pross lectures in public administration at Dalhousie University and has written previously in the fields of natural resource administration and the dissemination of public information.

policy dispute which occurred in Ontario between 1941 and 1946 over the correct administrative machinery to be used in the management of the province's forest resources. Ultimately, as most participants in the dispute realized, the quarrel over administrative structure determined the direction of Ontario's forest policy in the post-war years. Two factors give the case particular relevance. First, it provides a view of interaction not only between a department and a pressure group but amongst a department, antagonistic and friendly pressure groups, the media, and the political leadership. Second, this incident involved a question of fundamental policy, a policy which might have radically altered the structure of the department concerned. In other words, this issue more than most sparked the instinct for organizational survival that is so frequently noted in administrative behaviour.

The purpose of this study is to investigate the manner in which a senior administrator received and processed a specific series of policy demands. The documentation used is primarily the personal daily memoranda of this administrator, the Deputy Minister of the department, and consequently the case study itself concentrates on his perceptions. Not purporting to be a balanced account, it simply represents events as the senior official observed and responded to them both publicly and privately. The data are presented in chronological sequence with as little summarizing as possible and no attempt at analysis until the "story" has been recounted. Following this presentation, two levels of analysis are introduced. The first, primarily descriptive, adds supplementary information which could not be included in the presentation of the case, and ties together a number of the discrete events which occur in the evidence. The second, adopting a more abstract approach to the material, examines, in the light of this particular case, several hypotheses which occur in the literature dealing with Canadian pressure groups. Here the terminology of political science is applied to our analysis in order to increase the usefulness of its findings to current discussions of modern political systems. Hence we speak of pressure groups being concerned with obtaining satisfactory government responses to "input" demands—demands generated outside the political system in the economic or social systems and transmitted across boundaries by pressure groups acting as agents of political communication and conversion. We see governments processing not only these and other inputs, but also "withinputs", demands which do not enter the political system from the external world, but are generated within the system.[5] They may be the products of agency perceptions of shortcomings in existing policy; they may be logical consequences of existing structures and policies; or they may grow out of the innumerable rivalries which exist within complex organizations. Whatever their origins, withinputs are the contributions governments themselves make to policy deliberations. In a system that makes the bureaucracy "the core institution at the formulation stage of policymaking",[6] the interaction between withinput and demand inputs has to be critically important.

FIGHTING OFF "THE DELAHEY ELEMENT"

George Drew made the administration of Ontario's forest resources a major political issue early in his career as leader of the province's Conservative Party. When he entered the Ontario Legislature in the fall of 1939, his charges of corruption and maladministration of forest resources began his first major battle against Premier Mitchell Hepburn. Goading the Liberal government into establishing a select committee to inquire into the administration of the Department of Lands and Forests, Drew repeatedly claimed that the management of the province's renewable natural resources, particularly forest resources, had to be "taken out of politics". By the time the committee reported its findings, in the spring of 1941, he and his Opposition colleagues had crystallized their views into a proposal for the establishment of a commission form of administration, somewhat similar in concept to the Hydro-Electric Power Commission.[7]

A Forest Resources Commission, asserted the committee's minority report, should be the only body with the authority to make contracts for timber concessions. Completely divorced from politics and placed under the direction of men with "the highest type of business ability," it would administer and protect the forest resources and plan for full employment within the industry during the period of postwar rehabilitation. By turning over control of the forest resources to such a commission, many of the questions difficult to resolve—particularly such matters as the equitable distribution of cutting rights—could be easily settled. The commission would also be a fact-finding body whose capacity to co-ordinate information would facilitate more effective decision-making than had previously been possible.[8] Drew vigorously promoted the commission approach in the months following tabling of the report.[9]

In reply, the government adopted a position that became the core of the defence against the commission proposal until the idea was finally defeated in 1946. The Minister of Lands and Forests, Peter Heenan, stated that a commission would take administration of the resource away from the control of the elected representatives. "The commission would not be responsible to either the government or the House, consequently there could be no check on spending."[10] The people of Ontario expected a revenue from their forests; they did not want to be always pouring money into them. Moreover, the commission would not eliminate criticism of politics. "So long as there is a natural resource to be administered, there will be the cry of politics."[11]

Outside the legislature, editorials in the Fort William *Daily Times Journal* and the *Toronto Evening Telegram* supported the commission idea, while the *Canada Lumbermen* suggested that it warranted further investigation and agreed with *The Globe and Mail* that the administration of the province's forest resources should be more "open" and "businesslike."[12] Several representatives of forest interests also expressed support.

The establishing of an Ontario Forest Resources Commission became entrenched as Conservative counter-policy and was a prominent part of the party's platform in the 1943 election. Drew achieved a minority victory and although he appointed a Minister of Lands and Forests, W. G. Thompson, a western Ontario grain dealer and banker, he assured him that "he would be relieved of the Department before long,"[13] an indication that the commission scheme was to be implemented.

However, between 1941 and 1943, changes had taken place within the Department of Lands and Forests as well as on the political scene. Following the select Committee inquiry, Hepburn had replaced the Minister with N. O. Hipel, a leading member of his government and a capable administrator, and the Deputy Minister with F. A. MacDougall, the first professional forester to achieve the highest career position in the Ontario department. MacDougall had his own remedy for keeping the administration of the forest resource "out of politics" and in the two years since his appointment had made some progress in implementing his scheme.[14] Essentially it depended on erecting what he called "a technical umbrella" over Lands and Forests. By staffing critical positions with professional foresters and ensuring that they could not be intimidated by local timber barons, MacDougall hoped to gradually eliminate the inefficiency and illegality which had led to public criticism of the department. Eventually he hoped to create an agency able to effectively supervise "forest management" throughout the province. Though hampered by the demands of the war effort on scarce resources of men and material, MacDougall felt that the success of the reorganization, and the implementation of new policies intended to promote industrial management were sufficient to render unnecessary Drew's proposed further reorganization. Already alarmed at the tone of the Conservatives' campaign attacks on the department, MacDougall's first interviews with his new Minister after the Conservative victory of 1943 convinced him that the department was "fighting for its administrative life." He was astounded when Thompson reported Drew's comment that, "it was a quiet department": "I disillusioned him and told him that Lands and Forests was the Government of Ontario, particularly in the northern part of the province." More disquieting than Drew's ignorance was his hint that Thompson himself would soon be supplanted by the creation of the Forest Resources Commission.

For the moment, however, the new government concerned itself with settling into office and MacDougall directed his own efforts to establishing an effective working relationship with his new Minister. Thompson appears to have gone along with previously existing plans for the development of forest management in the province. Prominent among these was a new scaling manual, introduced shortly after he assumed office, that, in MacDougall's view, initiated a long battle with the industry since it brought to Ontario for the first time, a standard procedure for assessing the quantity of wood being removed from

Crown lands. At the same time, the government accelerated its efforts to introduce management clauses[15] into agreements with pulp and paper companies. Both steps signalled the end of the freedom of companies to determine for themselves the management policy that would be applied to land held from the Crown, and it was to them that MacDougall attributed the creation, late in 1943, of an industry organization, the Ontario Forest Industries Association (OFIA).

Manager of the new association, and prominent in its relations with the government, was Wallace A. Delahey, a professional forester who, MacDougall noted, was "strongly ensconced at Conservative headquarters." The Deputy Minister's terse summary of the fight over the scaling regulations suggests the department's antagonism to this group and to Delahey in particular: "When the manual came out we were immediately blasted by a delegation of lumbermen to have the manual changed or abolished. A fight covering several months developed with Delahey heading the attack. The department finally won out."

Opposition to the new policies encouraged support for the commission scheme. A 1945 review of departmental policies and activities refers to the fact that "following the election, [the commission proposal] became a very contentious matter. The minister found himself faced with numerous nominations for the commission jobs. Behind each of the nominations was a group, usually of industry or other faction, that might benefit from gaining control of the forest resources of the province." The most consistent attempt, conducted by the group that Mac-Dougall labelled the "Delahey element," aimed at installing Major-General Howard Kennedy as chief commissioner. Early in November it became clear that Drew, encouraged by Delahey, was seriously considering Kennedy's appointment and by mid-month the Minister advised MacDougall that Kennedy would be chairman of the commission and that the Premier was in the process of trying to negotiate Kennedy's release from his current employment.

This news did not deter members of the department from attempting to influence the decision. E. J. Zavitz, an influential senior member of the department with extensive political connections, took advantage of a field trip with the Minister to discuss with him the pros and cons of the commission idea. Zavitz reported to MacDougall that he had stated his opinions frankly; that he had argued that the commission idea, certainly not a novel one, would mean no spectacular changes in forest administration; that the real road to improvement lay in hard work.

Outside the department, professional friends revealed that they were willing to enlist public opinion in support of MacDougall's position. On November 20, Gordon Cosens, Dean of Forestry at the University of Toronto, called, indicating that he was "greatly concerned about Drew's commission . . . and Howard Kennedy." Cosens maintained that the Kennedy appointment would be ill-advised and "wished to know if the southern Ontario section [of the Canadian Society of

Forestry Engineers] should put on a dinner for [MacDougall.] If it would help in any way." MacDougall told him he "was not in favour of things like that. And that what Drew did was government policy and the civil servant could accept it or resign if he didn't like it." He noted, however, "that it is evident that Drew's commission idea is creating a great deal of concern in professional forestry circles. The problem is how to do anything constructive without looking as though one is opposing the commission idea."

These appear to have been days of considerable introspection and rumour-mongering within the department. MacDougall's diaries note daily discussions with key subordinates concerning the latest information or rumour. Some professionals favoured abandoning the civil servant's rule of self-effacement and taking a stand publicly on the issue, and one conversation indicated that at least a few foresters had talked of resigning if Drew's proposal was put into effect. MacDougall himself was inclined to discount talk of this type, arguing that few members of the department would risk their careers if it came to "a showdown." Not all of the advice he received, however, was encouraging and not all of his information indicated whole-hearted support within the department. On November 17 he noted that "several times during the last few weeks it has been intimated to me that I was getting in wrong with the lumbermen. In short if I valued this job it would be well to get in better standing with them. For changes seem evident from those above. First, the reforms of the last three years haven't been taken . . . with any too good grace by those who have been affected and who may have been getting something for nothing in the past. Second, there has been some undercutting going on from within. Napoleon's maxim of pulling one's friends in to assist still holds in modern life." The same day he derived some comfort from a report in *The Globe and Mail* to the effect that "in our zeal to bring about reform we may overreach and embrace unsound [changes] that will bring the very chaos we are trying to arrest." On November 23, 1943 MacDougall was visited by a professional forester whom he equated with the "Delahey element" and whom he considered to be "on a fishing expedition." The man apparently left with very little information, but reinforced MacDougall's view that Delahey himself was anxious to be appointed to the commission, though his main object remained to establish Kennedy as chief commissioner.

The flurry of activity over the nomination of commissioners was not the only pressure on the department that MacDougall perceived emanating from the "Delahey element." On November 23 Delahey himself visited MacDougall to discuss various matters involving the OFIA, and in the course of conversation suggested that he would like MacDougall to meet Clarke Davis, the President of the OFIA, who "thinks we should trust each other better and discuss more mutual problems off the record. I don't like off the record talks on government business. But told Wallace we should be glad to meet Clarke sometime if no business was discussed." Less easily handled was Delahey's attempt to bring professional pressure to bear on the department. He introduced a critical motion at a regional meeting of the Canadian Society of Forestry Engineers and the Society went so far as to appoint a committee to discuss forest policy in Ontario. Some members of the department apparently felt that it should have representation on the committee, but MacDougall considered that the civil service should not involve itself in attempting to influence, directly at least, the position that would be taken by the Society. MacDougall's records make no further reference to the Society's committee and presumably it died a quiet death after an innocuous life.

Throughout this period MacDougall, with his supporters in the department, had been conducting a steady lobby of the Minister. His daily memos during November and December refer several times to the fact that he was writing "notes on commission administration." They also refer to discussions with the Minister "re . . . the formation of the commission." A summary of suggestions was produced indicating "how a commission form of administration . . . may be obtained with little cost to the province, and yet solve the commission policy in a manner that should have the support of all those interested in the well-being of Ontario's forest resources." As well as including comments on various types of commission structures and recommending a type utilized in Great Britain, "where ten members represent all parties, but where sectional interests are not represented," the document underlines the necessity for continuing existing departmental policy initiative. However, while purporting to support the commission proposal, and actually suggesting a commission structure, the document presents a good deal of negative evidence. A report on the Minnesota Conservation Commission, obtained from the Ontario-Minnesota Pulp and Paper Co. Ltd., painted a particularly damning portrait of that State's experience, suggesting that the commission's administrative independence had been abused—in the interests of patronage—to such an extent that it eventually had to be abolished. A similar story was told in a long excerpt, quoted from a *Saturday Evening Post* article, criticizing the New Jersey political system and particularly the practice of conducting the State's business through independent and semi-independent boards and commissions. According to the *Post*, independence in New Jersey meant that commissioners were free to ignore the wishes of elected officials.

Thompson's response to this memorandum is not available, but despite his readiness to promote the established policies of the department, he evidently continued to accept the Premier's view that the existing form of organization would be replaced with a commission structure. Enabling legislation approved by the Legislature during the spring 1944 session, provided for creation of a five-man Forest Resources Commission with power to do "such things as it deems necessary or advisable to protect and utilize to the best advantage the forest resources of Ontario."[16]

The issue, however, was not dead. Legislation had been enacted, but the commission had not been formally created. The flow of memoranda continued as did the manoeuvrings within and beyond Lands and Forests. The spring session of the Legislature was followed by a summer campaign on the part of the department intended to convince Cabinet members that the department was well and efficiently operated. In particular, Cabinet ministers visiting northern Ontario were encouraged to take notice of Lands and Forests operations and were supplied with information concerning the development of projects and the institution of new policies.

Lobbying of the department and within the department concerning various policies must have been quite intensive, for during the summer the Minister "greatly worried about all [the] bickering and high-pressure lobbying . . . desired to resign, and finally sent in his resignation." Drew at first persuaded him to remain in office for the duration of the summer, and in the fall, when Thompson renewed his request to be relieved of his responsibilities, refused to let him go. MacDougall notes that, while the Minister's restlessness was the cause of some concern, after it became clear that he would have to stay in office Thompson "resigned himself to staying and became more interested in the department and its affairs."

In February 1945, Drew addressed the annual meeting of the Ontario Forest Industries Association, greeting the delegates warmly and encouraging them to feel that they had the ear of the Premier:

> Already you have been of great assistance in offering me suggestions of benefit, not only to the industry but to the province generally, and I can assure you that the stronger and more representative your association becomes the more pleased I will be.[17]

MacDougall viewed such events as part of a pattern: "While in the first year many problems were met, not the least troublesome was that of trying to keep the P.M. out of hot spots created by ill-advised suggestions and advisors. They were mixed with the routine of the department and other special problems and created much unnecessary work and much confusion and delay and stalled progress in forestry materially. For we had to unwind many crackpot schemes. In effect it often put the department in the precarious position of having to try and take the government out of difficult positions." In his view, the "boost to the O.F.I.A." was typical of the problems Drew created for himself and for the department.

It is interesting, but probably coincidental, that shortly after Drew's speech to the OFIA, the Opposition again raised the question of the creation of a forestry commission, asking when the Forest Resources Commission would be set up.[18] The government did not reply immediately, but a week later the Minister received from his deputy a statement concerning "misconceptions about a Forestry Commission" which recapitulated information presented in earlier memoranda. On March 19 Drew, replying to a further question, stated "that until wartime controls were off, nothing further would be done."[19] Early the next month, the department forwarded to Drew a brief, similar to the one prepared for Thompson in March, outlining the case against the commission proposal. To reinforce the contention that the department was just as capable as any commission, given professional personnel and adequate resources, a lengthy résumé of "things done in forestry since August, 1943" was attached.

Evidently these arguments prevailed and the Minister accepted the position put forward by the department. As well, he was temporarily successful in persuading his colleagues, and particularly the Premier that the department's view should prevail. The new position was set out in a draft of Thompson's 1945 speech on the departmental estimates:

> In the field of administration you will recollect a year ago I brought in a statute amendment concerning a commission.
> For the legislation and for the action on it since last year, I take full responsibility. When I introduced it, I considered it a step or one part of the whole phase of forest management.
> Immediately there arose the assumption that by some administrative change we would, overnight, achieve forest management.
> Now the problems in forestry are too complex and of too great magnitude to be so lightly brought to a solution.
> Now the question will arise as to what I intend to do with that legislation, or why have I delayed? I could spend a considerable time analyzing the question but I would prefer to answer the question in these words.
> The Crown forests, the streams with their water powers and the Crown lands of the province of Ontario are now in the control of and under the guidance and direction of this House. I do not propose, lightly and without proper safeguards, to pass over these resources to any outside control that might jeopardize these holdings of the people of Ontario.

The issue receded, and many must have felt that it no longer would recur. However, a new crisis was precipitated on January 3, 1946, when "after work, the minister told me he was handing in his resignation . . . because his own business affairs were suffering. He did not feel he was giving the department the support he should be giving it . . . I assured him emphatically that he was doing everything that could be done to support the department." Although pressed by his colleagues, including the Premier, Thompson appeared determined to carry through his resignation, and the search began for a replacement. The next day Thompson told MacDougall that Harold Scott, a colleague in the Cabinet, would be his successor. But on January 5, MacDougall received a telephone call from Gordon Cosens at the School of Forestry who reported "that the P.M. had called him and mentioned that he was getting Howard Kennedy to come in and asked Cosens about him." Evidently the department's attempt to persuade Drew that it was pursuing reorganization and reform effectively had not been successful, for the Premier "told Cosens he had the hardest time getting anything forward out of the department. Cosens told him he had the best Minister and a good department behind him and all he had to do was to give the go ahead signal."

Drew's conversation with Cosens suggests that Thompson's resignation had reminded Drew of his earlier difficulties with the department and had revived his conviction that the province's forest resources were best managed through an independent forestry commission. It seems that Kennedy was only one of a group of individuals being considered for the post. On the afternoon of January 7, the Minister mentioned the names of three additional candidates, and added that his own resignation was being deferred until February. The candidates, however, seem not to have been approached at all by Drew, and at the end of the week, MacDougall noted that "information started drifting into the department . . . that Kennedy was coming into the department." The information triggered new speculation and new rumours; MacDougall himself wondered whether the newly instituted management clauses would be modified or interpreted less stringently than he would interpret them. He also tried to anticipate the approach industry would take to the new administration, surmising that the OFIA would promote the view that forest management could best be entrusted to the corporations using the resources. This approach, MacDougall reasoned, would be most likely to assure industry of effective control of the forests.

The issue came to a head on January 9th, when a friendly journalist reported to MacDougall that Drew had called Gordon Hogarth (his press secretary) from New York to dictate a statement announcing the appointment of Major-General Howard Kennedy as chairman of a Royal Commission to examine Ontario's forest resources and their sale. Claiming that the statement had been seen by a colleague, the reporter said that after its study was completed, the Royal Commission was expected to develop into the agency to take charge of lands and forests promised by Drew in his election platform. Evidently Thompson had not been consulted by Drew who reportedly stated that the Minister "had done a very good job, but that the time had come to have a committee of experts to advise," and went on to instruct Hogarth to get in touch with Thompson before the story was released. Apparently Thompson was angered by the news, stated that he had never discussed the matter with Kennedy and refused to approve the release of the statement until he had considered it. An embarrassed Hogarth was forced to retract the statement and promise its release the next day.

The next morning, MacDougall was relieved to note, "the announcement did not appear. Thompson will not approve it unless a rider is added." In the late afternoon Hogarth had to tell the press, "there will be no announcement. The announcement is postponed indefinitely and it might or probably would never be given."

Nevertheless sufficient information had leaked to the press and to the forestry community to arouse considerable speculation. MacDougall received several telephone calls fishing for information, while on January

12, a member of the department reported that he had been contacted by Delahey who asserted that Kennedy was being considered for the job of commissioner and reportedly showed him the dispatch from Drew.

The announcement appeared to throw the Cabinet into turmoil. Drew had dictated the original press release from New York, and had proceeded from there to a holiday in the southern United States. Thompson felt strongly about the issue and rallied support within the Cabinet. It was significant that that support appeared to include Leslie Frost, Drew's lieutenant and eventual successor, who stated on January 11 that no announcement concerning the appointment of a Forestry Royal Commission would be made at that time.

The Premier's continued absence meant that rumours circulated almost without check. It became apparent that officials of the Ontario Forest Industries Association had known of the proposed Kennedy appointment prior to many members of the department, probably including MacDougall and Thompson. On January 14, the news reached George McCullagh, the influential publisher of *The Globe and Mail.* McCullagh discussed it with members of his staff who, in reporting to MacDougall, advised him to "sit tight" and indicated that McCullagh was going to see Drew and would oppose what had been going on. Support also manifested itself within the industry; not all industry representatives were anxious for a change in management, and the group opposed to it apparently included the President of the OFIA, Clarke Davis, who on January 21 told MacDougall "that he had always been with us," a remark which, MacDougall noted, confirmed the earlier departmental view that Davis "was satisfied with things as they are."

On January 23, Thompson decided to withdraw his resignation. MacDougall's significant note, "cabinet behind him," indicates that the discussions within the Cabinet had brought about a confrontation with the Premier, who was still in the United States. Although rumours continued to circulate concerning the appointment of Kennedy, who had resigned from the position he was holding, the Minister made it clear that he "was not walking out on the fight," and as the Cabinet strongly supported Thompson, he had had the best of the discussion with Drew. A compromise was worked out, and though a Royal Commission was appointed to inquire into forestry and forest management in Ontario, there was an understanding that it would be a Royal Commission and nothing else. On February 6 MacDougall noted "minister and p.m. discuss [commission] and some announcement will be made soon, but nobody, I believe, will be hurt. Minister cannot talk on the matter." The Kennedy Royal Commission was appointed on April 16th, 1946 and reported on May 12, 1947. MacDougall's notes record occasional recurrences of interest in the commission idea in the intervening period, but they appear to have led to nothing. The final report of the Royal Commission recommended some structural changes in the department, primarily to achieve the devolution of responsibilities to the field, but specifically rejected "any other fundamental changes." The legislation empowering the Forest Resources Commission to undertake the management of Ontario's forests was quietly repealed in the 1946 session.[20]

POWER RELATIONS AND THE COMMISSION ISSUE

The most striking feature of the case is the success of Lands and Forests' resistance to a clear demand from the political leadership for a change in administrative policy. This change, moreover, could have been effected without reference to the department, and it had both a measure of public support and the backing of reputedly powerful interests. Whatever the merits of the commission proposal, its supporters should have had every reason to expect its successful implementation. Among those reasons were the following:

First, the department did not enjoy a favourable public reputation. The select committee inquiry of 1939–1940 had revealed an inept, bungling organization which, if not corrupt, was too influenced by purely political considerations. The intervening years had seen important changes within the organization itself, but these were not of the sort that would bring about a dramatic alteration in the public's view of the department. The general preoccupation with World War II also hindered a public reassessment, and simultaneously imposed personnel, financial and material constraints on the implementation of policies intended eventually to achieve sound management of the forest resources. Furthermore, it must be remembered that while the modern community is cynical about the possibility of taking major resource policy decisions "out of politics," the public of the 1930s and 1940s was often ready to entrust essentially political decisions of wide significance to agencies such as the Hydro-Electric Power Commission, police commissions, and the like. Its faith in businesslike methods of organization and decision-making exceeded its confidence in the political accountability of government. In the context, then, of Lands and Forests' poor public image and the acceptability of semi-independent management of the public domain, the Forest Resources Commission must have seemed an appropriate, conventional solution to the problem of creating an organization which could properly manage Ontario's forests.

To appreciate the significance of this climate of opinion we must remember that though public attitudes provide support for the demands of political actors, they are always implicit in the political situation. They attain significance only through the interaction of pressure groups, politicians, government officials and others involved in the processes of political communication. The Conservatives created that interaction in the realm of forest administration, focused public discontent and provided an alternative to existing policy. Although electoral support did not necessarily imply that the public enthusiastically endorsed the commission proposal, it did suggest some support for the party's platform as well as its leadership. The proposal, ranking fairly high in the platform's list of priorities, was not a minor election promise. The government possessed a modest mandate for its implementation.

A third reason for expecting implementation of the commission scheme was the fact that George Drew's particular association with it gave it a prominence far beyond a mild public dissatisfaction with the department, or even beyond apparent electoral approval of a proposed new policy. Simply because he was the newly elected provincial Premier, Drew should have found creation of a Forest Resources Commission an objective reasonably easy to attain. He had been deeply involved in the proposal's early formulation by the minority group in the select committee. In the Legislature and on the hustings, Drew had made the commission scheme a prominent part of his campaign against Hepburn, and after coming to power he seems to have indicated to Thompson that he intended to go ahead with it. He actively considered filling the position of principal commissioner and had legislation introduced creating a Forest Resources Commission. In the second phase of the dispute, Drew not only showed that he continued to support the plan, but his comments to Cosens and his press release reference to the need for expertise in forest management suggest that he had not revised his opinion of the capacity of the department. Given this sort of support on the part of the Premier, it is extremely significant that the plan was not implemented, for when a politician of Drew's prominence identifies so closely with a particular policy, an attack on that policy becomes an attack on the leadership itself. Drew might have been expected to react strongly to the failure to implement the scheme and to use his extensive powers to ensure the creation of the Forest Resources Commission.

Furthermore, Drew initially possessed significant political support for his position and could count on meeting serious opposition only from the Department of Lands and Forests itself. He had selected a Minister whose knowledge of the department was very limited and who had apparently no preconceived objection to his plans. More importantly, he was supported by a group of forest resource interests, whom Mac-Dougall called "the industry gang," reputed to be powerful politically. An indication of their influence with the Premier is found in the fact that they frequently appeared to be better informed about the Premier's intentions than was MacDougall or even Thompson. For example, Clarke Davis, president of the OFIA apparently knew before Drew dictated his abortive press release that a major change was about to take place.[21] Thompson was not informed until several hours later when he was asked to approve the release and announce it to the press.

Three factors could explain Drew's failure: (1) the OFIA, despite Wallace Delahey's vigorous support of the scheme, was internally divided; (2) the length of time which elapsed between Drew's appointment of Thompson, the introduction and passage of enabling legislation and the search for a suitable commissioner, permitted Thompson to familiarize himself with the department and to become convinced that the department's position was a correct one; (3) the department was able to rally support of its own, chiefly through its association with the forestry profession, but also through the co-operation of friendly industrialists and, somewhat unexpectedly, a powerful media interest.

At times, MacDougall seems to have felt that the entire Ontario forest industry was opposed to the structure and administration of the department. As we have noted, he felt that particular sore points were the introduction of the new scaling manual and the inclusion of management clauses in agreements with pulp and paper companies. Formation of the OFIA permitted the industry to bring concerted pressure to bear on the department at both politicial and administrative levels. (MacDougall's notes indicate that contact between representatives of the association and members of the departments occurred almost daily, at social gatherings, professional meetings, formal conferences and in the course of ironing out minor problems in administering the timber regulations.) However, the alliance, though it had periodic successes, could not hold fast when a number of inherent internal divisions began to appear.

A significant weakening factor was the tendency of several key participants to put their own interests ahead of the alliance's. The Ontario Paper Company was especially noted for this. During the depression it had refused to co-operate with other pulp and paper interests in the establishment of a pro-rata system designed to keep the industry alive by sharing out the work that was available. At the same time it was anxious to obtain great cutting areas, and applied extensive political pressure to obtain them. In MacDougall's view, Drew's commission scheme offered the company an opportunity to forward this end by ousting the "technical foresters" who had recently gained control of the department, and by installing instead its own affiliate, Kennedy. In consequence, Ontario Paper was not popular with the rest of the industry.[22]

More fundamentally divisive than the tendency of specific participants to give their own interests priority was a split between the two wings of the forest industry, the sawlog operators and the pulp and paper industry. The focal point of the division was the Lakehead, where E. E. Johnson's Great Lakes Lumber and Shipping Company was constantly in need of new cutting areas, frequently areas that had been assigned to other operators or to pulp and paper companies. Johnson had excellent political contacts and used them. More noisy, though by no means as skilful, was the effort made by another Lakehead figure, Charles W. Cox, to obtain cutting rights on territory assigned to the Brompton Pulp and Paper Co. Trailing behind Johnson and Cox were the "whole element who had been denied timber concessions in Hipel's time."[23] The disputes at the Lakehead over the division of the declining supplies of sawlog timber eventually led to the establishment of a Commission of Inquiry.[24]

The problems at the Lakehead, while they contributed to dissatisfaction with the department, were equally vexing to the OFIA; at one point, Delahey, waiting for an appointment with the Minister, was reported to have remarked to a colleague that the OFIA knew how to deal with Johnson, hardly an indication that the association saw eye to eye with an important figure in the industry.

These and other divisions caused industry representatives to advise the department, either directly or through the Faculty of Forestry, of the latest moves on the part of the Premier or "the Delahey element." An unidentified informant apparently associated with the OFIA reportedly had the impression "that . . . something was going to happen which would intervene with management, and . . . he would like to see us go ahead and was tipping us off." Again, MacDougall seems to have accepted at face value the OFIA president's remark "that he [the president] had always been with us." The precise extent and political impact of such support is difficult to gauge. Possibly messages of support strengthened the Minister's hand in bargaining with his colleagues, while the division within the OFIA may have blunted the thrust of Delahey's campaign and some dissidents may have expressed their doubts to Drew in much the same way that Cosens and, reportedly, McCullagh had. Perhaps the most striking view of industry reaction was that allegedly put forward several years later by E. E. Johnson's lawyer, McTague, who argued that the forest commission was not set up because the pulp and paper concerns had threatened to cut off campaign funds if Drew went ahead with his scheme.

However obscure and uncertain the support of the friendly elements within the industry, there can be no doubt that the key to eventual success lay in the effort made to persuade the minister that the proposed policy was ill-advised and should be abandoned. Thompson had to be persuaded on two points: first, that the department had reformed itself after the 1940 report of the select committee and second, that the commission scheme itself would present no advantage over the existing arrangement for forest management administration. In achieving these objectives, the department acted very much like an ordinary pressure group, with the significant exceptions that it had much readier access to the Minister and to an extent controlled the Minister's sources of information. So, for example, the deputy minister's papers for the period 1943 to 1946 contain copies of innumerable notes, newspapers clippings and records of conversations with the Minister dealing with items of information, both significant and insignificant, relevant to the issue. Lengthier, more formal memoranda provided the opportunity, as we have seen, to attack the proposal both directly and obliquely. MacDougall did not carry on this campaign alone, for influential colleagues like E. J. Zavitz seized appropriate moments to reinforce their chief's arguments.

Nor did members of the department confine their attention to Thompson. A department such as Lands and Forests, which is responsible for the administration of the province's wildlife resources and amenities like Algonquin Park, and possesses a fleet of bush planes capable of whisking a weary Cabinet Minister from his Toronto office to the well-stocked lakes and rivers of northern Ontario, has innumerable opportunities to encourage, quietly and unobtrusively, those same Cabinet Ministers to identify with its programs and aspirations. It is difficult to say how effective such contacts were, but they may have been partially responsible for the support which Thompson was able to gather from his colleagues in his January 1946 confrontation with Drew. It appears that the Premier himself was one of the few members of the Cabinet not wooed and won by the department. He emerges from the MacDougall papers as unwilling to consider revising the opinion of the department that he had formed in 1939. MacDougall evidently came to see him as a victim of his own distrust of Lands and Forests and his corresponding confidence in the spokesmen of industry. On the other hand, the Premier complained that he "had the hardest time getting anything forward out of the department," and did not hesitate to voice his dissatisfaction publicly.

Professional ties offered MacDougall a diffuse, indirect source of support that was quite different in kind, yet nearly as important as the support he received from his Minister. MacDougall's appointment to the position as deputy minister had been one of the most significant events in the development of the forestry profession in Ontario. It represented the culmination of several decades of work directed towards the attainment of an influential role for the profession in the determination of resource management policy in the province.[25] MacDougall's first years in office indicated to his colleagues, both inside and outside the department, that he fully intended to implement the policies that foresters in general considered necessary for the proper management of Ontario's woodlands. Such sentiments were part and parcel of the professional ethics of the province's foresters during this period and represented the sense of interdependence and mutual support which pervaded the Ontario profession.

Professional involvement consequently was a bond that superseded loyalties to other organizations and institutions. It encouraged informal supportive action from individuals whose companies were attacking the department. More important, it enhanced loyalty to MacDougall himself within the Department of Lands and Forests, since it provided not only a common background of training and norm inculcation, but also a sense of fighting for a common cause. Though MacDougall pooh-poohed suggestions that several foresters would resign if the government's policy were implemented, such talk was nevertheless a significant departure from the normal attitudes of civil servants faced with the prospect of having to implement a policy that was distasteful to them. In short, because the Department of Lands and Forests was essentially controlled by a group of men who shared a strongly felt professional ethic, and because the group saw itself and its objectives threatened by the commission movement, MacDougall could count on its continued support during the years of crisis. Other factors contributed to his success—influence with the Minister, continuing control of the vitals of the organization, and division within the ranks of his opponents—but the unusually high level of professional commitment to MacDougall and his policies must have been critically important.

Beyond the department, professional feeling aroused support in three areas: within the industry itself, within professional organizations and at the University of Toronto Faculty of Forestry, a centre of information and a guiding force in the creation of professional opinion. Dean Cosens of the faculty was probably MacDougall's most frequent and most reliable external source of information. It was he who suggested that the Ontario section of the Canadian Society of Forestry Engineers should publicly support MacDougall by throwing a dinner in his honour. Others advocated making overt use of the sentiment within the profession in MacDougall's support. Interestingly, MacDougall exercised considerable restraint in rejecting these offers, being careful to observe the boundary which he felt demarcated his zone of permissible action. The civil servant, he felt, was quite entitled to follow Napoleon's maxim and rally his friends, but he had to do so without appearing to pit the government's administrative arm against its executive centre. Not only would such an action offend the professional ethic of the civil service, it would be a strategic mistake.[26] The necessary support, then, could be encouraged only with great subtlety and could not be manifested in an overt form.

The role of George McCullagh, one of the most influential figures in the political life of Ontario at that time, is impossible to determine. It may have been crucial. Evidence suggests that he periodically interested himself in the department's affairs, but there is no conclusive indication of whether he did so on this occasion.

These, then, were the factors which in MacDougall's mind weighed for and against Drew's scheme to create a Forest Resources Commission. Whether or not they were crucial factors it is impossible to say, given the limited data now available to us. However, the information we have has enabled us to piece together a reasonable picture of the events. It also provides us with a base from which to proceed to a more abstract interpretation, one that will attempt to test some of the assertions commonly made about the relationships between government agencies and pressure groups.

INPUT AND WITHINPUT: PRESSURE GROUPS AND CANADIAN PUBLIC ADMINISTRATION

The tendency of Canadian pressure groups to establish close and amicable relations with relevant government departments is perhaps their most frequently noted characteristic, as a review of the contributions to this volume and of the literature in general will amply demonstrate. However, it is one thing to know that reciprocity exists, but quite another to state precisely how mutually supportive relationships operate and to what extent they assist either side to achieve desired objectives. Even the form of interaction is obscure. The literature offers some illustrations of devices employed to engage governmental sympathy and support for group objectives. These include frequent formal and in-formal contacts between group representatives and agency officials; group participation in governmental advisory boards; performance of quasi-administrative activities by professional bodies in gathering of intelligence for official use; dissemination of propaganda; and inclusion of public officials in groups' general membership and decision-making bodies. Until recently, evidence and commentary have suggested a rela-tionship in Canada like that which exists between British pressure groups and governmental organizations. There "the habit of consulta-tions is very strong . . . , indeed the ease with which affected interests and relevant expertise can be co-opted into the decision process has largely compensated for lack of subject specialization in the permanent administrative machinery."[27] Although Canadian pressure groups do not appear to have supplanted the intelligence function of administrative structures, students of their behaviour have agreed that, as in Britain, "the departments and the interest groups both have what the other requires, and both require what the other has."[28] In S. E. Finer's terms, for each the relationship provides information, consent, and administra-tive convenience.

An important modification of this view has recently been put forward by Anderson, who suggests that "in Canada the relations between civil servants and pressure groups are usually dominated by civil servants."[29] The case study supports this contention by depicting a series of events through which a governmental agency successfully repulsed an in-fluential group's attempt to exploit a commitment by the political leadership to change basic policy. In this case, at least, the agency's success may be attributed to its internal cohesion and its capacity to influence the external environment, first by winning over critical support within the political leadership, and second by determining the nature of support offered by friendly groups and individuals.

This becomes particularly important when we recall that the case study emphasized the extent to which considerations, related to the internal needs of the administrative agency, affected the discussion, formulation and implementation of policy. It is sometimes argued that it is the duty of the senior public servant "to support his Minister by giving him the best advice of which he is capable and by ensuring that the decisions ultimately reached are put into proper effect."[30] Practice falls far short of this ideal because the public agency, possessing organ-izational drives similar to and just as powerful as any possessed by the various bodies with which it must deal, modifies the intelligence it transmits. Consequently, when we examine pressure group–agency rela-tions we must bear in mind the probability that the agency's treatment of group demands will be conditioned by its perceptions of its own needs as well as by external factors. Our analysis, then, of the way in which agencies process pressure group demands will be facilitated by an understanding of the organizational forces at work within the agency.

Organization theory offers us numerous useful approaches to such an understanding. For example, our case study offers a classic illustration of Downs's proposition that "the larger the costs of getting an organization to adopt a new behaviour pattern, the greater will be the organization's resistance to it, other things being equal."[31] Downs goes on to argue that "each official's resistance to a given change will be greater the more significant the required shift in his behaviour . . . [and that] the more officials affected, the greater will be the resistance."[32] His discussion of the life-cycle of organizations, though impressionistic, is replete with observations—for example, his discussion of functional rivalry between established and fledgling agencies—which could explain many of the events we have described. Other scholars propose equally tempting hypotheses which could be applied profitably to a discussion of agency processing of pressure group demands.[33] For our purposes, however, the approach presented by Daniel Katz and Robert L. Kahn in *The Social Psychology of Organizations*[34] has a particular appeal, since its use of systems analysis permits us to relate the interactions of agency and group sub-systems to the processes operating within the political system itself.

This approach maintains that organizational structures develop goals beyond those formally assigned to them by the community. "The dynamic of a structure derives . . . from the common interests of its members sharing a common fate, from the common norms for carrying out their functions, and from the common values which rationalize and provide a rationale for their activity."[35] Through this interdependence a structure becomes a system, surrounded, in turn, by a range of appropriate systemic and sub-systemic roles. At its heart are the "productive system", concerned with creating a product or service, and the "supportive system", which ensures a flow of human or physical material needed to support production and which disposes of the final product.[36] Surrounding these are sub-systems growing out of the main system's need to secure for itself a safe external environment and a dependable internal one. The most prominent is the "maintenance system" which is "concerned with inputs for preserving the system either through appropriate selection of personnel or adequate rewarding of the personnel selected."[37] Such rewards may be tangible or intangible, deriving their significance from the complex of values and norms which constitute an organization's culture or climate, itself an important supportive element in the maintenance system. Providing overall direction and co-ordination of the internal organization is the "managerial system," and closely related is the "adaptive system" which is concerned with generating "appropriate responses to external conditions"[38] either by seeking change in the outside world or by helping the organization itself to modify its behaviour. Each of these systems plays a role in supporting the prime, or productive, function of the organization, but in order to perform that role each develops further roles that are more supportive of the organization and its other systems, than of the productive system itself. When role-playing of this type imposes on the organization and on the outside world demands that have nothing to do with any input demand from the external world, we can call those demands "withinputs".

Of the various functions performed within these organizational sub-systems, the case study has illustrated most completely the adaptive function. For the most part we have been concerned with the role played by F. A. MacDougall. During the early years of his tenure (1941–1943), he was primarily concerned with modifying the internal structure of Lands and Forests, attempting, through the reorganization and development of new forest management policies, to promote the department's capacity to meet the demands of a changing world, demands registered in the hostile political milieu of the late 1930s. Later, however, MacDougall's efforts were aimed in the opposite direction and he attempted to manipulate the external environment in order to protect the organization and to push forward the policies with which it had become identified.

In a sense the successful adaptation of Lands and Forests triggered the attempt on the part of the forest industries to promote the commission proposal. In MacDougall's view—and the activities of the OFIA seem to bear him out—the department's more effective management of the forest resource threatened various concerns which, rather than effecting internal adaptation, sought to remove the threat by persuading the government to revert to an earlier style of administration. This group's failure to secure an adequate maintenance system—one which ensured the support of all members—contributed largely to its eventual defeat.

A formidable maintenance system supported MacDougall, however. It consisted of several elements: the creation of an appropriate organizational climate deriving from the implementation of new policies and the introduction of new productive and support systems; the infusion of a professional ethos that bound foresters within the organization and created allies externally; and finally the investment represented by departmental adaptation itself. These, of course, were interrelated. Reorganization not only created the productive system—a new field service, in particular—for a new policy; it also introduced supportive systems, such as the professional values of the foresters who were now in charge, and fostered indigenous ones like those that protected individual officials from political pressure. By 1943, department members were committed to these values and to the structures they supported. Consequently, the proposed Forest Resources Commission loomed as a threat to them as well as to MacDougall. In other words, a maintenance system was securely in place and could not be shifted easily to a new adaptive posture. The only course open to the department in 1943 was to adopt an aggressive stance and to work towards modifying the external rather than the internal environment.

MacDougall's position, then, was primarily a withinput response deriving its impetus from the conviction that the department was "fighting for its administrative life." His success, however, depended upon more than the resources he could muster within the department, and emphasizes the fact that in this case, at least, the input-withinput relationship was extremely subtle. Points of interaction between the principal conflicting organizations were numerous, and as few individuals played only one role, the consequent confusion of values and norms led to contradictory behaviour patterns, particularly on the part of professional foresters employed by industry. Similarly, the fact that many values were shared by individuals in conflicting systems contributed to a blurring of distinctions between input and withinput demands, even though many of the issues initially appeared to be clear-cut. Frequent interaction at many levels caused a confusion of values and thus a breaking down of systemic boundaries, creating problems of role identification for individuals responsible for formulating pressure group policy.[39]

Analysis of the case study in terms of organization theory sheds some light on agency–group relations. It is clear that the agency's internally-generated demands conditioned its perception of the Drew–OFIA scheme. It is also clear, however, that external support for Lands and Forests was derived in part from a shared value system. Whether or not the department would have survived without that support is impossible to guess. In an earlier confrontation the department had been forced to reorganize itself, and it is quite possible that if the department had again found itself without a strong ally, it would have succumbed to the external pressure. As it happened, the department asserted its dominance while demonstrating its dependence upon supportive reciprocal relations with at least some elements of the external environment. In this respect, Lands and Forests' experience may be representative of that of most agencies faced with threatening input demands. That is, where major policy issues are involved, civil servants may require the support of external groups to achieve desired goals. Dominance in such cases is not complete, and without requires input support.

NOTES

1. Porter, 1965, pp. 425–26.
2. J. E. Hodgetts, "Challenge and Response: A Retrospective View of the Public Service of Canada" *Canadian Public Administration* VII (1964) pp. 409–21.
3. See Guy Dusseault of the Federated Council of Sales Finance Companies in *Financial Post*, Nov. 25, 1972. Similar comments are quoted by Engelmann and Schwartz, 1967, p. 105.
4. David M. Kwavnick, Other contributions to this aspect of the literature are referred to elsewhere in the present volume, particularly the introduction and the bibliography.
5. The term 'input' is too widely used to require definition here. 'Withinput' is less generally discussed, but was introduced by David Easton as follows: "Insofar as things happening within a system shape its destinies as a system of interactions, it will be possible to take them into account as they are reflected through the inputs of the members of a system . . . we might call them "with-

inputs". *A Framework for Political Analysis* (Englewood Cliffs, N. J.: Prentice-Hall, 1965) p. 114. This definition is potentially too inclusive (e.g. if pressure groups are seen as part of the political system, how does one determine which of their demands are "withinputs" and which inputs), and it is used here to describe demands originating within the governmental system exclusively.

6. Dawson, (1967), p. 454.

7. A general account of these events will be found in Richard S. Lambert with Paul Pross, *Renewing Nature's Wealth: A Centennial History of the Public Management of Lands, Forests and Wildlife in Ontario, 1763–1967*, (Toronto: Copp Clark for the Ontario Department of Lands and Forests, 1967), pp. 313–424.

8. Ontario, Legislative Assembly, Select Committee Inquiry into the Administration of the Department of Lands and Forests, 1939–1941. *Proceedings and Reports*, printed in Ontario, Legislative Assembly, *Journal* (henceforth, *JLAO*) Vol. LXXIV, 1939–1940 and Vol. LXXV, 1941, App. 1. The committee's majority report generally supported the Department's defence of its administration but is of little interest to us here since the minority report provided the touchstone for Drew's later actions.

9. See *JLAO*, 1941, pp. 246–47, and *The Globe and Mail*, 10 April, 1941.

10. *The Globe and Mail*, 10 April, 1941.

11. *Windsor Daily Star*, 10 April, 1941.

12. On 14 and 17 April, 1 May and 10 April, 1941, respectively.

13. *MacDougall Papers*. Unless otherwise indicated, the following account is based on the personal papers of Mr. F. A. MacDougall, Deputy Minister of Lands and Forests from 1941 to 1966.

14. See Lambert and Pross, *op. cit.*

15. Management clauses, which were attempts to specify the rates of use and replacement of forest resources, were first introduced into agreements with forest users before 1940, but had not been enforced because of lack of knowledge of the resource and insufficient manpower to enforce the regulations. By the mid-1940s, with the end of World War II in sight, there were real prospects that companies would be forced to adhere to the requirements.

16. Statute Law Amendments Act. 8 Geo. VI (1944) c. 58, s. 4.

17. *MacDougall Papers*, Newspaper clipping, source unknown, dated February, 1945.

18. *Ibid.* Transcript of question by E. B. Joliffe, CCF leader, 22 February, 1945.

19. *Ibid.* Memo to Minister, March 20, 1945.

20. See *Ontario Royal Commission on Forestry* (Toronto: King's Printer, 1947) The Statute Law Amendment Act 10 Geo. VI (1946) s. 20, ss. 6, permitted the Ontario Forest Resources Commission to continue in existence, but removed all of its powers.

21. J. F. Sharpe, head of the Timber Management Division, told MacDougall that Davis seemed ready to divulge "something important" during a conversation on the day Drew's press release was to have been released. *MacDougall Papers*, Note, 13 Jan. 1946.

22. *MacDougall Papers*, notes dated Jan. 1946, headed "The Industry attempts to take over our forests".

23. *MacDougall Papers* "Commission résumé" probably written 1946.

24. See: Inquiry into the requirements of Great Lakes Lumber and Shipping Limited, *Report* (Toronto: King's Printer, 1945).

25. See Pross, 1967.

26. Reflections of this sort occur repeatedly in MacDougall's daily notes and résumés.

27. R. G. S. Brown, *The Administrative Process in Britain* (London: Methuen, 1970), p. 165.

28. S. E. Finer, "Interest Groups and the Political Process in Great Britain" in Henry W. Ehrmann, *Interest Groups on Four Continents*, (Pittsburgh: University of Pittsburgh Press, 1958), pp. 117–44, 130.

29. Anderson, 1970.

30. Mitchell Sharp, "The Bureaucratic Elite and Policy Formation" in W. D. K. Kernaghan *Bureaucracy and Canadian Government* (Toronto: Methuen, 1969) pp. 82–87, 85.

31. Anthony Downs, *Inside Bureaucracy*, (Boston: Little, Brown & Co., 1967), p. 196.

32. *Ibid.*

33. See Herbert Simon's various contributions to the literature, M. Abrahamson *The Professional in the Organization* (Chicago: Rand McNally, 1967); Philip Selznick, *Leadership in Administration* (Evanston, Ill.: Harper & Row, 1957); and Victor A. Thompson, *Bureaucracy and Innovation* to name only a few of the most obvious sources.

34. Daniel Katz and Robert L. Kahn, *The Social Psychology of Organizations* (New York: John Wiley & Sons, 1967).

35. *Ibid.*, pp. 84–85.

36. *Ibid.*, p. 39.

37. *Ibid.*, p. 41.

38. *Ibid.*, p. 39.

39. *Ibid.* p. 51. The problem of boundaries within the organization is similar to the problem of boundaries within and between larger systems described by Easton and others. This particular aspect of our discussion casts doubt on Easton's view that demands that "emerge out of political roles themselves [withinputs] . . . differ from . . . inputs . . . in that the latter are shaped by such parameters as culture, economy, social structure, and the like . . ." (*Systems Analysis*, 55) Interdependence of role within organizations, together with the multiple role-playing of organization members in carrying on their business and private lives, ensures the transfer of values between systems and a consequent blurring of distinctions between input and withinput. The point is amply demonstrated in Michel Crozier's *The Bureaucratic Phenomenon*. (Chicago: University of Chicago Press, 1964).

8.

The adaptive capacity of pressure groups has been a recurrent theme in this collection of studies. Whether because of shifted jurisdictional responsibility or of modified relations between the executive, the legislature and the bureaucracy, Canadian groups repeatedly have had to change their tactics and sometimes their organizational structure in order to successfully exert influence on governments.

As several writers have suggested, changes in the policy system have occurred at an unusually sharp pace in the last ten to fifteen years. At the federal and provincial levels, extensive government re-organization has occurred partially in the wake of re-assessments of government organization, like the Glassco review of the federal government, but also as a result of attempts to deal with the problems of policy fragmentation. The results are embodied in conglomerate agencies—such as Environment Canada; co-ordinative and policy-oriented ministries—such as the Ministry of State for Urban Affairs, and in the strengthening of central policy structures. Simultaneously, the activities of pressure groups have received heightened media attention; pressure group formation appears to have accelerated, and there is apparently a greater tendency than in the past to attempt to influence government activity by exciting public interest in specific issues.

In the following article Peter Aucoin attempts an assessment of some of these trends. Focussing on developments at the national level, his analysis suggests that while institutional groups will likely continue to be the most effective pressure groups in the policy system, their relations with government will henceforth tend to be given greater publicity and be increasingly subject to challenge by competing issue-oriented groups. As well, the latter groups are likely to play a more prominent *part in public debate, with their role receiving growing recognition as a legitimate one. In broader terms, if we can speculate on the basis of a strictly tentative assessment, it may be we are experiencing a broadening and diversification of Canadian political communication processes reflected in altered pressure group behaviour and that our entire policy system is becoming more open, more competitive and more dynamic.*

Peter Aucoin is Associate Professor of Political Science, at Dalhousie University, and the co-editor of a leading collection of studies of the structure of policy-making in Canada.

Pressure Groups and Recent Changes in the Policy-Making Process

Peter Aucoin

Students of pressure groups in Canada have enriched our understanding of Canadian political processes principally by indicating the extent to which public policies are shaped by the interactions of members of the political executive and members of the civil service. Their studies have increased, in particular, our awareness of what can be called the "departmentalization" of public policies, a phenomenon which has resulted, in large part, from the tendency of governments to deal with specific policies within the confines of the department most responsible for administering them. This diffusion of responsibility has been facilitated by the growth of governmental activity in recent years, a growth which has produced new institutional interests to be protected and promoted.

In the 1960s federal governments in Canada initiated a number of changes in an attempt to limit some of the most undesirable consequences of this departmentalization of policy-making. These changes relate to the co-ordination of policy formulation by the government, the integration of government spending and program priorities, and parliamentary scrutiny of government policies and administration. Specifically, government initiatives for these purposes have included: first, the expansion of the Privy Council Office (PCO) and the Prime Minister's Office (PMO), the reorganization of the Cabinet committee system, the creation of policy ministries within the Cabinet, and the use of task forces; second, the establishment of a separate Treasury Board and secretariat and the introduction of the Planning, Programming, and Budgeting System (PPBS); and, third, the reorganization of the Parliamentary Standing Committee system and the use of the white papers.

To date, analyses of these changes have not paid much attention to their effects on pressure groups, or, perhaps more important, the possible consequences they may have for the policy process in the future. A few observers have suggested that they will make politicians in particular and the public in general more aware of what groups are actually involved in the formulation and execution of public policies. But, for the most part, pressure groups have not been singled out for investigation. This essay will describe in a general way the changes that have taken place in the Canadian policy process in order to determine their actual and possible consequences for the structure and functioning of pressure groups in Canada. In addition, it will attempt to indicate the reciprocal effects these consequences might be expected to have on the political system, given what we know of the changes and their consequences to date. The recent changes found in the structures and functioning of government and pressure groups in Canada may, in fact, be part of a larger context of political change in this country. This larger context of political change—one in which paramount emphasis is placed on the active participation of a greater number of individuals, especially those belonging to traditionally unorganized groups, in determining the fate of their political communities—is not the subject of our discussion. But it does follow, of course, that if some significant alterations are in the offing, students of pressure group behaviour must be alerted to them as they affect the conventional processes of public policy-making.

REFORMING THE POLICY-MAKING PROCESS

The recent changes in the structure of the Canadian government will be described only briefly here. Various scholars, including Doern, Franks, Hockin, Hoffman, Johnson, Hicks, Mallory, Smith and Schindeler,[1] have studied them in some detail, focussing for the most part on the Prime Minister and his Cabinet as the elected executive responsible for the formulation of public policy; the elected Members of Parliament as the representatives of the people who possess the final authority in legislating public policy; and, the appointed bureaucrats as the actual administrators of government policies. Their observations provide the principal basis for the following description of the changes in the policy-making process.

In the first place, the executive branch of government in Canada has in recent years placed considerable emphasis on the establishment of policy advisory units separated from the regular public service and attached to the Prime Minister and his Cabinet. Among other developments, the Prime Minister's Office and the Privy Council Office have been expanded in terms of staff, reorganized along broad policy lines, and freed from concentrating exclusively on purely administrative or partisan matters. These units are meant to offer general policy recommendations based on their analyses of departmental and independent advice, thus co-ordinating all suggestions regarding departmental program requirements and the political needs and aspirations of the governing party.

The major aim of these innovations was to reassert the primacy of the political executive—the PM and his Cabinet—in the setting of the government's objectives and especially in the monitoring of its policies. Much attention has been given by the mass media to the effects the changes are supposed to have had on executive-legislative relationships. Thus they have partially distorted the issue by their focus on the influence of an executive "super group" in contrast to the importance of our national Parliament.[2] As Doern and Schindeler have pointed out, however, these changes were designed primarily to alter existing executive-bureaucratic, not executive-legislative, relationships.[3] The PMO and the PCO were expanded for two basic reasons. In the first place, it was considered important that the Cabinet be afforded the opportunity to have the advice it receives from individual departments and agencies assessed by units not committed to the institutional concerns of the regular departmental civil service. This assessment by the PMO and PCO, it was felt, would counter what had been regarded as a near monopoly over the flow of expert advice and information to the Cabinet by upper echelon civil servants in various departments and agencies, especially in relation to on-going or established policies.[4]

Secondly, the Prime Minister's Office and Privy Council Office were to provide advice *across* departmental lines, thus enabling individual Cabinet members to evaluate the advice they received from their own departmental specialists in the context of broader policy concerns. On both counts the dependence of the executive, individually and collectively, upon the regular bureaucracy was to be reduced.[5] An "executive-bureaucracy" was created, not to counter the regular bureaucracy in every respect, but rather to assist the Cabinet in formulating policies that are consistent with each other and are more than a reflection of the particular interests of specialized groups in the regular bureaucracy.

Paralleling developments in the PCO, the Federal Cabinet committee system was reorganized in the 1960s, first by Pearson and again by Trudeau, in an effort to focus the attention of Cabinet members on the interrelationships of their individual departmental concerns, especially in broad policy areas.[6] The Cabinet was accordingly divided into a small number of committees both to bring together those Cabinet members responsible for departments having common or related interests—social policy, for instance—and to co-ordinate those dimensions of government policy which affect many departments—for example, federal-provincial relations. The two major committees were thus two of the co-ordinating committees: the Priorities and Planning Committee which was to be responsible for providing direction to government policies and determining their relative importance; and secondly, the Treasury Board, the committee of Cabinet which was to propose the general pattern of spending on government programs. The PCO, therefore, was reorganized along the lines of Cabinet committees with a group of PCO officials constituting the support staff for each of the committees, while the Treasury Board staff was hived off from the

Department of Finance and a new Cabinet portfolio was created, the Presidency of the Treasury Board.

At the same time, the policy influence of the regular departments and agencies was not to be reduced simply by ignoring expert opinion and relying primarily upon policy laymen or party influentials.[7] Rather, individuals were to be recruited, especially by the PCO and the Treasury Board, not only with expertise in particular policy fields but also with the skills necessary for integrating broad policy concerns. The "modern generalist" was to be the new kind of policy advisor and hence emphasis was given to the analysis of total "systems", that is the bringing together, if only conceptually, of all those individual policy fields which are interdependent or interrelated. The policy advisors recruited by the central agencies were thus a mixture of systems analysts, communications experts, economists, organization and management experts, and the traditional generalist with a professional training—the lawyer. As Bruce Doern has noted, this orientation was expected to facilitate "rational policy-making" and "comprehensive planning",[8] two major features of the general political philosophy of Prime Minister Pierre Trudeau, the executive leader most responsible for these developments.

Another change in the executive process in the 1960s was the increased use of the task force device. This instrument, by employing both governmental and non-governmental consultants, was to be the executive's equivalent to a Royal Commission which by tradition and law has been a public mechanism of enquiry. Task forces, such as Grey task force on foreign investment in Canada or the Hellyer task force on housing, were created to assist the executive in tackling political issues which, it was felt, could not have been examined adequately either by departments alone or by central advisory bodies. They were to further enhance the command of the Cabinet over difficult and controversial policy questions, both during and after the investigation. The task force instrument was to differ from the Royal Commission in that it was to be more closely tied to the political executive and comprised of personnel closely affiliated to the executive, with a clear interest in subsequent policy formulation.[9]

At the bureaucratic level, changes took place in the budgetary process to complement the alterations in the executive branch. The major innovation was not so much the establishment of the Treasury Board portfolio as its acceptance of what came to be called the Planning, Programming and Budgeting System. Besides the more technical goals PPBS was designed to achieve,[10] this budgetary approach was supposed to promote a central role for the political executive; that is, the Cabinet was to establish "priorities" among broad fields of government expenditures, thus setting the general government objectives to be pursued through the spending of public monies.[11] In effect, PPBS was to create a "top down" expenditure process, as opposed to one in which initiative came from the "bottom". The Cabinet, not individual government departments, was to take the initiative for decisions respecting government resource allocations.

A second complementary feature of PPBS was its emphasis on the evaluation of public expenditures in meeting established objectives. The primary aim of this exercise was to determine the effectiveness of specific government policies in light of the expenditures devoted to them. The more traditional emphasis on controlling the costs of policies was thus to become a secondary, although still important, concern. Attempts to evaluate the effectiveness of policies were to complement "rational policy-making" and "comprehensive planning" better than attempts simply to control their costs. In other words, *how well* public monies are spent, in terms of government priorities and policies, was to be considered more important than *how much* is spent. Determining the former is a task for top management and thus required the strengthening of the central management team of elected and appointed officials.

The third major development in the Canadian federal political system involved changes in the legislative process. A restructuring of the system of standing committees in the Canadian House of Commons also took place in the 1960s.[12] This was to enable Members of the House, individually and collectively, to participate more actively and meaningfully by giving them greater opportunities to gather information and opinion on both existing government programs and policy proposals. MPs were to have more interaction not only with departmental staff but also with members of the Cabinet on questions of public policy. Their roles were thus expanded in the deliberative stages of policy-making by the placing of a greater emphasis on a forum suitable for serious scrutiny and discussion.

The reorganization of the standing committees of the House of Commons, along the lines of the major policy concerns of the national government and with smaller memberships for each, was the principal means employed to effect changes in legislator participation. In addition, the federal government increased its use of white papers, that is, the issuing of "general statements of the government's thinking on a particular subject".[13] The Trudeau government viewed the white paper process "an integral part of the reform of parliamentary procedures designed to strengthen the institution and adapt it to modern conditions" by aiding Parliament's scrutiny and control of public policy; and, secondly, "as a means of increasing the knowledge of Parliament so that its final legislation would be improved".[14] Through the white paper process, legislators were to consider general policy questions *before* being presented with drafted legislation.

The rationale for these developments was that they would encourage those members of the legislative body who are not members of the executive to play a more significant role in evaluating the activities of the bureaucracy and to become more knowledgeable about the policy proposals of the Cabinet. This was to produce two results. The first was to coincide with the changes in the executive system, giving the elected official and public representative increased control over the appointed official and the civil servant. The second effect was to complement PPBS somewhat, by affording the legislature the opportunity to assess the performance of existing policy programs administered by government departments and agencies in relation to stated government priorities, objectives and financial commitments.

In sum, the changes in the executive–bureaucratic–legislative sectors were intended: (1) to bring about a more open, comprehensive, and visible policy-making process; (2) to promote a greater awareness in the political sector of the issues and interests involved; and (3) to facilitate greater involvement by the political sector, executive and legislative, in all stages of public policy-making.

CONSEQUENCES OF REFORM

In light of the objectives of the past decade's changes, what important consequences for pressure groups can be expected from the described alterations in policy-making structures and processes? In the following discussion, we will attempt to outline the possible impacts on the traditional models of pressure group-government interaction presented more fully in previous essays in this book. These changes in the executive branch of government, including the expansion of the PMO and PCO, the restructuring of the Cabinet committee system, the creation of policy advisory councils reporting to Cabinet members, and the increased use of task forces closely tied to the political executive, reflected a growing concern that there was not sufficient public exposure of the functioning of the bureaucracy and its programs. In part they also pointed to the political sector's ignorance of the actual roles and interests of various non-governmental groups, that is pressure groups. The changes in the policy process at the executive level hence can affect pressure groups in two ways.

The new or expanded units of policy analysis and advice have imposed yet another layer in the hierarchical structure of policy-making, or at least a source of countervailing inputs. Pressure groups are now faced with the possibility of being dropped one step in the hierarchy, as the influence of the regular department diminishes somewhat, given the competing advice presented to the political executive from well placed advisors not closely linked to group organizations or constituencies. The new or enlarged organizations give advice to the executive which is more or less independent of the traditional sources of demand inputs. Pressure groups and departments, while by no means excluded from the advisory process, are not to be given *a priori* the opportunity to dominate the input stages. The executive has sought to institutionalize or at least regularize the flow of advice from other than traditional sources, in much the same way as governments often did in the past, albeit in an *ad hoc* way, with Royal Commissions.[15]

Pressure groups are also affected in another way by these same changes. In creating or expanding central advisory agencies, the government, in addition to seeking more advice, also has sought to obtain advice which is comprehensive in nature. Most pressure groups now find themselves confronted by government advisors who, in performing their duties, must attempt to see beyond the concerns of individual groups. In effect, the establishment of these central advisory agencies gives formal recognition to the inefficiency of elected political leaders attempting, by themselves, to aggregate the whole host of individual group demands made on them. Pressure groups, as a result, are given further incentive to show how their interests are in the "public interest" and to do so in a way that presents their arguments in a more than superficial manner.[16]

The possible effects on pressure groups of internal changes in the bureaucratic sector are also of importance. In establishing the Treasury Board as a separate organization, and in implementing PPBS, it was not manifestly intended that they have a major impact on the non-governmental sector. Nevertheless, they have significant latent consequences for pressure groups, especially those affected by government expenditure policies. Since the new budgetary system was expected to relate policy objectives and spending of public monies in a more systematic and explicit way than had been done previously, pressure groups obviously must be interested in the manner in which government priorities and program expenditures are to be connected. These relationships are critical insofar as the interests and demands of recipient groups are now examined not only by the departments but, more importantly, by another central agency, the Treasury Board, through its program evaluation staff. This has introduced an additional set of expert policy advisors, also independent of the departments and groups affected and connected to the executive.

The new budgeting process requires departments to submit their proposed expenditure needs in a way that relates, in a detailed fashion, their public expenditures proposals to government objectives. The Cabinet, assisted by the PCO, establishes its general priorities and they are used by the Treasury Board to evaluate the importance of departmental programs. The Treasury Board is placed in a position where it must assess, not only the programs of the departments, but also the demands of pressure groups served by departmental programs. Thus the Treasury Board is to identify the groups or constituents benefiting from existing or proposed programs and to determine the government's commitment to them, either by reference to the stated policy intentions of the government or by referring such questions back to the PCO and the Cabinet. A major potential consequence for pressure groups of the introduction of PPBS and the role of the Treasury Board is, therefore, the exposure of the many groups which *compete* for government expenditures.[17] Analysts of the budgetary process have noted the change in orientation on the part of government decision-makers that is promoted by this new system. Decision-makers, it is argued, are now more conscious of the need to *redistribute* financial support rather than simply to distribute more and more of it in order to bring about policy changes. The austerity practised in government spending in the past few years has undoubtedly promoted an increased awareness that public monies are not unlimited. While this point may seem obvious to political economists, given the perpetual state of monetary scarcity, it is important to realize that in the past two or three decades governments often have acted as if this condition of scarcity did not exist; witness the increases in federal government spending in the fields of post-secondary education, science, and health, for instance.[18] Pressure groups in several policy fields thus were able to make demands on government without arguing explicitly that they deserved a greater allocation of public monies than groups in other fields. PPBS, it was advocated, would develop both the procedures and the philosophy to bring about changes in process and orientation. The PPBS approach contributed to this change in orientation because it presumes a scarcity of resources to be allocated; hence the necessary exercise of determining who shall be indulged and who shall be deprived.

Pressure groups were to be similarly affected by the restructuring of the legislative process. Both the committee system of the House of Commons and the use of white papers were to promote a more rigorous consideration of the substance and process of policy-making in a number of broad policy fields. They were meant to give the non-Cabinet MP, among other things, the opportunity to confront directly those groups affected by government programs and activities. Pressure groups, by appearing before committees in specific policy fields, were to be brought out into the open to a greater extent than they had been previously. Committee members could then examine the relationships between various groups and departments, assess the demands made by these groups and determine the importance to be attached to each of them.

Canadian pressure groups, accustomed to concentrating their efforts at the executive-bureaucratic levels, are now to be compelled to interact with the elected representatives of the people. The traditional structure and functioning of the Canadian party system has not been conducive to the alignment of pressure groups with individual political parties; at least not the two major parties in national politics. The logic of the Canadian system of Cabinet government has necessitated a focus primarily on the party in power, and only secondarily on the party in opposition, irrespective of which major party occupied each position at any point in time. Canadian legislators have seldom been regarded as constituting cliques which would or could exert significant influence in the policy process on behalf of pressure groups.[19] Party discipline usually has erased attempts at differentiation along group-affiliated lines within or between parties. Secondly, Canadian legislators have been considered "representatives" of their constituencies with responsibilities to follow party lines, rather than "delegates" who should act as spokesmen for their constituents.[20] This view has reinforced the party role of the MP, given the realities of power, but it also has reduced possible conflicts or strains in the members' perception of their proper role. Thirdly, when MPs have all, on occasion, clustered together to represent interests they have usually done so over regional, as opposed to socio-economic, concerns.[21] The representation of regional interests by MPs has been perhaps the major hindrance to strict party discipline, although it has been limited somewhat by the representation of regional interests in the federal Cabinet itself.

Providing a forum for more regular contact between pressure groups and MPs thus was to signal a change in the position of the legislator. His position was to be altered because he was to be given the chance to scrutinize and evaluate the proposals and goals of pressure groups, irrespective of whether or not he was approached by or supported them. This should remove some of the secrecy associated with pressure group-bureaucratic interaction and thereby enhance the amount of information on programs and their purposes available to the legislator. Secondly, it should assist the legislator in becoming more aware of the relevant policy issues and group interests at stake in various fields and at an earlier stage in the policy-making process.

The manifest consequence of these changes for pressure groups is not only that they are to be faced with another set of participants to persuade, but that this is to occur within the confines of committees with legitimate powers of enquiry. Pressure groups, under such circumstances may no longer have the advantage of initiative on their side. The changes in the standing committee system and the increased use of white papers should require that pressure groups be more visible, a requirement unfamiliar to many groups, accustomed as they are to the informal surroundings of the upper echelons of the bureaucracy.

A MORE PUBLIC ROLE FOR PRESSURE GROUPS

The preceding discussion suggests some possible general consequences of the recent changes in the Canadian system of government for pressure groups operating in the national political arena. Since pressure groups attempt to be very much involved in policy formulation and implementation, changes of the kind we have described should have an impact on the roles played by pressure groups, even if the policies actually affecting their constituencies are not altered substantially in the short run. In other words, changes in the policy-making process need not lead to significant changes in policy outputs, at least not of the allocative variety.

It is now obvious to observers that the structural alterations of the past few years have not completely rearranged the old order. The political executive has reasserted its legitimate dominance over the bureaucracy,[22] but in many policy fields, especially those out of the public limelight, departmental programs remain much the way departments want them. PPBS, while it has contributed to the Treasury Board's evaluation of most government programs in terms of expenditure policies, has not brought about the millennium in "rational" policy-making. In many cases it has simply prompted changes in the "rationalization" of existing programs without altering their policy direction or even the level of spending for them.[23] And, at least according to Franks, the major "dilemma" of the standing committees of the House of Commons still exists.[24]

There are, nonetheless, some changes to be found in the way pressure groups now interact with the executive, bureaucratic, and legislative sectors of government. Increasingly, many pressure groups are finding that: (1) they can no longer rely as exclusively as they once did on their contacts with departmental bureaucrats but must also attempt to penetrate central advisory mechanisms, such as the PMO, PCO and Treasury Board; (2) they must be prepared to present more formal presentations, based on the views of their own experts, rather than simply communicate their demands in friendly chats with bureaucrats or Cabinet members; (3) they must formulate their demands in a way that enables the political and bureaucratic sectors to compare them to demands from competing groups and to assess them in terms of government priorities; and (4) they must be more willing to engage in public discussion, at least in the forum of legislative committees. It must be noted the foregoing are statements of tendency. Still, while perhaps the majority of pressure groups have not drastically altered their behaviour, many are beginning to realize that changes in the policy-making process, even if they have not radically altered the outputs of the process, do mean a shift away from the more traditional pattern of informal, secretive and restricted face-to-face contact with the upper echelons of the executive-bureaucratic arena.

These tendencies have not been caused only by changes in governmental policy-making structures and processes. The mass media, especially with their new emphasis on "investigative reporting", various radical and reform movements (within and outside political parties), and generally increased public demands for accountability in our governing system have led to an increasing exposure of pressure groups. The "politics of low profile", if not extinct, has at least become suspect.

The most noticeable impact can be observed in the realm of pressure group–legislator interaction. Studies of legislative behaviour, especially by Hockin and Presthus,[25] point to the significant number of pressure groups now appearing before standing committees of the House of Commons and/or presenting briefs to them. In spite of the criticisms directed towards the structure and functioning of the committee system itself,[26] the changes described here have increased the need for continual activity on the part of pressure groups if their written and oral presentations are to promote their interests or, and perhaps more important given the continuing dilemma of the committee system, at least not to harm them. Pressure groups must spend more of their resources on gathering data, assembling them into a presentable form, and preparing their spokesmen for Committee appearances. Insofar as pressure groups have accepted these tasks, they now pay greater attention to the organizational changes necessary to accomplish them. The main point, it must be stressed, is not that legislative committees under the new system have substantially affected government policies as a result of pressure group participation, but rather that the committees, simply by conducting hearings and receiving briefs, have imposed increased demands on the personnel and resources of these groups.

The way in which the white paper device has been used in the past few years is further testimony to the new demands placed on pressure groups. The Doerr study of the white paper on taxation provides much evidence of its impact on affected groups.[27] The House of Commons standing committee which received and heard briefs on its proposals noted that, "The degree of public participation in the formulation of tax policy, as far as your Committee is aware, is unparalleled."[28]

As Doerr notes, this participation emanated mainly from the "articulate, the financially well-endowed, and the organized." The white paper, nevertheless, was a device *par excellence* for bringing out into the open the organized groups with a vested interest in taxation policy. Moreover, it did this in a way that required the expenditure of considerable effort on the part of many groups, given not only the complexity of the issues involved but also the number of groups participating, including provincial governments.

At the executive level, the increased use of task forces has likewise required pressure groups to expose themselves to the political sector. For instance, the Hellyer Task Force on Housing, irrespective of the difficulties it created (especially for its chairman), was instrumental in shedding some light in public on the network of relationships, involving various pressure groups, that determined the kind of housing policies being pursued in this country.[29] The publicity given this enquiry drew attention to a field of public policy which hitherto had been the concern of a small cluster of very low profile bureaucrats and interest groups. The subsequent creation of a Ministry of State for Urban Affairs and Housing was in part a recognition by the government of a need for greater and more centralized governmental authority in this field.

This development is also a good illustration of the government's attempt not only to integrate those policy concerns which are interrelated and interdependent, but also to co-ordinate the many groups— government agencies and private organizations—involved in the provision of housing and other urban-centred services. Rather than setting up a new department, the Trudeau government sought to overcome the "departmentalization" of public policy by locating policy formulation outside the confines of traditional organizations. The new ministry does not have functional program responsibilities but it is to scrutinize the operations of programs in this field and formulate policy on the basis of such investigations. In so doing, the ministry's scope of enquiry is extended to all those groups—governmental and private—which affect or are affected by housing and urban policies. In one sense, the establishment of the Ministry of State for Urban Affairs was the institutionalization of the Hellyer Hask Force and therefore allows for an on-going examination and evaluation of pressure groups operating in this field.

A somewhat similar illustration of the effects of task forces can be found in the field of health policy, long a field of interest to pressure group analysts.[30] Here two government-initiated study groups, the Task Force on the Cost of Health Services and the Community Health Centre Project, have been very much responsible for contributing to our knowledge of the various group interests—industrial, professional, organizational—at stake in present health care policies.[31] Their analyses have presented the political sector with a better appreciation of not only these group interests in themselves but, more importantly, the extent to which they might be related to the public interest through possible alternative policies. By so doing they have encouraged a number of the groups involved to consider their positions from the perspectives of government priorities. Furthermore, they have provided the government with the necessary information to evaluate the demands being made by many of these groups, especially in the context of existing health care programs. Pressure groups in this highly sensitive policy field, notably the medical profession, can no longer argue that only they possess all the relevant expertise needed for formulating government policies.[32]

Still at the executive level of government, the various expanded advisory units have further affected the roles of pressure groups. One good example can be found in the field of science policy. As Doern's study of this policy area shows,[33] the initiatives of the PCO, the Science Secretariat and the Science Council began a series of reviews and evaluations which brought the scientific and technological community in Canada under considerable public scrutiny, a position it had not been in since the late 1920s and early 1930s when the National Research Council's research establishments were created. The central position of these new advisory agencies afforded them the opportunity to assess Canada's science policies and the role of the scientific community in dealing with problems ranging from the state of the scientific disciplines, through industrial research and development (including the question of foreign ownership) to the deployment of science and technology in reaching socio-economic goals. In response, the scientific community revaluated its position *vis-à-vis* government in particular and the public in general and realized the extent to which changes in the policy-making process required changes on the part of the organizations representing them. Various "public policy committees" were established by scientific groupings and even a new national pressure group, SCITEC, was established to represent all the scientific and technological communities in Canada. The initiatives of policy advisors in the executive sphere had in effect, disturbed the arm's-length relationships which existed previously between, on the one hand, the autonomous government research agencies and the scientific community, and, on the other hand, the same agencies and the public treasury. This new era of science policy thus has witnessed the creation of the Ministry of State for Science and Technology, illustrating the degree to which science has become a salient policy question for the political sector. Scientific pressure groups, as a result, have found themselves in a much different position from that of even ten years ago.

The impact of changes in the bureaucratic sector on pressure groups, especially those relating to PPBS and the Treasury Board, is more difficult to document. This is due, in part, to the fact that the consequences of these changes are bound to be indirect, at least insofar as pressure groups work through the departments most relevant to their demands. The central position of the Treasury Board in the determination of the annual expenditure pattern and the role of its staff in using PPBS to evaluate departmental and program demands is well appreciated within the bureaucratic sector, including pressure group spokesmen conversant with the budgetary process. (In one policy field there was even opposition by pressure groups to the implementation of PPBS.[34])

To many observers this approach simply cannot measure up to the standards set for it by several of its early proponents. Hence, notwithstanding the obvious importance of the Treasury Board and its staff, some would argue that pressure groups should not be concerned about PPBS. Yet, in spite of the analytical and methodological problems encountered in the implementation of this system, PPBS has, according to Doern,

> generated an increased feeling of political control over the major priorities. . . . This has been especially so among officials at both the political and bureaucratic levels in the central agencies of the federal government.[35]

It is this new sense of confidence and posture of aggressiveness on the part of the central agencies, particularly the Treasury Board, that has led departments to be more conscious of the position of their programs in the pecking order of government priorities. Pressure groups, therefore, not only must attempt to show how their proposals are in the "public interest", they must also argue that they coincide with "national priorities". Hence the increasing demands by department officials that pressure groups present proposals based on well-documented evidence.[36] Faced with the requirement of annually justifying their programs and proposals before the Treasury Board, government departments expect pressure groups to do the same before them. PPBS, then, is part of the government's attempt to have all demands for allocation exposed to serious scrutiny, and as such has contributed to a general expectation that those making demands will present them with some clarity and precision. Again, this demands a greater expenditure of resources by pressure groups than was previously required.

While the foregoing examples and suggestions of ways the changes in the Canadian system of government have affected some pressure groups cannot be considered verification for any hypotheses regarding the changing roles of pressure groups in Canada, they do lend support to the accuracy of the tendency statements found at the beginning of this section of our analysis. Of course, some pressure groups have been little affected by these changes, either because their demands are being met and thus there is little need for publicly articulated presentations, or because they operate in policy fields where issues have not become politically salient and controversial and thus they can behave as they have in the past. The latter condition is more crucial perhaps insofar as all policy fields are not exposed to continuous and penetrating examinations during any one period. And, as Simeon has pointed out, some areas of Canadian government activity exhibit a policy-making pattern involving federal and provincial executives which does not provide procedures for continuing interaction between these executives and affected pressure groups.[37] These groups have been virtually frozen out of the policy-making process by another recent development in the Canadian system of government—the increased use of federal-provincial executive meetings to settle broad policy matters.

ENHANCING PARTICIPATION IN THE POLICY PROCESS

In the preceding section we have noted some of the consequences for pressure groups of the recent changes in the Canadian system of government. We shall conclude our discussion by pointing to a number of consequences for the policy-making process resulting from the ways pressure groups themselves are changing.

Perhaps the major impact to date has been the extent to which the political sector, and the public have generally become more consciously and knowledgeably aware of the many interests involved in the making of public policies. Pressure groups have always been an important part of the structures of policy-making in Canada but often little was known of them, except by the departments involved. Generally their existence was explicitly recognized only when policy issues in their fields of interest became highly controversial. (For example the Canadian Medical Association achieved prominence in the debate over medicare.)[38]

Presthus, for instance, in his study of the interaction between MPs and pressure groups, notes the extent to which elected representatives depend upon the new committee system to obtain information from groups presenting briefs to and/or appearing before committees.[39] This new channel of communication must be considered a major innovation in the policy-making system, as information is a prerequisite for meaningful involvement by MPs. That this opportunity has been restricted somewhat by the interpretation of the proper structure and functioning of committees by both government and opposition party leaders is, however, the main hypothesis of Franks. Change, nevertheless, has occurred insofar as the committees have brought together in a regular format two sets of political actors—legislators and pressure groups— which previously interacted only intermittently, even if, as committees, they have not had a major impact on government legislative proposals.

Pressure groups, by responding to the demands of this new committee system, now assist this organizational mechanism in providing for two important requirements of a democratic political process. Without them, legislators and the general public must depend on the operating departments of government, the mass media, and their own investigative resources for information and group opinions. These are the conditions under which Canadian legislators traditionally have had to function.

Secondly, pressure groups, insofar as they now have been encouraged to participate more openly in the political and thus public arena, have a greater incentive to provide expert or specialized advice and to translate this advice into laymen's language. In so doing, they contribute to the presentation of alternative interpretations of complex policy questions. The policy attitudes of government bureaucrats thus can be countered in public, not merely confined to the council chambers of executive-bureaucratic structures. In this sense pressure groups constitute a regular source of alternate expert opinion.

Thirdly, pressure groups assist in the determination of priority issues in the formulation of public policy by competing more explicitly with one another over the allocation of public resources and positions of authority in the polity.[40] Given the increasing concern of governments to determine, in a rational and deductive manner, the distribution of resources and influence, pressure groups are beginning to focus on the merits of their demands compared to those of other groups. All demands cannot be met simultaneously; all interests cannot be in the public interest; all goals cannot be given a high priority; and finally, all groups cannot be afforded the same authority vis-à-vis each other. This change in form is, of course, a relative one. But the attempts of contemporary governments, especially to redistribute their authority and resources, are assisted to the degree that pressure groups articulate competing demands in a way that helps to crystallize the essence of political conflict and the nature of the decisions to be made. Rational planning and policy-making mean nothing in a political context if there is governmental and public confusion over the interests and goals contained in the issues to be decided upon by policy-making structures.

Finally, by altering their structures and activities to changes in governmental processes, pressure groups facilitate the expansion of individual and group participation in political matters. By attaching more importance to the public articulation of group interests, active pressure groups stimulate similar activities on the part of other groups. The proliferation of pressure groups in the past few years, especially those organizing sections of the community previously without mechanisms for mobilization, illustrates the growing awareness in many people of the need for concerted action to promote their causes. The new demands placed upon pressure groups, new and old, also have encouraged the participation of greater numbers of people. The face-to-face contacts of the traditional pressure group/executive–bureaucracy model required only a handful of well-placed, influential notables. By "opening up" the process, so to speak, opportunities for meaningful political activity by more individuals are enhanced. Not only are there the enlarged responsibilities for the preparation and presentation of group demands, but also the number of government councils, boards, and committees involving non-governmental personnel has increased greatly in the past few years, and organized groups have a role to play in providing personnel for them.[41] Through such methods, pressure groups have contributed to increased participation in the policy process.

Changes in pressure groups, therefore, have produced additional developments in the political process. They have provided for more information, more expert opinion, a greater clarity in the dimensions of policy issues, and a greater degree of participation in the policy-making process. Having stated this, one should point out, however, that the changes are relative in degree and, in many cases, difficult to evaluate. More information, for instance, may not mean better information. A greater number of expert opinions may not include the necessary solutions. Greater clarity in the dimensions of issues may, in fact, promote a greater polarization of the community. Lastly, more individual participation need not greatly affect the structure of power in the polity. On each of these counts, pressure groups have had a mixed record. This results partly from the logic of the parliamentary system of responsible government found at present in Canada, and partly from the existing distribution of resources at the disposal of all groups.[42] It must be noted, moreover, that the changes which have taken place and their consequences have more to do with the *process* of policy-making than with the *outputs* of these activities, especially the allocative outputs. The latter have been affected, but not in a radical way. This is to be expected, however, since the alterations to the policy-making process were designed primarily to redress the imbalance between the executive, bureaucratic, and legislative branches of government, not to bring about a new pattern of policy outcomes. Finally, pressure groups have been affected by, and have contributed to, changes in the policy-making process, but not to the point where the student of pressure group activity can disregard the traditional model of pressure group/executive-bureaucracy interaction. As the other essays in this book make clear, the Cabinet remains the final source of policy decisions and departments and agencies still exercise considerable influence in the way policies are shaped and then implemented.

NOTES

1. See G. Bruce Doern, "The Development of Policy Organizations in the Executive Arena", and "The Budgetary Process and the Policy Role of the Federal Bureaucracy", in G. Bruce Doern and Peter Aucoin (eds.), *The Structures of Policy-Making in Canada*, (Toronto: Macmillan, 1971), pp. 39–78, 79–112; C. E. S. Franks, "The Dilemma of The Standing Committees of the Canadian House of Commons", *Canadian Journal of Political Science*, vol. IV, December 1971, No. 4, pp. 461–476; Thomas A. Hockin, "The Advance of Standing Committees in Canada's House of Commons: 1965 to 1970), *Canadian Public Administration*,

Summer 1970, Vol. XIII, No. 2, pp. 185–202; David Hoffman, "Liaison Officers and Ombudsmen: Canadian MPs and their Relations with the Federal Bureaucracy and Executive," in T. A. Hockin, ed., *Apex of Power*, (Scarborough: Prentice-Hall, 1971), pp. 146–162; A. W. Johnson, "The Treasury Board of Canada and the Machinery of Government of the 1970's", *Canadian Journal of Political Science*, vol. IV, September 1971, No. 3, pp. 346–366: Michael Hicks, "The Treasury Board and its Clients: Five Years of Change and Administrative Reform, 1966–71", *Canadian Public Administration*, 1973, Vol. 16, No. 2, pp. 182–205; J. R. Mallory and R. A. Smith, "The Legislative Role of Parliamentary Committees in Canada; The Case of the Joint Committee on Public Service Bills," *Canadian Public Administration*, Spring, 1972, Vol. 15, no. 1, pp. 1–23; and Fred Schindeler, "The Prime Minister and the Cabinet: History and Development," in Hockin, *op. cit.*, pp. 22–50.

2. One such analysis can be found in Walter Stewart, *Shrug: Trudeau in Power*, (Toronto: New Press), 1971.

3. Doern, "The Development of Policy Organizations in the Executive Arena," and Schindeler, *op. cit.*

4. The classic statement on the role of senior civil servants is found in Porter (1965), Chapter XIV, "The Federal Bureaucracy," pp. 417–456.

5. For two "inside" accounts of these developments, see Gordon Robertson, "The Changing Role of the Privy Council Office", and Marc Lalonde, "The Changing Role of the Prime Minister's Office," *Canadian Public Administration*, Winter, 1971, Vol. 14, No. 4, pp. 487–508, 509–537. These were written when the former was Clerk of the Privy Council and Secretary to the Cabinet, the latter, Principal Secretary to the Prime Minister of Canada.

6. For a discussion of some of the factors responsible for these changes, see Gordon Robertson, "The Canadian Parliament and Cabinet in the Face of Modern Demands", *Canadian Public Administration*, Vol. 11, 1968.

7. See Doern's assessment of the Diefenbaker approach to the matter of policy advice, one which exhibited a bias against the use of the kind of expertise now found in the PCO and PMO, in his "The Development of Policy Organization in the Executive Arena," especially pp. 42–46.

8. *Ibid.*, pp. 60–68. Also see Bruce Thordarson, *Trudeau and Foreign Policy: A Study in Decision-Making*, (Toronto: Oxford University Press), 1972.

9. On task forces in general see V. Seymour Wilson, "The Role of Royal Commissions and Task Forces", in Doern and Aucoin, *op. cit.*, pp. 113–129.

10. For a description of the general and specific objectives of PPBS by the Secretary of the Treasury Board, see Johnson, "The Treasury Board of Canada and the Machinery of Government of the 1970s".

11. See Doern's "The Budgetary Process and the Policy Role of the Federal Bureaucracy", for an analysis of the relationship between the budgetary and political processes.

12. On the standing committee of the House of Commons, see T. A. Hockin, "The Advance of Standing Committees in Canada's House of Commons: 1965 to 1970", and C. E. S. Franks, "The Dilemma of the Standing Committees of the Canadian House of Commons".

13. A. D. Doerr, "The Role of White Papers", in Doern and Aucoin, *op. cit.*, p. 185.

14. *Ibid.*, pp. 186–187.

15. An examination of some of the issues involved here can be found in Fred Schindeler and C. M. Lanphier, "Social Science Research and Participatory Democracy in Canada", *Canadian Public Administration*, Vol. XII, No. 4, Winter, 1969, pp. 481–498, and J. E. Hodgetts, "Public Power and Ivory Tower", T. Lloyd and J. McLeod, eds., *Agenda 1970*, (Toronto: University of Toronto Press, 1968), pp. 256–280.

16. D. C. Corbett examines the relationship between group interests and the public interest in his essay, "The Pressure Group and the Public Interest" (1953).

17. See, again, Doern's "The Budgetary Process and the Policy Role of the Federal Bureaucracy".

18. That political analysts have not been sufficiently concerned with matters related to public spending, is one of the main questions examined by Richard Bird in *The Growth of Government Spending in Canada*, (Toronto: Canadian Tax Foundation, 1970), especially pp. 123–138.

19. At this point it is becoming a tradition to quote a pressure group observer who once wrote, "When I see members of Parliament being lobbied, it's a sure sign to me that the lobby lost its fight in the civil service and the cabinet". Quoted in Engelmann and Schwartz (1967), p. 105.

20. On the question of the role perceptions of legislators, see Robert Presthus (1971), p. 449, and David Hoffman and Norman Word, *Bilingualism and Biculturalism in the Canadian House of Commons*, (Ottawa: Queen's Printer, 1970), pp. 66–69, 77–80.

21. On this point see Porter, *op. cit.*, and A. C. Cairns, "The Electoral System and the Party System in Canada", *Canadian Journal of Political Science*, Vol. 1, No. 1, March, 1968.

22. It could be argued perhaps the Trudeau government never quite succeeded in convincing the interested public that his reorganization of the executive was for the purpose of more effective direction of the administration of government. Opposition politicians, the mass media generally, and even some government supporters kept insisting he was constructing a technocratic elite in the executive arena to control, not the bureaucracy, but Parliament and other traditional sources of political influence, the Liberal party and its supporters for instance. The post-1972 election personnel changes in the PMO and the PCO have been considered by some to constitute a recognition by Trudeau of the need for closer liaison between the Cabinet, the government party in the legislature, and party supporters. The PMO and PCO remain, nevertheless, institutions of policy advice strategically located at the "apex of power".

23. The new budgetary system, although it may not be a substitute for the making of hard political choices about government spending, has still strengthened the Treasury Board's position in the formulation of public policy. Observers may scoff at attempts to find quantitative formulae to determine policy priorities and objectives, but they cannot dismiss the Board as a central agency of policy-making. See Hicks, *op. cit.*

24. Franks, *op. cit.*

25. Hockin, "The Advance of the Standing Committees in Canada's House of Commons", and Presthus, *op. cit.*

26. Franks, *op. cit.*

27. Doerr, *op. cit.*

28. Quoted in *Ibid.*, p. 192.

29. See Lloyd Axworthy, "The Housing Task Force: A Case Study", in Doern and Aucoin, *op. cit.*, pp. 130–153.

30. See, for example, Taylor, (1960).

31. See R. L. Jones, "From health insurance to a health system—the Hastings Report", *The Canadian Forum*, December, 1972, Vol. LII, No. 2623, pp. 13–15.

32. These two study groups conform to the model of the task force in that they conducted their investigations chiefly within the confines of the executive-administrative and interested constituency arena, they employed a number of personnel already involved in the formulation and execution of public policies, and the executive determined the kinds of specific questions to be pursued. In these ways the two groups differed significantly from the Royal Commission on Health Services (1964, 1965) which, while comprehensive in its recommendations, found policy-makers interested only in that aspect of its report, i.e. medicare, which they had decided *a priori* they would accept.

33. G. Bruce Doern, *Science and Politics in Canada*, (Montreal: McGill-Queen's University Press, 1972).

34. Groups representing the Indian Community of Canada have objected to the use of PPBS in the Department of Indian Affairs. Cf. Doern, "The Budgetary Process and the Policy Role of the Federal Bureaucracy", p. 105.

35. *Ibid.*, p. 103.

36. See Bruce Little, "Ottawa's Quiet Persuaders", *Financial Times*, September 25,

1972, p. 16. The point was also made to this writer in interviews with a number of senior government officials.

37. Richard Simeon, *Federal-Provincial Diplomacy: The Making of Recent Policy in Canada*, (Toronto: University of Toronto Press, 1972). pp. 280–283.

38. See, for example, B. R. Blishen, *Doctors and Doctrines*, (Toronto: University of Toronto Press, 1969).

39. Robert Presthus, *op. cit.* Presthus found that the information function performed by pressure groups for MPs was considered the most important by the greatest number of legislators in his sample, pp. 448–449.

40. For a discussion of the distinction between allocative and positional policies see my "Theory and Research in the Study of Policy-Making", G. Bruce Doern and Peter Aucoin, *The Structures of Policy-Making in Canada*, pp. 10–38. An excellent analysis of a pressure group's concern with positional policy demands, as opposed to allocative demands, can be found in Kwavnick (1970).

41. This point is further developed in Dion. (1968).

42. For a critique of the established group bias of Canadian politics, see Charles Taylor, *The Pattern of Politics*, (Toronto: McClelland and Stewart, 1970), and Robert Presthus, *Elite Accommodation in Canadian Politics*, (Toronto: Macmillan, 1973).

Selected Bibliography

Canadian Pressure Group Studies

Anderson, J. E., (1970) "Pressure Groups and Canadian Bureaucracy", in W. D. K. Kernaghan and A. M. Willms, eds., *Public Administration in Canada: Selected Readings*, 2nd ed. (Toronto: Methuen), pp. 370–379.

Armstrong, R., (1969), Pressure-Group Activity and Policy Formation: Collective Bargaining in the Federal Public Service" in W. D. K. Kernaghan, ed. *Bureaucracy in Canadian Government*, (Toronto: Methuen), pp. 120–128.

Baird, R., (1970), "Interest Groups and Departments in Alberta," *Proceedings*, Canadian Political Science Association, Winnipeg, June, 1970.

Barry, D., (1971), *Interest Groups in the Canadian Foreign Policy Formulation Process: The Case of Biafra*, unpublished M.A. Thesis, Dalhousie University.

Belanger, M., (1969), *L'Association volontaire: le cas des Chambres de Commerce*, Unpublished Ph.D. dissertation, Laval University.

Byers, Roddick, (1971), "Executive Leadership and Influence: Parliamentary Perceptions of Canadian Defence Policy," in Thomas A. Hockin, ed., *Apex of Power*, (Scarborough: Prentice-Hall), pp. 163–182 .

Brownstone, M., (1968),"The Canadian System of Government in the Face of Modern Demands," *Canadian Public Administration*, XI, No. 4 (Winter, 1968), 428-439.

Bucovetsky, Meyer Wilfred, (1971), *Tax Reform in Canada: A Case Study of the Mining Industry*, Unpublished Ph.D. dissertation, University of Toronto.

Campbell, Colin, (1972), "Canadian Senators as Appointees to a National Legislature: Group Consultants, the Lobby Within, and Social Reforms", *Proceedings*, Canadian Political Science Association, Montreal, June, 1972.

Canada, Library of Parliament, Research Branch, (1970), "Pressure Groups in Canada," *The Parliamentarian*, LI, No. 1 (January, 1970), pp. 11–20.

Clague, Michael, (1971), "Citizen Participation in the Legislative Process," in James A. Draper, ed., *Citizen Participation: Canada*, (Toronto: New Press), pp. 30–44.

Clark, S. D., (1938), *"The Canadian Manufacturers' Association: A Political Pressure Group"*, in Canadian Journal of Economics and Political Science, v. 4.

Clark, S. D., (1939), *The Canadian Manufacturers' Association*, (Toronto: University of Toronto Press).

Corbett, D. C., (1953), "The Pressure Group and the Public Interest," in J. E. Hodgetts and D. C. Corbett, *Canadian Public Administration*, (Toronto: Macmillan), 1960, pp. 452–462.

Curtis, James, (1971), "Voluntary Association Joining: A Cross-National Comparative Note," *American Sociological Review* 36, (October, 1971), 872–880

Dalhousie Institute of Public Affairs and Richard H. Leach, (1970) *Interprovincial Relations in the Maritime Provinces*, (Fredericton: Maritime Union Study).

Dawson, H. J., (1966), *Agricultural Interest Groups in Canada and Great Britain,* unpublished thesis, Oxford University.

Dawson, H. J. (1963), "The Consumers Association of Canada," *Canadian Public Administration,* VI, No. 1, pp. 92–118.

Dawson, Helen Jones, (1960), "An Interest Group: The Canadian Federation of Agriculture," *Canadian Public Administration,* III, No. 2 (June, 1960), pp. 134–149.

Dawson, Helen Jones, (1967), "Relations between Farm Organizations and the Civil Service in Canada and Great Britain," *Canadian Public Administration,* X No. 4, pp. 450–471.

Deveaux, Bert and Kaye, (1971), "The Enemies Within Community Development," in James A. Draper, ed., *Citizen Participation: Canada,* (Toronto: New Press), pp. 93–105.

Dion, Léon, (1967), *Le bill 60 et la société québécoise,*" (Montréal: Editions HMH).

Dion, Léon, (1968), "Participation in the Political Process", in *Queen's Quarterly,* v. 75. No. 3.

Dion, Léon, (1969a) "Politique consultative et système politique, *Canadian Journal of Political Science,* II, No. 2 (June, 1969), pp. 226–244.

Dion, Léon, (1969b), "A la recherche d'une méthode d'analyse des partis et des groupes d'intérêt," *Canadian Journal of Political Science,* II, No. 1, pp. 45–63.

Doern, G. Bruce (1970), "The National Research Council: The Causes of Goal Displacement," *Canadian Public Administration* XIII, No. 2, 140–185.

Doern, G. B., (1969) "Pressure Groups and the Canadian Bureaucracy: Scientists and Science Policy Machinery" in W. D. K. Kernaghan, ed., *Bureaucracy in Canadian Government,* (Toronto: Methuen), pp. 112–119.

Doern, G. B., (1972) *Science and Politics in Canada,* (Montreal: McGill-Queen's University Press).

Eggleston, Wilfrid, (1953), "The Cabinet and Pressure Groups," *Proceedings of the Fifth Annual Conference, The Institute of Public Administration of Canada,* Toronto, IPAC, pp. 156–167.

Englemann, Frederick C. and Mildred C. Schwartz, (1967), *Political Parties and the Canadian Social Structure,* (Scarborough, Prentice-Hall), (Particularly chapter 5, "Organized Interest Groups," pp. 92–114.)

Frechette, W. D. H., (1969), "The CMA-Spokesman for Industry," in Paul Fox, ed., *Politics Canada,* (Toronto: McGraw-Hill, 1970), pp. 172–175.

Grayson, L. M., and J. Paul Grayson, "Interest Aggregation and Canadian Politics: The Case of the Central Bank," in *Canadian Public Administration,* Vol. 16, No. 4, pp. 557–572.

Hagy, James William, (1969), "Quebec Separatists: The First Twelve Years," in W. E. Mann, ed., *Social and Cultural Change in Canada,* (Toronto: Copp Clark, 1970), pp. 288–295.

Hannam, H. H. (1953), "The Interest Group and Its Activities," *Proceedings of the Fifth Annual Conference, the Institute of Public Administration of Canada,* Toronto, IPAC, pp. 171–181.

Hawkins, Freda, (1972), *Canada and Immigration: Public Policy and Public Concern,* (Montreal: McGill-Queen's University Press), (Part Five, "The Voluntary Sector", pp. 291–322, contains two useful chapters on the role of government and voluntary associations in developing immigration policy and in providing services to immigrants.)

Hodgetts, J. E., (1957), "The Civil Service and Policy Formation" in *Canadian Journal of Economics and Political Science,* V. XXIII, No. 4, pp. 467–479.

Horowitz, Gad, (1968), *Canadian Labour in Politics,* (Toronto: University of Toronto Press).

Isbister, Fraser, (1968) "The CNTU Comes of Age," in W. E. Mann, ed., *Social and Cultural Change in Canada,* (Toronto: Copp Clark, 1970), pp. 261–274.

Jacobs, Dorene E., (1971), "The Annex Ratepayers' Association: Citizen's Efforts to Exercise Social Choice in Their Urban Environment," in James A. Draper, ed., *Citizen Participation: Canada,* (Toronto: New Press), pp. 288–306.

Johnson, P. G., (1969), "The Union of Nova Scotia Municipalities," Unpublished M.A. dissertation, Dalhousie University.

Johnson, P. G., (1970) "The Union of Nova Scotia Municipalities as a Pressure Group," *Proceedings,* Canadian Political Science Association, Winnipeg, June, 1970.

Kernaghan, W. D. K., (1969), *Bureaucracy in Canadian Government,* (Toronto: Methuen).

Kwavnick, David, (1972) *Organized Labor and Pressure Politics*, (Montreal: McGill–Queen's University Press).

Kwavnick, David, (1973), "Pressure-Group Demands and Organizational Objectives: The CNTU, the Lapalme Affairs, and National Bargaining Units," *Canadian Journal of Political Science* VI, No. 4 (Dec. 1973), 582–602.

Kwavnick, David (1970) "Pressure Group Demands and the Struggle for Organizational Status: The Case of Organized Labour in Canada," *Canadian Journal of Political Science*, III, No. 1, pp. 56-72.

Lamontagne, M., (1968), "The Influence of the Politician," *Canadian Public Administration*, XI, No. 3.

Lemieux, F., (1966), "Lobbying Plus . . . the CMA" in Paul Fox, ed., *Politics: Canada*, (Toronto, McGraw–Hill, 1970).

Lenoski, J. Gerard (1972) "Interest Groups and the Canadian Legislative Process: A Case Study of the Canada Water Act," Unpublished M.A. dissertation, Carleton University.

McGillivray, Don, (1964), "Lobbying at Ottawa," in Paul Fox, ed., *Politics Canada*, (Toronto: McGraw-Hill, 1970), pp. 163–172.

Manzer, Ronald, (1969), "Selective Inducements and the Development of Pressure Groups: The Case of Canadian Teachers' Associations," *Canadian Journal of Political Science*, II, No. 1, 103–118.

Meisel, John, (1965), "Recent Changes in Canadian Parties," in Hugh G. Thorburn, ed., *Party Politics in Canada*, (Scarborough: Prentice-Hall, 1967), pp. 33–54.

Meynaud, Jean, (1968), "Groupes de pression et politique gouvernementale au Québec," in André Bernard, ed., *Réflexions sur la politique au Québec*, (Montréal: Sainte Marie), pp. 69–96.

O'Riordan, Timothy, (1970), "Toward a Strategy of Public Involvement," in W. R. Derrick Sewell and Ian Burton, eds., *Perceptions and Attitudes in Resources Management*, Ottawa, Policy Research and Coordination Branch, Canada Department of Energy, Mines and Resources.

Ouellet, F., (1959), *Histoire de la Chambre de Commerce de Québec, 1809-1959*, (Québec: Université Laval).

Porter, John, (1965), *The Vertical Mosaic: An Analysis of Social Class and Power in Canada*, (Toronto: University of Toronto Press).

Presthus, Robert, (1971), "Interest Groups and the Canadian Parliament: Activities, Interaction, Legitimacy, and Influence," *Canadian Journal of Political Science*, IV, No. 4, pp. 444–460.

Presthus, Robert, (1973), *Elite Accommodation in Canadian Politics*, (Toronto: Macmillan).

Presthus, Robert, (1974), *Elites in the Policy Process*, (Toronto: Macmillan).

Pross, A. P., (1967), "The Development of Professions in the Public Service: The Foresters in Ontario", in *Canadian Public Administration*, v. X, No. 3, pp. 376–404.

Sewell, John, (1972), *Up Again City Hall*, (Toronto: James Lewis and Samuel).

Sewell, W. R. Derrick, (1970), "Integrating public views in planning and policy making," in W. R. Derrick Sewell and Ian Burton, eds., *Perceptions and Attitudes in Resources Management*, Ottawa, Policy Research and Co-ordination Branch, Canada Department of Energy, Mines and Resources.

Sharp, P. F., (1948), *Agrarian Revolt in Western Canada*, (Minneapolis: University of Minnesota Press).

Stairs, Denis, (1971), "Public and Policy-Makers: The Domestic Environment of Canada's Foreign Policy Community," *International Journal*, Winter, 1970–71.

Swettenham, John and David Kealy, (1970), *Serving the State: A History of the Professional Institute of the Public Service of Canada, 1920-1970*, (Ottawa: The Institute).

Taylor, Malcolm G., (1972), "Quebec medicare: policy formulation in conflict and crisis," *Canadian Public Administration*, 15, No. 2, pp. 211–250.

Taylor, Malcolm G., (1960), "The Role of the Medical Profession in the Formulation of Public Policy," *Canadian Journal of Economics and Political Science*, XXVI, No. 1, pp. 108–127.

Thorburn, Hugh G., (1964), "Pressure Groups in Canadian Politics: Recent Revisions of the Anti-Combines Legislation," *Canadian Journal of Economics and Political Science* XXX, No. 2, pp. 157–174.

Townson, Frank W., (1972), "The Labour Federations as Pressure Groups," in Donald C. Rowat, ed., *Provincial Government and Politics: Comparative Essays*, (Ottawa: Department of Political Science), pp. 495–520.

Van Loon, Richard J. and Michael S. Whittington, (1971), *The Canadian Political System: Environment, Structure and Process*, (Toronto: McGraw-Hill). (Particularly ch. 13, "Interest Groups in Canadian Politics," pp. 297–321.)

Verney, Douglas V., "The Role of the Private Social Research Council of Canada in the Formation of Public Science Policy, 1968–1974", *Canadian Public Policy*, I, No. 1, winter 1975.

Young, Brian J., (1967), "C. George McCullagh and the Leadership League," in Ramsay Cook, ed., *The Politics of Discontent*, (Toronto: University of Toronto Press).